HC440.C6 B45 2008

Bijapurkar, Rama.

Winning in the Indian
   market : understanding
      2008.

2007 10 31

WINNING IN THE INDIAN MARKET
Understanding the Transformation of Consumer India

D0560893

	DATE DUE	
MAR - 6 2008		
MAR 13 2008		

GEORGE BROWN COLLEGE
ST. JAMES CAMPUS
LIBRARY LEARNING COMMONS
200 KING ST. E.
TORONTO, ON
M5A 3W8

290301

WINNING IN THE INDIAN MARKET
Understanding the Transformation of Consumer India

Rama Bijapurkar

John Wiley & Sons (Asia) Pte., Ltd

Copyright © 2008 John Wiley & Sons (Asia) Pte Ltd
Published in 2008 by John Wiley & Sons (Asia) Pte Ltd
2 Clementi Loop, #02-01, Singapore 129809
All rights reserved.

No part of this publication may be reproduced, stored in a retrieval system, or transmitted in any form or by any means, electronic, mechanical, photocopying, recording, scanning, or otherwise, except as expressly permitted by law, without either the prior written permission of the Publisher, or authorization through payment of the appropriate photocopy fee to the Copyright Clearance Center. Requests for permission should be addressed to the Publisher, John Wiley & Sons (Asia) Pte Ltd, 2 Clementi Loop, #02-01, Singapore 129809, tel: 65-6463-24000, fax: 65-6463-4605, E-mail: enquiry@wiley.com.sg.

This publication is designed to provide accurate and authoritative information with regard to the subject matter covered. It is sold with the understanding that the Publisher is not engaged in rendering professional services. If professional advice or other expert assistance is required, the services of a competent professional person should be sought.

Other Wiley Editorial Offices

John Wiley & Sons, Inc., 111 River Street, Hoboken, NJ 07030, USA

John Wiley & Sons Ltd, The Atrium, Southern Gate, Chichester PO19 BSQ, England

John Wiley & Sons (Canada) Ltd, 5353 Dundas Street West, Suite 400, Toronto, Ontario, Canada

John Wiley & Sons Australia Ltd, M9B 6HB, 42 McDougall Street, Milton, Queensland 4046, Australia

Wiley-VCH, Boschstrasse 12, D-69469 Weinheim, Germany

Library of Congress Cataloging-in-Publication Data:
978-0-470-82199-2

Wiley Bicentennial Logo: Richard J. Pacifico
Typeset in 11/13 point, Garamond by ChungKing Data Systems
Printed in Singapore by Saik Wah Press Pte Ltd
10 9 8 7 6 5 4 3 2 1

For My Parents

Contents

Foreword   ix

Preface   xiii

Prologue   xv

Acknowledgments   xix

Introduction   1

1. The Mixed Messages from Consumer India   9

2. Why Bother with Consumer India?   23

3. Understanding Consumer India's Demand Structure   43

4. Just How Much Purchasing Power Does Consumer India Actually Have?   65

5. Schizophrenic India   85

6. Demographic, Psychographic, and Social Determinants of Consumption   101

7. Understanding the Process of Change   123

8. Cultural Foundations of Consumer India's Behavior   139

9. Young India, Woman India: A Closer Look   157

10. Rural Consumer India   179

11. Understanding the "Bottom of the Pyramid" Consumer India   191

12. Winning in the Indian Market   203

Bibliography   217

Index   219

Foreword

———»·•·«———

Few topics elicit as much unwarranted optimism or skepticism as the Indian consumer. Yes, the optimists say that India represents a huge, untapped, middle-class market; a market critical for a global firm. Yes, the skeptics say that India is still too poor by global standards—most getting by on less than three dollars/day/person. So this market is not critical for us and won't be for a long time. At a high level of aggregation both are right. However, as Rama Bijapurkar so ably illustrates in this book, any broad generalization about the consumer market in India is bound to be wrong. The market is complex. It is evolving rapidly in ways that few could have predicted, even five years ago.

First, from a consumer-market perspective, *there is no single India.* There are the very rich. There are the information technology/ pharmaceutical employees who aspire to global standards and have high expectations. Then there is the aspiring middle class. The self-employed India. The agriculture-dependent subsistent farmers. The urban poor. The rural poor. They all have different approaches to consumption. They construct their consumption basket in distinctly different ways. So firms are better off in creating their "own India" that they want to serve.

Secondly, *gross domestic product (GDP) per capita is not a good measure of the capacity to consume; much worse, it can be misleading.* Rama goes into depth in articulating a methodology on how to understand the propensity and the capacity of Indian consumers to consume using primary income survey data. This approach provides a new and broad understanding of the size of the market, once we know *which India* to go after. She also includes in her analysis an understanding of the demographic (a young India), psychographic and social determinants of the market in India. I believe that the psychographic and social determinants may have as much relevance as expenditure data in segmenting and sizing the Indian market. Such an analysis, therefore may give clues to which India a company should target. The interesting aspect of the methodology that Rama provides here is that it is helpful in identifying and sizing the market.

Thirdly, *rural India is not poor; nor is it totally agriculture-dependent.* This is an important insight. Rural India represents 50% of India's GDP (but 70% of its people) and 50% of rural GDP is non-agricultural: it comes from the self-employed in all kinds of services. Although they are rural they are not very different in their aspirations from the urban consumers. They like fast-moving consumer goods (FMCG) products, jeans and cell phones. They have their own logic for consumption.

Rama's analysis provides a focus on new questions, not just for multinationals entering India but for established Indian firms as well. India is like a kaleidoscope. Every time you turn it, you get a different perspective—enticing, different, and "real". The basic requirement for understanding Consumer India is to recognize that there are no simple algorithms to segment it. It is the methodological nuances that allow one to get at the heart of this opportunity. Rama has done a great service by capturing in this book her vast experience for all: from CEOs to market and business-development professionals.

While India is undoubtedly complex, there still are some simple truths that managers have to accept. Indian consumers are *very value-conscious. They may be poor, but they are not backward.* Even in media-dark India, consumers are well informed. They are not overwhelmed by western brands. *And they can make a difference to the global positions of individual firms.* Consider cell phones. The Indian market is growing at the rate of six million new subscribers per month. The market cap of the top five carriers in India is more than US$75 billion. There is a message for multinationals here. If you can understand the Indian consumer and create appropriate business models (including products), the Indian market will surprise you. You cannot expect to flog old and tried products in India and expect to create a mass base. Rama's prescription is clear. India is not an easy market to understand and operate in. But for anyone who does understand it, the prize can be very substantial. India is an investment opportunity. Therefore, think like a venture capitalist. Invest in innovation.

Rama has developed a very strong case for learning India on its own terms before investing. This book is a critical read for anyone considering building a large franchise for themselves in India.

C K Prahalad
The Paul and Ruth McCracken Distinguished University
Professor of Corporate Strategy
Ross School of Business
The University of Michigan

Preface

Developing economies, with India and China at the forefront, are set to give the world economy its biggest boost in the coming years. These nations are regarded not only as the sourcing and production bases for the entire world, but also as booming market places. It is estimated that, over the next decade, almost a billion new consumers from these countries will enter the global marketplace as their household incomes reach the threshold at which they would generally begin to spend on discretionary goods.

India's growth is described by economists as a consumption driven one. Though the average incomes of Indians are still low, the middle class is expanding very fast and creating a vast market, ready to absorb appropriate products and services. Also, there is a marked shift in the income patterns of rural India, with people moving from farm-based businesses to more highly remunerative, non-farm businesses. Encouraged by these trends, global firms view India as a key market in which they want to expand their presence and create an impact. However, on several occasions, the strategies they have adopted—the textbook ones or the ones they had followed in the developed markets—have been unsuccessful.

It is always possible to find facts and trends to justify a particular hypothesis on consumer profiles and behavior, and then use it, often wrongly, as the basis for a new argument. I find this very true in the current context of India. The global firms have steadfastly accepted the marketing and consumer behavior axioms that had worked in the developed markets. They use data to justify these axioms and try to replicate them in India. In doing so, quite often, they assume that the India of today is akin to a developed country at its early stages of development. Bereft of proper consumer insights, the strategies they develop don't yield positive results.

This book describes the Indian market as a collection of people with different expectations. It urges the development of a "made for India" customized strategy, by making the case that history is not repeating itself, that never before has the world seen such a consumer market, that we need to create new business models to win and that merely transplanting the old, tried-and-tested strategies does not work. Rama notes that the right question marketers should ask is not "what is the size of market that India offers for my global strategy?" But rather "what should be my local, customized strategy for the Indian market?"

Rama takes the reader at a brisk pace through the consumer perceptions, behavior, and wants, across several regions within India, leavened by interesting examples and anecdotes. The author has collected a wealth of material based on extensive research supported by relevant data and facts, and has presented them in a very cogent form. For example, Rama notes that the number of middle income households in rural India is around 27 million, while the corresponding number in urban India is just a bit higher at 29 million. Every chapter offers a vivid image or telling detail that captures the intricacies of the Indian market, and its consumer profiles and behaviors. The reader not only gets a potent sense of this market but also gets insights on how to approach it strategically.

All in all, this book is an engaging read that presents the socio-cultural perspective of the Indian market, and illustrates how firms should understand the heterogeneity of the market and develop their winning strategies accordingly. Thought provoking and topical, it will be of great value to a wide spectrum of people, most importantly to those global firms and their senior management who are looking for credible insights and data to create these winning strategies. It will also be of immense help to those management students and academic researchers who are interested in understanding the Indian consumer market.

N. R. Narayana Murthy
Chairman and Chief Mentor
Infosys Technologies Ltd., Bangalore

Prologue

———⟫◦⟪———

This book is the culmination of innumerable panel discussions, powerpoint presentations, and speeches that I have made around the world on the possibilities, perils, and paradoxes of the Indian market and the Indian consumer. The audiences included such diverse groups as the Young Presidents Organization (YPO), the British Business Group, the Alfred Herrhausen Society for international dialogue, students from leading American and European business schools, corporate business leaders and emerging market strategy teams from large global companies preparing for the new world, the Council for Foreign Relations, the Fortune 500 power women's forum, the advertising agencies association in France, board members of the Fletcher School of Law and Diplomacy, and, of course, lots and lots of fund managers, private equity investors and investment bankers from Mumbai to the Bahamas. Some totally agreed with what I had to say, some violently disagreed, some were blown away, quite a few were underwhelmed. But they always listened with a deep level of interest and engagement, remarking that what was new and different was the 360-degree view of the Indian market through the lens of consumers and people, and that it made them think differently about India, in the context of their own work. With such encouragement, I felt that this book could be of interest to a wider audience, especially at a time when India is attracting more and more attention in the world, and confusing more and more people with her oddities and contradictions.

My own consulting experience of the past decade has been very rich and rewarding in terms of lessons that it has taught me about Consumer India and what it takes to develop winning strategies for it. It has enabled me to examine strategic choices confronting a wide range of business contexts, sectors, company types and nationalities, and distill universal issues related to developing customer-centric business strategy for the new world. It has also come with its share of struggle —persuading Indian companies to become more customer-centric in their battle for dreams and markets, and persuading multinational companies (MNCs) to be more open to adopting a "made for India" business approach has not been easy.

I also confess that what goaded me to write this book was my near total disagreement with popular methods used by consulting firms and business analysts to evaluate the Indian market opportunity. Developed almost entirely using supply-side data, they relied heavily on analogies of how other markets had evolved in the past, assuming unquestioningly that a uniform looking world was inevitable and that there was only one model of evolution for the entire world. I, on the other hand, believed that the top line of a P&L statement was about consumer choices, not supply-side economics, and that analogies of the kind being used did not make much sense. I also believed that emerging markets are not like developed markets were in their infancy and that they would pursue a path of their own, as they got more prosperous. Furthermore, I did not agree with their theories about the magic number of per-capita income above which consumption in a country was supposed to "take off," when in fact, with low-priced innovations, it had already taken off at far lower income levels. I was puzzled by their analyses of how, if the per-capita consumption of a widget in the US or Brazil was 100, and in India it was 10, then the gap of 90 represented a huge opportunity waiting to happen. I thought that maybe Indian consumers will never use 100 units per capita of *this* widget because of environmental or cultural factors, or because they might have leap frogged to a more modern widget and have skipped this stage altogether.

The data and insights for this book have been drawn from a variety of sources—from highly formal survey research, lots of anecdotal and experiential consumer stories from the field, and the work of social scientists. The last source was particularly difficult to find, because in India, the world of social science and the world of business are totally separate and there are very few people and institutions that bridge the two. The world of economics was pretty challenging too, for me. During the first fifteen years of my working life, there was never any real need to understand macroeconomics in order to understand consumer markets since we lived in a closed and insulated economy. In a tranquil pond, there are no unpredictable storms caused by global trade or economic policy. I have often, this past decade, wished that there were a formal and well-established discipline called *macro-consumer,* that I could have drawn ideas and inspiration from. Akin in scale, scope, and ubiquity to macroeconomics, it would focus on the combined effects of macroeconomics, social development, politics, policy, cultural changes, and so on, in shaping consumer markets at a national level or regional level.

It is from this perspective that *Winning in the Indian Market* has been written—to provide a macro-consumer view of the changing Consumer India, for use as an input into developing winning "made for India" business strategy.

Acknowledgments

My thinking on Consumer India has evolved over the past decade, contributed to, in no small measure, by a whole host of people who have been fellow travelers on this road to discovery and clarity and who have generously shared their work and their thoughts. Consequently, the people that I need to acknowledge are sadly too numerous to individually name here. There are some, however, who I must specifically mention.

The biggest influence on my thinking has come from Professor C K Prahalad, my professor at Indian Institute of Management (IIM), Ahmedabad, who has remained my teacher ever since, through his inspirational work and the intellectual energy that he radiates.

Mr. S L Rao, a former director general of the National Council of Applied Economic Research (NCAER) was the first person to do serious macro-consumer research on Consumer India and put it in the public domain. He showed me what the territory of this could be, and has always been a thoughtful and constructive critic.

Dr. Rakesh Mohan (presently deputy governor of the Reserve Bank of India, and earlier, director general of NCAER) wrote to me when I published, with trepidation, my first big article on Consumer India based on NCAER data and his "cold call," with warm praise, gave me the confidence I needed to take larger steps on this journey. Since then, he has been a very helpful thought and discussion partner, patiently explaining the nuances of income distribution through squiggly graphs drawn on scraps of paper, and answering endless economics questions with simplicity and clarity.

While on the subject of economists, my first big revelation about the changing composition of rural India's gross domestic product (GDP) came from work that Subir Gokarn (chief economist, Credit Rating Information Services of India Limited (CRISIL)) and I did for Mahindra and Mahindra.

Subsequently, I worked further on this with Omkar Goswami and his team at CERG Advisory Pte Ltd, and I learnt a lot, even as we gamely traded economist and consultant jokes.

Laveesh Bhandari (founder, Indicus Analytics) helped me achieve a long-standing desire of linking survey income data to GDP by coming up with a conceptually elegant and wonderful piece of analysis that we wrote up in an joint article titled *Solving the Income Data Puzzle*.

Ashok Das (managing director, Hansa Research Group), in addition to being a special, longtime buddy, has been a very important research partner. He has always provided just the right kind of data to explore any hypothesis I might have, and he has also come up with several novel constructs and analyses to push my thinking further. His footprint is all over the chapter on purchasing power.

Santosh Desai (now managing director of Future Brands, formerly president of McCann Erickson) has added a significant dimension to my understanding of changing consumer values and attitudes and has been quoted frequently in this book.

And a special thank you to Arun Adhikari (presently chairman Nippon Lever, formerly director, Hindustan Lever) for his thoughtful and deep insights, over ten years, into whatever issue I was grappling with and needed help to think through.

I really owe Mythili Bhusnurmath, a longtime editor of my *Economic Times* editorial page column, for making sure that I captured my thoughts regularly over the years.

Also a big thank you to Tony Joseph and Indrajit Gupta (formerly with *Business World*), for allowing me to write cover stories on Consumer India, and helping me deliver work that got noticed and acclaimed.

Getting this book out has been quite a torturous process for me; but I suspect that it might have been more torturous for my many editors who worked hard to beat my manuscript into something fit to be published as a book. Thank you Nick and Janis at Wiley, and thank you Sharad Panse for going well beyond the call of duty and working so closely with me to produce something that was all mine in tone, yet so much better in the way it read.

And last but not least, I want to acknowledge those near and dear who have been there with me through the travails of writing this book. Lucy Sutari, at my office, kept track of every little detail of every part of the book, and never let me know even once, just how disorganized I was. Aparna, my daughter, gave me the best advice I got in the context of this book: "Mom, please stop trying to write the mother of all books. Just get on with it and write *a* book please." Ashoke, my husband, has lived through the house being invaded by untidy stacks of paper, and never once said anything rude when I ceaselessly moaned and groaned about "the damned book," as if it were his fault that I had to do it! My mother has been terrific—she sympathized when I needed sympathy, goaded me when I needed goading, and kicked butt when I was drowning in self pity as I faced yet another stack of editorial queries. The book started getting written at her dining table in Hyderabad, and finally got finished at my dining table in Mumbai, a year later. But she was there throughout it all for me.

Introduction

MADE FOR INDIA
The Context of Consumer India

India is undeniably an important future growth market of the world. It is large (it has the fourth-largest gross domestic product (GDP) in the world in purchasing power parity or PPP terms), it is young (it has 450 million people below the age of 21), and it is just beginning its consumption journey.

In 1991, India made a 180-degree turn in its economic ideology and started the process of economic liberalization. Until then, its consumer markets had been governed by the socialistic ideology of Jawaharlal Nehru, its first prime minister. There was a very strong focus on self-reliance and local production and a high degree of protection for small-scale producers. These ideas were partly the legacy of Mahatma Gandhi. During India's freedom movement, Gandhi had positioned British mill-made cloth as a symbol of colonial oppression, calling upon all self-respecting Indians to boycott it and wear Indian-made homespun or *khadi* fabric instead.

Nehru's socialistic model continued even after his death in 1964. Indeed, it reached its zenith in the days of his daughter Indira Gandhi, who was India's prime minister for 16 years in two spells, from 1966 to 1977 and then again from early 1980 to late 1984. She nationalized banks and with her slogan *garibi hatao* ("banish poverty"), she went to war against the rich. The nationalization of banks was one of the many measures she took to spread the tentacles of state ownership deep and wide through the economy.

Thus, until 1991, when India began its journey towards market capitalism, it was the government that was in charge of business. It was the government that largely decided who produced how much of what, quite unmindful of either the sense of business economics or the sensibilities of consumers. Prices of most items were so high that hardly anyone could afford to buy them and the largest components of those prices were taxes or import duties. Taxes were very high on whatever the government decided were luxury items, be it shoes, shampoos, light bulbs, and lipsticks, or air conditioners and branded apparel.

Television had arrived in India—in Delhi—as early as 1959. Its expansion, however, began only in 1972; but even in 1991, there were only two state-run channels. Very stringent currency regulations inhibited most people from traveling abroad. There were severe restrictions on the operations of multinational companies (MNCs) in the country and, as a consequence, most decided against it. So global brands were few and far between in India. To top it all, while agricultural income was tax-free in the rural hinterland, where people did not have much to buy, the urban Indian paid taxes upwards of 75%. There was an enormous and flourishing black economy, but this wealth could not be spent freely on anything conspicuous for fear of attracting the attention of the taxman.

High Hopes and Belied Expectations

The socialistic model failed miserably. GDP growth crawled for the first 35 years after Independence and the per-capita income was very low. The latter began to inch up a little in the mid-1980s when Rajiv Gandhi succeeded Indira Gandhi as prime minister and took a few faltering steps towards economic liberalization, but it was only in 1991 that an unprecedented financial and balance-of-payments crisis forced the Indian government to open up the Indian economy and initiate the process of liberalization and economic reforms.

Since then, there has been a jump in the GDP growth rate and a spurt in national income. In place of just two government-owned channels, there are now over 100 television channels, offered at throwaway prices, throughout the country, by private cable operators via a ubiquitous, low-cost distribution network. Consumer confidence and aspirations have also been upbeat ever since 1991, as consumers have been seeing visible and tangible improvements in their lives with each passing year.

That is the scenario on the consumer side. On the supply side, first and foremost, there have been drastic cuts in taxes and import duties. De-licensing has led to competition and a supply-side renaissance has occurred in category after category, at an amazing speed. There is now a lot more to buy, it is cheaper—and what's more—it is better than ever before!

The potential of a market of over a billion people, residing in the world's fourth-largest economy (in PPP terms) and consistently growing, should be the end of this story. "Consumer India integrates with the global consumer-market scene and is enthusiastically welcomed as a new source of growth by global corporations, smoothly rolling out their global strategies, duly adjusted for cultural sensitivity" is how the story ought to conclude.

Unfortunately, it doesn't. The conclusion actually reads something like this: "Consumer India has been the source of belied expectations and frustrating resistance to conventional global offerings. Never before has any market been so rebellious about what it will embrace and what it will not. Nokia wins. Coca-Cola and Pepsi struggle. Honda wins. Mercedes struggles. LG and Samsung walk away with the market. GE appliances don't. Levi's lags behind expectations. Nike limps along. Diageo does not make a big splash, Star TV has had many rethinks, MTV localizes, Kellogg's still struggles. Heinz ketchup doesn't catch on. Beware! Consumer India offers as much pain as gain and there will be no walkover for global big brands that don't think through their India strategy from the ground upwards."

Lessons Learnt

Over the past decade and a half, we have learnt many valuable lessons from watching new multinational entrants negotiating the slippery turf of Consumer India. Anyone aspiring to embark on this journey would be well advised not to lose sight of them.

The Nature of Emerging Market Economies is Fundamentally Different: Emerging market economies are large in their total size but small in terms of per-capita income, India being a prime example. And that is what makes all the global received wisdom, on price-performance points and margin-volume equations, ineffective in such markets. As far as India is concerned, a fundamental rethink around appropriate "made for India" propositions is needed, which must replace the conventional wisdom of "global standard" benefits at "global equivalent" prices.

In fact, the two interesting questions to think about, given the demographic and economic growth characteristics of India and China, are, "What exactly do we mean when we say *global standards*?"; and "Where is the *global* center of gravity going to be?"

Emerging Markets Need Not Be Virgin Markets:

• *Range of offerings available:* Even in an emerging market like India, there can already exist an array of home-grown options in many categories, which can offer incredibly tough competition to new entrants. Such options can be several and diverse, ranging from traditional solutions to hybrid blends of the traditional and the modern, as well as Indianized versions of international options—all available at several price-performance points.

One good example of this is the retailing environment in India. Street markets of every level of sophistication coexist here. There are the organized Mumbai pavement shops that locals refer to as "Fashion Street." They sell the "export surplus" stocks of the very latest fashions of big, international brands which, thanks to outsourcing, are now manufactured in India. They also sell jeans that are manufactured in India, but which are the exact replicas of the latest styles from Bangkok. Then, there are the mom-and-pop shops or stores ranging from the high-end, high-service shops to the "holes in the wall" existing alongside various shades and grades of local supermarkets and hypermarkets.

This range of competition proves to be a very challenging environment for global retailers, who always end up with a value disadvantage against existing options. And since most Indians shop at all options, the question "Why buy me?" becomes even more challenging for a global retailer to answer.

• *Sophisticated distribution and brands:* Until 1991, India was certainly not a market that had an ethos of modern consumerism as we know it the world over. Nevertheless, within the framework of the numerous constraints, business practices were quite modern and Indian consumers were exposed to a wide, deep and efficient distribution system comprising a network of over five million (and still growing) small retailers that dotted the country (and still do). Robust and sophisticated Indian brands were built, which had to compensate for the primitive products they represented. Advertising was therefore often the hero of the brand-building process and was very creative. The Indian market-research and advertising industry was extremely well-developed even by acknowledged international benchmarks. All this actually raised the bar for the new entrants into India.

The picture at the time of liberalization, therefore, was of a deeply inhibitive regulatory framework that repressed and suppressed all forms of consumption and product innovation, but within which, paradoxically, a sophisticated sales and marketing system existed and operated, doing its best to innovate, develop and tease out whatever consumption it could from the market; a market that was, still is, and will always be, mind-boggling in its linguistic, cultural and income diversity.

As I often explain to overseas business folks, Consumer India is like an experienced hire in an organization, while Consumer China is like a fresh hire. An experienced hire is more difficult to manage and mold, because he already has a set way of doing things that works pretty well and, therefore, needs a lot of convincing (by persuasion or clout) to adopt your ways of thinking or doing things. A fresh hire, on the other hand, has a clean slate as far as past experiences are concerned; at any rate, his past experiences are fairly primitive and, hence, persuading him to adopt your ways is comparatively easy.

Not only China, but also Russia or, for that matter, even most countries of Southeast Asia—when they were emerging—have been like new hires.

Today's Emerging Markets—Such as India—are Not What the Developed Markets Were in Their Infancy: Hence, the assumption that Indian consumers today are like American consumers were 20 years ago is deeply flawed. Consumers exist in real time and are confronted by all the forces of today, not yesterday. Moreover, they are products of their own unique consumer history and culture.

Let me illustrate this with an example. Indian consumers have not embraced the culture of drinking cola as many other emerging markets have. To begin with, water holds a pre-eminent place in Indian food and drink. Water is loaded with cultural meanings and is seen to be the elixir of life. Offering water to a stranger in the middle of the summer is the epitome of hospitality and kindness. Further, there is already a well-developed "in-home" beverage market of tea and coffee that coexists with a network of out-of-home, bottled-water distribution, as well as tea and coffee bars. Added to this is the fact that American popular culture, of which cola is a prominent symbol, has not had the same influence in this region as it has, say, in the Philippines. At the same time, all the discourse around the world on health concerns with colas is being transmitted in real time to consumers in India, as much as to consumers anywhere else. So the Indian consumer also knows that there is a move to ban colas in American schools.

If we keep this background in mind, it becomes rather obvious that neither Coca-Cola's current, global strategy nor its age-old, market-penetration strategy cannot win in India. The strategy necessarily has to be different, as cola companies are now discovering.

So would it be with Walt Disney, who must understand that the child of today's India has no parallel elsewhere. This child represents a poor country's Internet generation, its aspirations running riot in a milieu of very scarce opportunities: a situation that has not existed anywhere else, ever before.

To take another example, Intel will have to stop worrying about when personal computer (PC) penetration in India will hit the same levels as in developed markets—it will need to fight in an India revolutionized by cell phones, which are getting far more deeply entrenched than PCs in a much shorter span of time.

Countries Change Around Their DNA: And the Indian DNA is about continuity with change; it is about "THIS *as well as* THAT"; about cobbling together clever and low-cost solutions that are ingenious combinations and adaptations of products available in the market. As I often say, our faith in astrology does not decrease as a result of the rising levels of our scientific education; rather, as a consequence, we move effortlessly to computerized horoscope casting!

Products and services that understand all this, win. Those that don't are bewildered about why consumers process value the way they do and give a "thumbs down" signal to a product that has been successful elsewhere in the world.

Made for India

It is now fairly clear to all Consumer India watchers, that what we have here is a tricky and complex market. It demands strategic complexity and customization way beyond its current worth. The right question to ask here is not "What is the size of market that India offers for my global strategy?", but, rather, "What should be my local, customized strategy for the Indian market?"

As C K Prahalad says in a brilliant article in *Harvard Business Review*[1]: "While it is true that MNCs will change emerging markets forever, the reverse is also true. Many corporations are beginning to see that the opportunity that big, emerging markets represent, will demand a new way of thinking…requiring more than developing cultural sensitivity."

He goes on to urge MNCs to "rethink price-performance equations, rethink the cost of market building". I would add, rethink business definition and business models.

The Indian experience so far makes it pretty obvious that only those companies that leverage their competencies for creating businesses tailor-made for India are likely to win in India and benefit from its inevitable growth, rather than those who mechanically transplant their best-practice strategies from other markets.

As C K Prahalad says, it is not about "best practice." It's about "next practice."

In order to create this "made for India", "next practice" strategy which carefully balances the compulsions of global economics and the comfort of the tried and tested best practices with what is needed to unlock the potential of this distinctive market, a deep understanding of the market is absolutely essential. And the imperative is to gain this deep understanding through the discipline of shaping business strategy, not merely *adapting* existing marketing policies and programs that may be functioning, and functioning well, elsewhere.

That's what this book attempts to do, by presenting an in-depth analysis of what Consumer India is all about and of the resultant complications for business-market strategy.

Most investors and new entrants into India have a list of FAQs such as:

- Why bother with India when I have China?
- Is there enough evidence that India can be a consumption powerhouse?
- Tell us about the Indian middle class?
- What is the exact purchasing power of the market? Is there really a fortune at the bottom of the pyramid?
- Why are demand patterns so capricious?
- Is rural India a sophisticated or a primitive market?

This book addresses all these and more.

It looks at Consumer India through multiple lenses, and presents a zero base, consumer-centric view of India's demand structure and its drivers, the demographic, cultural and social trends, and the strategic themes and approaches that corporations must think about when addressing Consumer India, so that they may develop their own mental models of it.

ENDNOTE

[1] Prahalad, C. K. and Lieberthal, Kenneth, *Harvard Business Review* article reference R0308G, "The End of Corporate-Imperialism," originally published 1998, republished August 2003.

1

The Mixed Messages from Consumer India

THE STRATEGIC CHALLENGES OF CONSUMER INDIA

Global businesses haven't quite been able to make up their minds about the opportunity offered by the Indian market and what their strategy for it should be. That is understandable given the many mixed messages that Consumer India has been sending out.

Ever since India opened up its markets in 1991, Consumer India has been the source of a fair amount of heartache and headache even for the most seasoned global businesses, including multinational companies (MNCs). Almost all early entrants into the market, ranging from Coca-Cola, Kellogg's, and Seagram to Reebok and Sony to Mercedes–Benz and Booz Allen Hamilton, soon found their business expectations totally belied. So did a host of companies in the specialty chemicals, computers, confectionery, and cosmetics businesses, to name just a few. The conclusion was the same in each case, even if the specifics of the story were slightly different—namely, that the much touted, supposedly vibrant, hungry and desperate-to-consume, Indian market, the sleeping beauty just waiting to be awakened by the kiss of the multinational prince, was more mythology than reality.

Yet now, 15 years later in 2006, slow and steady economic growth has created the world's fourth-largest economy, having just under 6% of the, global gross domestic product (GDP) (on a purchasing power parity (PPP) basis). If you are a PPP non-believer, then, in US-dollar terms, India is today the eighth-largest economy in the world. Nearly 40% of its population, of over a billion people, is below the age of 21, a heartening statistic in an otherwise ageing world and one that would warm the cockles of all marketers' hearts. However, the fact remains that in per-capita income terms, the Indian market ranks 145th in the world.

The fact also remains that Consumer India lives in many centuries at the same time, and at many levels of affluence.

This paradox comes into sharp focus in the media coverage that India gets. For instance, take the period between, say, March and July 2006 and look at the montage of mixed messages put out by foreign and Indian media on India's future. *The Economist* did a cover story with a provocative editorial titled "Can India Fly?" and concluded, "…it has taken off at last. Only with further reform can it spread its wings and soar." It went on to state that such reform did not look like it was going to happen in a hurry. It elaborated: "India has been in fashion before, only to disappoint foreign and local companies alike. Despite its huge potential market…despite its wealth of English speakers…despite its vaunted 15-year-old reforms…"

Newsweek had a cover story called "The New India" where it examined the question "Is Asia's other powerhouse ready for its moment under the sun?" The article was brutally candid when it said that most people would find it hard to take India seriously despite all the threats to American jobs from the outsourcing by American companies to Indian IT companies. It went on to say: "Anyone who has actually been to India will probably be puzzled." "India," he or she will say, "with its dilapidated airports, crumbling roads, vast slums and impoverished villages? We are talking about that India?"

The article further states, however, that "the country might have several Silicon Valleys, but it also has three Nigerias within it, more than 300 million people living on less than a dollar a day," but concludes with a hugely positive pat on the back for the enterprising, energized, Indian spirit because of which "there is change that can be felt even in the slums."

During the same period, two consecutive cover stories in India's largest business weekly, *Business World*, made one wonder whether it was the same country that was being talked about. The first story was about the race that Indian pharmaceutical companies were running with their counterparts in the developed world to discover a new molecule, but at a fraction of the costs that the latter were incurring.

The second story asked the spine-chilling question: "*Will the Indian economy crash?*"

It is little wonder, then, that even as interest in India grows, skepticism about whether or not India will deliver the promised future remains, a fact that never fails to escape anyone who has been on a road show overseas to market India as an investment destination. An Indian diplomat posted in London summed up this "guilty until proven innocent" attitude towards India succinctly. He and I were on a panel at an India conference organized by the London Business School. The conference hall was in the building next door, the Royal College of Obstetricians and Gynaecologists. The diplomat, tongue firmly in check, informed his audience that it was ironic that the India conference was being held at that venue, as India had been shouting from the rooftops for the past few years that she was pregnant (with economic possibility) and about to deliver a new and attractive, long-term-growth market. But the world has mostly looked on impassively and said, "Please bring us more evidence that this is not a false pregnancy and that you are capable of delivering a fully-formed baby that will grow to be a healthy adult."

It is against this backdrop of mixed messages that businesses need to answer the question: "Just how much business interest and what kind of strategy does a market like this really deserve?"

STRATEGIC PERSPECTIVES ON INDIA ARE CHANGING, BUT STILL CONFUSED

The cautious companies (or are they the laggards?) which aren't here yet are reluctantly beginning to think that since India appears to be here to stay and set to grow on the world's economic and political stage, the Indian market merits a deeper investigation. Over and above the usual questions discussed earlier, they also grapple with some more fundamental questions: "Is India a 'nice to have in the portfolio' market, or a 'must have' market without which the future competitiveness of my businesses will be compromised?"; "Is the Indian market really ready for me, or should I wait till it gets more sophisticated, rich and ready to respond to my global strategy?"

Several global businesses are already here with varying degrees of strategic and resource commitment. They are beginning to realize that in order to fully exploit the demographics and the GDP of the Indian market, they need to do much more. Many of them have been cautious about investing in their businesses, which they operate with a global or a pan-regional strategy. In fact, they have been waiting for the turning point—when the market would evolve into something more recognizable and similar to the developed markets with which they are familiar. However, many of them now feel that the future is taking unexpected twists and turns and arriving at some place other than where it was supposed to. The turning point may, therefore, have to come for their strategy and not for the market!

This rather rare flash of realization has been further driven home by the transformational ideas emerging in business thinking during the past five years: the notion of the BRIC (Brazil, Russia, India, China) markets; the concept of the "fortune at the bottom of the pyramid"; the whole discourse around "disruptive innovation"; offshoring and so on. All this has helped deepen the thought that maybe the question to ask of the Indian market is not "When will the Indian market be ready for my global best-practice strategy?" but, rather, "When will I be ready to create the next-practice strategy for the Indian market?"

It is therefore not surprising that we now see a flurry of emerging market-strategy teams in Fortune 500 boardrooms, more and more board and leadership group meetings held in India and the return of some of the more high-profile, Indian diaspora to work in India. Yet, on the other hand, it is also not surprising that the state of India's airports, the ubiquitous stray buffalo in the middle of a main street in Delhi or Mumbai, the profusion of mom-and-pop shops cheek by jowl with glass-encased malls, the world-class PowerPoint presentations from Indians interrupted by other-worldly power cuts, make them all wonder whether this market would ever merit more than a token presence!

THE CONSUMER DEMAND JOURNEY: 1991 TO DATE

So has India been crying wolf? Is there really a market waiting to happen? In all fairness, some of the world's skepticism is well founded. The roller-coaster nature of Consumer India's progress is best described by Professor S L Rao, an economist and former Director General of the National Council for Applied Economic Research. He uses a delightfully accurate analogy and says that it is "like the walk of a drunken man. You know he will get home eventually, but it will be two steps forward, two steps sideways, one step backwards."

As a result, over all these years, there have been several wrong judgments and major disappointments, as well as some pleasant surprises, but not enough understanding of the pattern of this apparently random progress. It is therefore useful, with the benefit of hindsight, to review Consumer India's demand story since 1991. It may perhaps help in putting some past bogeys to rest, as well as in providing a realistic understanding of the future.

The First Few Years of Hyped Expectation: When India first started marketing itself as an investment destination in the early 1990s, soon after the liberalization of the economy began, it had the unenviable task of combating the dominant image the world had of it—that of a country of snake charmers, temple elephants, the Taj Mahal, and millions of people living in poverty. Needless to say, India's chief competitor in attracting foreign direct investment was China, with its image of a communist superpower now determinedly and efficiently turning capitalist. If one image was exaggerated in its backwardness, the other was exaggerated in its forwardness! Although the size of its economy was a mediocre US$100 billion and its per-capita income was abysmal at less than US$10 per month, India portrayed itself as an emerging, consumer-market powerhouse, an enormous juggernaut marching towards consumerism, but did not bother to put a timeframe on when this would really happen.

The Early Demand Boom: The market growth in the first five years after liberalization was phenomenal and, in retrospect, a red herring. The growth rates for practically every product on offer, from cars to shampoos, were explosive: 20–30% volume growth and 15–20% value growth were seen as the new "Hindu rate of growth" (the Indian equivalent of the golfing term, "par for the course") for consumer markets, in an unshackled economy that had, at last, unconstrained supply.

Market analysts and business strategists extrapolated these early growth rates into the future and the myth of the "Great Indian Middle Class" was born. Supposedly numbering 250–300 million consumers, it was perceived to be a homogeneous, consumer juggernaut rolling on towards mega-consumerism, delivering double-digit growth in all categories for many years to come.

The Subsequent Demand Stagnation: Based on this view of the market, the mid-1990s saw large-capacity investments and grand business plans. The only trouble was that this large and mean consumption machine failed to materialize. The late 1990s saw disappointment and frustration made worse by monsoon seasons with below-average rainfall leading to poor crops and retarded rural demand. The market did not yield the expected or predicted results. Not surprisingly, the first among the new entrants who had set up shop in India went through a lot of turmoil. Over the first decade, Coca-Cola ran up losses far exceeding its equity investment of US$268 million, presumably incurred in their effort to get to an equivalent top line. Procter & Gamble reduced the number of stockkeeping units it offered, cut its distribution width and depth, and shrank in order to be beautiful and profitable. Even the consulting firms had their share of trouble. Booz Allen closed shop, though McKinsey hung in there and waited for the market to mature—and maybe is still waiting! Despite many of the new MNC entrants declaring that they were in the Indian market for the long haul and would do whatever it took for long-term market development, CEOs' heads rolled, business cases were furiously reviewed, and the Indian market got a bad reputation for being fickle and for being more hype than reality.

Ironically, even in China the expected volumes and profits did not come in. But given its higher income levels and higher GDP growth rate, with all the visible signs of westernized development, the future seemed more real and more comprehensible there.

The Lessons Learnt

The Dangerous Delusion of Pent-Up Demand: The boom-extrapolation-stagnation cycle has since been repeated many times. It is now clear that there is always an initial starburst of demand as a result of a confluence of one-time events or phenomena, such as the release of pent-up demand from the rich who always had the money and the desire but had nothing much to buy; a television category promotion boom, where for the first time the category is being highlighted on the consumer radar screen; a distribution boom that brings the sought products and services within easy reach; a lowering of a price point with the launch of the miniature pack (the sachet) strategy or installment schemes that decrease the unit price and make a range of products affordable to more people.

The Rock Table: After mopping up pockets of pent-up demand or just-below-the-surface demand, the market always hits a rock table. To continue the growth trajectory, what is needed is not a mop but actually a powerful drill fashioned from a good market strategy; and over time the next round of growth begins. At this stage, what makes more sense is searching for weak areas of weathered rock in the rock table, rather than flogging the sales team with targets based on historical growth.

Zigzag Economic Growth Gives Zigzag Consumer Market Growth: Given the large number of variables, from politics and geopolitics to meteorology, each of which has some differential impact on the many sub-economies that make up its economy, India's exact economic growth cannot be taken for granted. Between 1994–95 and 1996–97, the real GDP growth ranged from 7.3% to 7.8%, breaking the "under 6%" jinx of many years before it. However, the folly was to assume that it would continue that way. In 1997–98, GDP grew at just 4.8% in real terms, and while in the next two years it was at 6.5% and 6.1% respectively, it again plummeted to 4.4% in 2000–01, went up to 5.8% the next year and crashed to 4% in the following year. In 2003–04 it was 8.2%, in 2004–05 it was 6%, and from the following year on, it has been at 8% and beyond.

Income Growth Does Not Always Keep Pace With Supply-Side Renaissance: Despite several years of good economic growth, there was a very important trouble-making factor that most of us watching the market had somehow overlooked. With many new product categories entering the market for the first time, there was an explosion on the supply side. Added to this were the many supply-side revolutions in quality, price and distribution, as well as the sudden easy availability of consumer finance. Therefore, the number of things that consumers could buy increased exponentially, while their income did not. As a result, "category-collide" or inter-category competition became very strong. The choice now was between paying for a cell phone for yourself and paying for high-quality shampoo and ketchup for the family. It was a real one.

The fast-moving consumer goods (FMCG) business, for example, was hit hard by this. As one small-town consumer told us, since a refrigerator in one's home or a second-hand car for one's family were such visible signs of status and indulgence, why would one want to use an expensive brand of shampoo that promised the same? Further, with the rise in consumer credit, many households had committed the bulk of their future income to pay for homes and consumer durables that they had acquired; and the residual money available had to be stretched to run the home and handle the "revenue" expenditure. So began the paradox of increasing consumer income and sophistication, but, at the same time, consumers adopting the practice of "down-trading" (shifting to a lower price performance point brand) in several categories. In the late 1990s and early 2000s, in the midst of all this churn, the theory of a huge, homogeneous mass market, made up of the "Great Indian Middle Class," which would be a tireless engine of growth, was officially buried. Companies resigned themselves to very slow top-line growth and focused on the middle line of their P&L— operational performance improvement and financial restructuring—in order to shore up their bottom line.

But Consumer India has always been pretty tricky to second guess. Not only has the real GDP grown at a spanking pace since 2003–04 (8.5%, 6.9%, and 7.5% respectively in succeeding years), and with it the national income, but by 2005, a lot of consumption-friendly little changes were also taking place in Consumer India. Each change, when viewed in isolation, could easily be rejected as not being particularly significant. But taken together, they have provided a critical mass of overall change and created a deep and distinctive consumer market: a market that now has more cell phones than bank accounts, more color televisions than toilets. And this is a market whose potential and desire to consume have perhaps moved way ahead of marketers' and investors' mental models of it. The number of cars has exploded faster than the roads to drive them on, airports cannot cope with the sharp increase in the number of flights and passengers, restaurants and movie theaters are full, and recovering from bypass surgery is now a fairly common middle-class pastime.

Prognosis

Good News: Consumer India is a market that has evolved into an economy that has increased its average per-capita income more than five times since 1991 and more than doubled it in the eight years from 1997 to 2005, when the market was written off as a mirage of hype and hope. Therefore, it is a market that is very high on consumer aspiration and consumer confidence, which is about believing that it's all right to spend and make merry today because tomorrow will definitely be better than today! So, are happy times here again, once marketers scramble and catch up with the consumers who have moved way ahead of them? Almost, but not quite!

Bad News: **DANGER! DIVERSION! ROAD UNDER REPAIR!** It is often said of the Indian cricket team that they are experts in snatching defeat from the jaws of victory. They throw away a winning position, paint themselves into a corner, and end up struggling with a "win some–lose some" nail-biting finish. So too, it would seem, with the Indian market.

Trouble seems to be looming ahead and a supply and infrastructure breakdown may dampen consumption. If the demand slowdown of the 1990s was about too much supply and not enough demand, the demand slowdown that may happen now is too much demand, with the groaning infrastructure yielding poor-quality supply. Calls are dropped as cell phones outstrip network capacity; flying is a nightmare because of air-traffic delays and small airports, so why bother to pay more for business class and arrive in terrible shape anyway; and a long, long line of cars snakes along a very slow path into the mall parking lots, resulting in irritated shoppers in terrible moods—which, as any retailer will tell you, is bad for business.

Even at the top end of pricing, there are not enough hangars for private planes, few as they may be given the size of the population; no jetties for the private yachts that lie anchored off the Gateway of India in Mumbai; and no five-star hotel rooms to be had for love or money in the big cities. Real-estate prices climb dangerously as there is not enough high-quality supply of apartments in the market; the stock market is forever yo-yoing; and investor confidence is becoming adversely affected by left-leaning, anti-free-market coalition politics.

Add to this list of woes the rising petrol prices and rising interest rates affecting consumer credit, and you have a slowing down, temporarily at least, of demand growth.

Yet, when the supply constraints ease and the politics settle down, there will be a return to high-consumption growth rates again. It seems quite clear that once again, Consumer India will outsmart its analysts.

It is a bit like those "good news–bad news" game shows on television that go a bit like this: "Contestant Bernice, we are happy to inform you that you are the winner of the grand prize in this spelling bee contest. The good news, Bernice, is that you get two first-class tickets to Rome—Rome, USA, that is. However, the tickets come to you in the pocket of a beautiful mink coat, here it is—the coat, by the way, is 100% fake mink…" Unable to take the pressure of this roller-coaster ride, contestant Bernice faints, only to be revived and then told that "the prize also comprised a million-dollar check placed in the other pocket of the coat. However, the rules of the contest say that in order to get all this, you have to remain conscious throughout the contest!"

As a Fortune 500 CEO once said to me after a particularly stressful session on the future of Consumer India, "I have no doubt at all that in the long run, I will be fine. But unfortunately I have to first survive in the short run!"

This is the exact opposite of China, where the long-term stability and continuity of policies of a non-democratic regime are in doubt, but in the short run, economic growth is steady and encouraging.

DEVELOPING A PERSPECTIVE ON CONSUMER INDIA

A Mosaic of Tradition and Modernity

India is a confusing market, which exists in many centuries, and at many levels of affluence, at the same time. We call it the "bullock cart to business class" economy—except that in India, consumers are forcing business class to get cheaper and demanding bullock carts that are more technologically sophisticated! Modern influences affect different parts of India in different ways and produce a mosaic of modernity that is sometimes quite unexpected and startling.

For the last decade, there has been, so to speak, an economic and sociological food processor on full churn in India, with some pretty powerful forces operating the controls and some pretty stubborn contents inside. The resulting compound is yet to be identified—all we can bet on is that it will scarcely be like anything we have seen before in the more developed markets.

India is a land where contradictions abound and will continue to abound, because there are many Indias being touched, with different levels of intensity, by different forces of globalization and they are responding to them in different ways. Consider these examples of progress and *status quo* coexisting. India is a nuclear-capable state that still cannot build roads that will outlast their first monsoon. It has eradicated smallpox throughout the length and breadth of the country, but cannot stop female feticide and infanticide. It is a country that managed to bring about what it called the "green revolution", which heralded food grain self-sufficiency for a nation that relied on external food aid, and yet it is a country that has easily the most archaic land and agriculture laws in the world, with no sign of anyone wanting to reform them anytime soon. It has hundreds of millions of people who subsist on less that a dollar a day, but who vote astutely and punish political parties ruthlessly. It has an independent judiciary, that once set aside even Indira Gandhi's election to parliament, and yet many members of parliament have criminal records and still contest and win elections from their jail cells. India is a significant exporter of intellectual capital to the rest of the world—that capital being spawned in a handful of world-class institutions of engineering, science, and management, yet it is a country with primary schools of pathetic quality and where retaining children in school is a challenge. India truly is an equal-opportunity employer of women leaders in politics, but it took over 50 years to recognize that domestic violence is a crime and almost as long to get tough with bride-burning. It is the IT powerhouse of the world, the harbinger of the offshore-services revolution that is changing the business paradigms of the developed world, but regrettably, it is also the place where there is a yawning digital divide.

And obviously, as a consumer market too, India is no less a land of conflicting truths. India's domestic demand for everything from motorcycles to color televisions to cell phones has surprised a lot of people who think of the India market in terms of its abysmal per-capita income of US$538. Equally, there are enough people buying American upper-end labels, imported Mercedes–Benz cars, and drinking the finest Scotch to justify all these companies setting up shop here and having their very modest expectations exceeded. The other aspect of consumer complexity is the way Indians belong culturally to many centuries at the same time. A farmer who understands ecological balance and the power of the Internet coexists with a nuclear scientist who insists that he needs a son to light his funeral pyre, so that he is not trapped in yet another cycle of birth and death.

A Strange Amalgam of Old and New

India's small-scale marketers and service providers design their offers for this strange amalgam very well indeed. My favorite example is the story of a business that a young lady who worked in a beauty parlor narrated to me. The institution of arranged marriages is still prevalent in India. Typically, there is a "girl viewing" ceremony where the boy's side comes to the home of the girl, bringing with them not just the immediate but the extended family, who have to be treated to high tea. The girl, formally dressed and coiffured, is made to serve the guests, so that her gait, posture, and gracefulness can all be critically examined. Then she is asked a few questions about herself and her abilities, maybe asked to sing if she is musically inclined, or about her "adjustability" if she is an "office working girl," and then the "viewing" comes to a close.

Someone decided that the cost and embarrassment of doing all this were too much—especially for a middle-class family, particularly if there is a fussy girl who would need to see several candidates. So a marriage broker built a business on the back of this. They would videotape a mock "viewing ceremony", with just the girl and her family (and himself, for his own brand awareness to increase), and would show it to prospective candidates, so that they could decide whether or not to move to the next step. It was a big hit, because this solution recognized the acceptability of technology, gender-driven decision-making (let the boy decide first, then the girl will), and the need to reform the process but not re-engineer it.

And here's another sobering, though controversial, thought about the analogy school of predicting market evolution that multinational marketers and big consulting firms are so fond of. It has not been and isn't going to be much help in understanding the future of Consumer India. The notion that as GDP per capita increases, all countries will demonstrate a predictable pattern of market structure and consumer behavior has been disproved already. The fact is that never before in the history of humanity have so many poor and illiterate people been provided with so much real-time exposure to the developed world, via television and the Internet, and never ever before have so many Indians, rich and poor, seen their incomes grow so fast.

And never before have they had so many things to buy and so friendly a consumption discourse. And unlike China, Indian consumers have a halfway-house experience of modern consumerism and are constantly benchmarking what they see new with what they have always been used to—and the new option is not always the better choice. For example, a mom-and-pop shop in India provides such sophisticated customer-relationship management and free services, like home delivery and replenishment on telephone orders, as would be hard for a Tesco or a Sainsbury to match. And the many housewives in large cities supplying home-cooked, ready-to-eat lunches and dinners at low overheads, high hygiene and low cost, with home delivery, are already inhibiting the growth of the packaged processed-food industry.

Define Your Own India

How, then, should businesses be making sense of all this? Shashi Tharoor, the well-known Indian author, gives us the first clue in his book, *India: Midnight to Millennium*, where he tells of how Winston Churchill once remarked "India is merely a geographic expression. It is no more a single country than the Equator." That's what I tell my clients—that the onus is on them to define what their India is, and translate the geographic idea into a well-defined construct of a consumer market.

Tharoor goes on to say "any truism about India can be immediately contradicted by another truism about India. The country's national motto, emblazoned or its governmental crest, is *Satyameva Jayate*, ("Truth Alone Triumphs.") The question remains, however, "Whose truth?" Again, the message...

The most important thing about dealing with the Indian market, therefore, is to figure out how to think about it in the context of your business strategy, and develop a mental model of what "my target India" is, and then proceed with the rest of the questions.

2

Why Bother with Consumer India?

—————⋙⋅◇⋅⋘—————

Most market analysts and business strategists bark up the wrong tree when they set out to evaluate the India opportunity by asking, "When will India have the per-capita income and infrastructure of China, the westernization and per-capita consumption of Brazil, the education levels of Russia, and the institutional framework and maturity of the USA?" In seeking such information, what they are actually asking is, "When will India become like someplace else?"

The correct answer to this incorrect question is "probably never"; certainly not in the lifespan of most people reading this book. That is the most important truth about India. To use a popular Indian phrase, "We are like that only! Mind it!" (loosely translated, this means "deal with it!"). Evaluating India through a comparative lens will lead to the inevitable conclusion that "now" will never ever be a good time to enter a market of a billion young consumers, US$785 billion gross domestic product (GDP) and growing at 6–8%, because it will probably never catch up with the benchmark "someplace else."

However, when evaluated through the "stand-alone" lens, and there are no surprises here, it leads to a mixed verdict. The glass of market attractiveness is both half full and half empty. However, there are several signs that would lead one to believe that the glass is filling—maybe not as fast as we would like it to, but it is definitely getting more full with each passing year.

THE DARK CLOUD AND THE SILVER LINING

Here's something that I call "Consumer India 101." These are a few indisputable truths about Consumer India that will endure for a long time to come and which must form the backdrop against which all mental models about "my target India" must be built: Consumer India is large, it is mostly poor, it is getting richer and less poor, and it is totally schizophrenic. Not surprisingly, it calls for unusual strategic complexity.

Consumer India is Large: With over one billion people and still growing at about 1.6% annually, India adds to itself a population equivalent to that of Australia each year. It will comprise 18% of the world's population by the year 2030. This is certainly something that global marketers cannot ignore, because in terms of sheer numbers, the center of "global" gravity has to shift towards the location of the consumers.

It is Mostly Poor, But is Getting Less Poor: Unfortunately, these billion people are mostly poor. The good news, however, is that they are getting less poor by the year, as economic growth fuels income growth. This can be seen from the increase in the per-capita income from a meager US$120 in 1991 to US$720 today. Despite the fact that the fruits of the new, improved economy—the fruits of liberalization— have gone far more to the rich and the educated than to the mostly illiterate poor, the bottom of the well of poverty is rising. Between 1993–94 and 2004–05, according to the National Sample Survey (an official government survey), the percentage of people below the poverty line has dropped from 36% to 22%. This is a significant reduction by any standard, even if the measure of poverty is a very cynical one based on the number of calories consumed, (that is, whether the person has had enough to eat to stay healthy). But the growing population has neutralized the percentage reduction and the number of the poor has roughly remained the same, at about 230 million.

It Has Some Rich People, Increasing in Number, Getting Richer: As we said earlier, the early fruits of liberalization have gone more to those who were already in a position to take advantage of it. Since 2001, the average annual growth rate of high-income households has been double that of any other income group. The top 10% of India's population has per-capita income levels that are at 60% of those in Malaysia and 80% of those in Brazil—the perpetual Indian number trick of even a small percentage of a large population being a large number of people! And these 100 million people are, by themselves, equivalent to three times the total population of Canada, five times that of Australia, a little less than double that of France, and about 60% of the population of Brazil.

Consumer India is Totally Schizophrenic: Words like "heterogeneous" and "plural" do not even begin to convey the extent of India's diversity and the varied dimensions or aspects of that diversity. And it's not just the 23 languages, the geographic and climatic diversity, the different religions living together, and the many shades of rich and poor people that exist, or coexist, in this vast, continental country. India has 28 states, and there are wide income and social-development disparities among them. Jean Drèze and Amartya Sen, in their book *India: Economic Development & Social Opportunity*, say that some states of India are worse off than sub-Saharan Africa, while others are better off than China. Rural and urban India are at different stages of evolution; even within rural India, often within the same state, there are oases of development poised to leapfrog and become more modern than even urban India.

Broadly speaking, India has two totally distinct age groups that coexist in sizeable numbers, but whose consumption ideologies are totally different. One is the isolated, post-Independence generation brought up in, even conditioned by, the Nehruvian socialistic milieu; the other is the free-market, globally integrated, post-liberalization generation. We shall return to this topic in more detail later.

Finally, as many as four separate economies, with startlingly different characteristics, can be said to coexist in India, ranging from the globally competitive infotech economy, which earns in dollars from overseas markets, to the totally uncompetitive (even in India) agricultural economy that is heavily dependent on the monsoon season.

Multiply all these different variables and you have a bewildering patchwork quilt with no apparent grand design or explainable pattern.

And to go back to what Shashi Tharoor says—everything you say about it and its opposite are both true! As different parts of India get exposed to different economic, social, political, and global forces to different degrees, I see this present level of schizophrenia getting worse, not better.

Requires Strategic Complexity: One of the most common complaints about India from global companies is that doing business in India demands far greater strategic complexity than any other market of equivalent size.

A "GUARANTEED TO HAPPEN" SNOWBALL/INITIAL PUBLIC OFFERING (IPO) TYPE OF OPPORTUNITY

So let us get back to the question we began with: "Why should global businesses bother with Consumer India, an ugly duckling that may never become a beautiful swan?"

As we saw earlier, India is hardly likely to become like "someplace else" in a hurry. But on its own terms, it still offers a fertile ground for long-term, sustainable growth, which is now "guaranteed to happen," even if it takes the meandering path of the walk of a drunken man. In short, India offers a large and "must-exploit" opportunity to global businesses for long-term value creation.

"Guaranteed to Happen" Growth Story: India is a large economy and a large consumer base, slowly and steadily growing at a modest and sustainable pace, and a proven environment for "guaranteed to happen" growth. Between 1992–93, when the economic reform process had just begun, and 2005–06, India's worst real annual GDP growth rate was between 4% and 4.4%: in 1997–98, 2000–01 and 2002–03; and the best was close to 8% (between 7.8% and 8.5%), in 1996–97, 2003–04 and 2005–06. On average, the 1990s achieved a real GDP growth rate of 6.3% per annum and since the new millennium began, it has been 6.2%. This rate of growth has survived three federal governments, countless changes in state governments, the communist parties as central government coalition partners, six years of negative growth in agriculture, (a sector that accounts for a quarter of the economy) and an Asian meltdown. So it seems to be pretty much sustainable, no matter what. With apologies to Shakespeare, "politics cannot wither her nor change in custom stale her infinite variety."

Young People, Virgin Market: For those operating in developed markets that are ageing and saturating, Consumer India offers a guaranteed growth source of 400 million people below the age of 21, and over 20 million new babies each year. Further, since incomes are increasing steadily, each year there are more and more new consumers just entering consumption, resulting in significant market expansion.

Low Risk from Government Policy Changes: In addition to interesting demographics-economics, India is a story of inclusive growth that is de-risked politically and socially. These are the fruits of being a democracy. There are several discussions amongst the intellectual elite in India about whether democracy is an asset or a liability for India. The inevitable answer that eventually emerges is that while democracy does derail us at times in implementing progressive plans, clearly it also de-risks us. While the wages of democracy are sometimes hard to deal with, if and when the party does happen, everyone will be invited to it and have a stake in it. Consequently, abrupt about-turns in economic or social policy are not a real threat to worry about.

Strong Institutions: Another aspect of a country de-risked for investment is that there are well-developed institutions, with a clear separation between the legislature and the judiciary. Furthermore, there is a continuous strengthening and modernizing of these institutions, as they are being tested constantly and, consequently, strengthened by the process. The Supreme Court has become more activist in recent times, the Election Commission has been getting tougher, the glare of the totally free electronic media enables a variety of voices and viewpoints to be widely heard and voters are becoming more punishing, even if they are not becoming more discerning.

Change Confluence: There is a "change confluence" that is happening, which is creating the tipping point for a vibrant consumer market, where we will see exponential changes in market growth and sophistication. This will be described in greater detail at the end of this chapter. In summary, the average Indian's income is growing, strong India is getting stronger and is unlikely to be derailed by the several-times-larger weak India, while rural India is decreasing its dependence on agriculture. The self-employed population dominates the process of making India a vibrant nation of strivers, not time-servers in sleepy large companies or government jobs and consumption is now a huge engine of growth. Unlike China's 42%, 67% of India's GDP comes from private consumption.

China 2005=India 2015: In 2015, India will have the same per-capita income that China had in 2005 and if China is currently being considered a hot and attractive consumer market, then India will be just as hot in 2015.

As I often tell multinational companies(MNCs) trying to make their India investment decisions, taking all these factors together, the best way to think about the Indian market is to think of it as an IPO or a snowball. For growth-hungry corporations, India is the second-biggest game in the world (after China), with entry tickets still going cheap. Hence, it is like an IPO: you invest in it early and get in on the ground floor of a "guaranteed to happen," long-term growth opportunity that is built on solid foundations. Or picture a snowball: it starts off modest in size, but grows at an ever-increasing pace over time. In short, India is likely to offer similar long-term benefits or returns to those who are willing to come in now and be there for the long haul.

It makes sense to pause and examine the journey so far and ask whether there is sufficient evidence to justify the confidence that the promised future will happen, even the way we have just visualized it. How have 15 years of a liberalized and 6%+ growth economy changed Consumer India? What is the change confluence that is now happening, which leads us to believe that Consumer India's tipping point is here, and that the change from now on will be both dramatic and irreversible?

CHANGE CONFLUENCE CAUSING THE TIPPING POINT IN CONSUMPTION

C K Prahalad, management guru and author of the book *Competing for the Future*, often says that in order to see the future and not miss fundamental changes that are about to happen, one needs to look at all the weak signals of change collectively—signals which, when viewed individually, can easily be dismissed as of not much consequence but which, when viewed collectively, give a clear message of change. Applying this to Consumer India, it is obvious that it is now fortuitously at the confluence of several changes (see Figure 2.1), the coming together of a diverse set of economic, demographic and social change waves, all

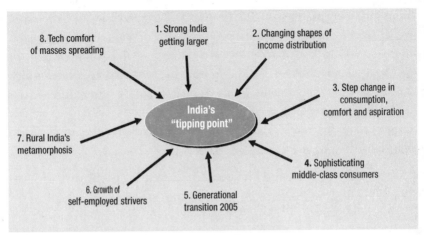

Figure 2.1: Consumer India's Change Confluence

pointing towards the fact that a brave new market is here—a market of a billion consumers, a very fertile ground to sow the seeds of future business creation.

The pace of change is slow, and it is a long-haul market, but the fact that the future will happen and Consumer India will keep its promise is now a concrete reality, not merely a creation of hope and hype.

The rest of this chapter describes the individual change waves that are causing the change confluence, which has resulted in the tipping point for Consumer India.

Strong India Getting Larger

In January 2000, P Chidambaram, India's Finance Minister since 2004, gave a talk at the University of Michigan. In his speech, titled *Of Elephants and Tigers: India's Place in an Asian Century* he said:

Reforms as implemented thus far have brought to the fore two faces of India. One that is vibrant, full of entrepreneurial and managerial energy, and eager to generate wealth through the use of technology, trade, finance, and markets. This India is eager to compete, win, and join hands with the best and the brightest in the global market place. It is keen on both learning and teaching, and dealing with the world on its own terms. But there is another India that is lonesome, sad, and sunk so deep in deprivation and misery that its quest for mere survival has doused any flicker of aspiration that it may have nurtured by mistake. Unfortunately, the second India is many times bigger than the first. Even more worrisome is that these two Indias seem to be moving on parallel tracks. Or to put it in current jargon, there is a strong "disconnect" between the two. I have no doubt that the first India will participate in and gain from the forthcoming Asian century. But what about the second India? Will it or will it not? Our reforms have still not provided a clear answer to this question. However, one thing is clear: that unless the "disconnect" is eliminated the second India will limit the promise the first India sees for itself in the Asian century.

The worry, which Chidambaram expressed in 2000, that the weak India will swallow the fledgling strong India, has now been proved to have been unwarranted. True, weak India will slow down strong India, but the evidence shows that strong India has now grown large enough and strong enough to be here to stay and grow steadily, as it has been between 2000 and 2005. This strong India, comprising Indians with economic opportunity, who have experienced visible improvement in the quality of their life in education, healthcare, housing, and so on, has grown significantly. By my estimate, this now comprises about 60% of urban India and about 12–15% of rural India, numbering almost 285 million people. This rural number varies significantly by state, with strong India being much larger in states like Himachal Pradesh, Gujarat, Maharashtra, and Tamil Nadu, but being much smaller in states such as Bihar and Uttar Pradesh. In fact, strong India has realized that it is in its own interest to help weak India rather than ignore it. Therefore, we are seeing a greater push in corporate social responsibility, in public–private partnerships, in innovations in education, healthcare, and financial-service solutions for the bottom of the pyramid via self-help groups as well as organized charity—again a set of weak signals, but taken together, giving an unequivocally clear message.

Changing Shapes of Income Distribution

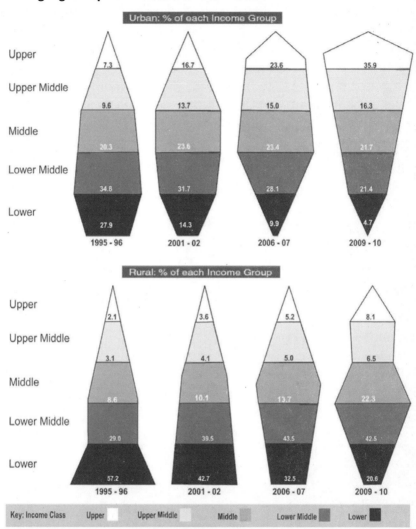

Figure 2.2: Changing Shapes of Income Distribution

Source: NCAER

Figure 2.2 is a graphical representation of a very interesting metric, the shape of income distribution; that is, what percentages of the population are at each of five levels of income, ranging from lower to upper incomes, and how this has changed over time. This is an interesting indicator because changes in the shape herald changes in consumption patterns: an idea not intuitively difficult to understand, because as these shapes change, the center of gravity or the reference point of the "average" consumer behavior also changes, as also do the reference points and role models where poor consumers peg their aspirations.

Figure 2.2 plots the changes in the shape of income distribution, based on data from the Market Information Survey of Households (MISH), survey of the National Council of Applied Economic Research (NCAER). Since the data was obtained from the same survey and is inflation-adjusted, it is comparable over time.

Between 1992–93 and 2005–06, the shape of income distribution in urban India changed from the traditional poor country shape of a pyramid (indicating far more people at the bottom rung of income than at the middle rung and even fewer at the top rung) to a diamond, with fewer people at the very bottom income level and several more in the middle and very top.

In 2001–02, the shape of urban income distribution was a pyramid but with the middle being low slung, that is, more in the lower-middle income level than the middle or upper-middle level. By 2005–06, this changed to a diamond shape for all the middle-income groups. At a 6.5% rate of growth of the economy, NCAER projects that the shape will become a cylinder standing on a narrow base, with equal numbers in the top four income groups and very few at the lowest income group. This means a sharp increase in demand for the higher performance offerings, even at higher prices. Never before in the history of the country has this shape of income distribution been achieved.

The shape of income distribution in rural India has also changed for the better over the years. From a very bottom-heavy triangle in 1992–93, it changed to a better-proportioned triangle by 2002–03. By 2005–06, it has begun to acquire the dimensions of a diamond shape—with more people at the income rung above the bottom rather than at the absolute bottom. By 2009–10, we will see a distinctly more diamond-shaped income distribution, with a further narrowing of the bottom. The point that ought never to be forgotten is that even a one percentage point improvement on any count in rural India accounts for six million people; so the 8% increase in the proportion of rural population in the middle income group, on the increased population base of 2009–10 of rural India, would be an addition of 14.5 million households, which is almost 90 million people. A state-by-state look at rural income distribution shows that in many states, the shape of income distribution has already changed to that of a diamond and, in some states, even to that of an inverted triangle, suggesting that parts of rural India are poised for a quality consumption boom, if only quality supply can be made available.

Step Changes in Consumption, Comfort, and Aspiration Level

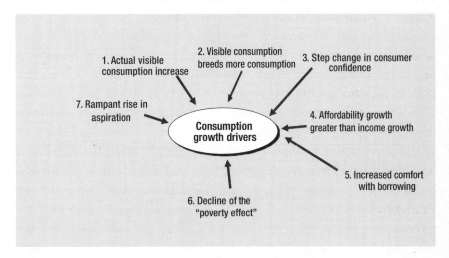

Figure 2.3: Drivers of Consumption Comfort

Actual Visible Consumption Increase: Between 1995–96 and 2003–04, car and two-wheeler (motorcycles, motor scooters and mopeds) sales more than doubled, and those of cell phones increased more than fivefold; today there are more cell phones than bank accounts in India. These categories are the best combination of functionality and status enhancement and have continuously been making efforts to drop price thresholds—indeed, they are great examples of how responsive the Indian consumer market can be to real value propositions. They also highlight the fact that it is Nokia's and Honda's experience that defines this market, rather than that of Kellogg's or Coca-Cola.

Business Today and *Business Standard*, two of India's leading business publications, also reported that there was a purchasing boom in the smaller towns, outside the large cities. For example, towns that were ranked number 60 and below in population terms, accounted for 20% of the sales of Maruti, India's largest car maker, and registered a growth of 33% in 2003–04

If we consider the 250 million-plus population or the 50 million-plus households of urban India, the increase in penetration is across the board for all sorts of products. Between the years 1990 and 1999, television penetration in the country increased by 20% and in the lowest income groups of urban India, it increased by 24%. In the highest income group, washing machine penetration increased by 20%. Most of urban India, rich and poor, acquired food mixers. Food mixers' penetration increasing by 16%, uniformly across all but the lowest income group. It was the same story for liquefied petroleum gas (LPG) cylinders used as a medium for cooking. Like televisions, pressure cookers increased their penetration in the lowest income groups by 17–20%.

In rural India, motorcycles penetration is quite stunning. Of the top 20 million households of rural India, 27% own a motorcycle. The bulk of this penetration happened in just a decade.

Visible Consumption Breeds More Consumption: Nothing breeds the desire to consume more than consumption itself. For someone who has not taken the consumption road yet, there is less desire and aspiration to consume. But with someone who is well on the consumption road, there will be more consumption. Urban India has increased ownership of durables quite significantly, in all socio-economic classes. How has enough of a base of consumption, and enough comfort with it, to act as a springboard for it to jump to the next stage of its consumption lifecycle.

The current level of penetration in a market influences the pace of future penetration. Penetration increases are not linear, but they accelerate as base penetration increases, up to a point when saturation sets in. If only one out of 20 households in a given affluence grade has a washing machine or a motorcycle adoption will be slow. But when this figure gets to one out of every 10 households, it appears on the aspiration radar screen of the rest. And when it gets to one in five, while it appears to be merely 20% penetration, it actually serves to rapidly penetrate the balance of households, for whom it becomes a "must have now" consumer durable. Given the current levels of penetration in the upper income group (enough as a springboard, but far from saturated), there will be a greater penetration increase in this group than in the middle.

Step Change in Consumer Confidence: Consumer confidence is all about the belief a person has that tomorrow's income will be greater than today's; and this has been the visible pattern for most Indians over the past 15 years. The biggest social implication of income growth has been the rapid change in the standard of living in just under one generation. In just nine years between 1990 and 1999, an average household saw its nominal income increase by a factor of 2.4, and with it came the climb on to the next rung of the economic (and hence social) ladder, and to a new self-image and new aspirations. Typically, as people will tell you, "in the old days, I could only hope to start my life at half the lifestyle that my father enjoyed when he retired. Now I start my life at a point above where he ended." And when people see this steady progress over the last decade in their own homes and the homes of those around them, it unleashes a huge amount of consumer and consumption confidence. Imagine the change wave of all this happening in a country of over a billion people who have seen steady income growth for a decade and a step change in their spending power.

Affordability Growth Greater Than Income Growth: This consumer confidence has been further fueled because affordability growth has been greater than income growth for this past decade, due to a sharp drop in prices with an increase in performance, thanks to the pressures of competition, falling interest rates, and easier consumer credit.

In real terms, the prices of everything—cars, shampoo, air conditioners, telephones, refrigerators—has actually come down, and as competition intensifies, fresh capacities increase, and the "low-cost business" learning improves amongst suppliers, this trend will continue. The prices of many consumer goods have actually fallen, both in real terms and in nominal terms, and the average price-performance points are unlikely to rise disproportionately beyond the income growth.

Increased Comfort With Borrowing: At last, consumer comfort with borrowing to fund future consumption is on the rise. Being in debt has always been an area of high discomfort for everybody other than the very poor who have no choice but to borrow for survival. And for a long time in the early years we wondered if this would ever change. However, three things have helped change this. One is the sheer confidence, based

ST. JAMES LIBRARY LEARNING COMMONS

on past experience, that tomorrow will be better than today. Therefore, being a borrower is now a sign that you are confident about your income rather than that you are living beyond your means (and that's a "no-no" in this country). The second is the low interest-rate regime; consumers feel that it makes far more economic sense to buy a home at these rates of interest, rather than renting one. The third is the concept of equated monthly instalment (EMI), which is the most popular form of repayment. EMI acts like magic at legitimizing borrowing, especially for funding future consumption—it creates a sensible and disciplined borrowing method, with predictable and planned outflows. Small wonder, then, that the average age of the home-loan taker has come down by 10 years in a period of just five years.

Of course, all this would not have happened had it not been for increased lending comfort from the banks. They survived the early phase of taking a leveraged bet on the Indian economy, betting that the potential risks of write offs from liberal loan policies would be more than offset by the increase in the number of higher-quality borrowers— not unreasonable, given the higher-than-average growth predicted of households in the upper income group.

This comfort with lending and borrowing is now well internalized socially, and can only increase, on a trend basis, as data on white goods purchases and consumer credit off-take has been showing.

Decline of the "Poverty Effect": Economists talk about the concept of the "wealth effect," according to which it takes some time before consumption decreases in response to decreasing income. Equally, it takes a while for comfort with consumption to happen, and consumption increase lags behind income increase, especially in a country that has been proudly poor and celebrating abstemiousness for so long. It also takes a supply explosion to spark the desire to consume and to translate it into actual action. Both events have happened.

Rampant Rise in Aspiration: The connectivity, communication, and literacy leap that India has gone through during this last decade has been a major driver of aspiration. Much has been said about these and how they drive aspiration. The most lucid explanation for this comes from the well-known anthropologist Arjun Appadurai, presently with The New School in New York:

Imagination is not about individual escape. It is a collective social activity. Informational resources are needed for people to even imagine a possible life, weave a story and a script around themselves, and place products in emerging sequences. Imagination may not always lead to action, but it is a prelude to action.

Consumer India now has enough informational resources to concretely imagine or visualize a better life, inspired both by the real and the make-believe world around it.

Sophisticating the Middle Class

The performance of the mid-price or "popular" segment products has improved dramatically, almost beyond recognition, in the past five years. This has been a long-delayed epiphany for both multinational and Indian businesses, underscoring the fact that volumes lie in middle-income urban and rural India and that unless prices drop to a level this India can afford, volumes will not pick up and markets will not be created. There is also the discovery across sectors that the arithmetic of lower margins being more than compensated by increased volumes does actually work. And finally, the supplier mindset of "rubbish at low prices" has changed, especially after a few resounding failures due to middle-income consumer rejection of what manufacturers thought would be adequate quality for the price. The moped category died and the chunky cell phone did not move off the shelf, but motorcycles with premium styles and popular price points were winners. Budget hotels of high quality, budget airlines, budget apparel brands, pre-paid cards for budget cell phone users, low-price basic handsets, budget retail formats that are hybrid superstore-hypermarkets, and high-end banking facilities for mid-level customers have appeared on the scene. And as this formula becomes more widely accepted, as more success stories emerge, and more and more lessons are learnt from them, we will see a whole slew of such new entrants. The result? A middle majority becoming sophisticated and discerning customers and joining the consumerism game.

Generational Transition: Liberalization Children Come of Age

Liberalization marked the ushering in of a non-socialist, consumption-friendly ideology. The post-liberalization generation is coming of age—the first non-socialist generation of India. Children born around 1990 will be entering the workforce shortly. Again, while this will be discussed in detail in a later chapter, there are 100 million 17–21-year-olds (source: Indian Readership Survey, 2003)[1]—indeed, six out of 10 households have a liberalization child. All these youngsters have grown up with no guilt about consumption, since they have never seen the bad times that the generation before them saw. Most importantly, these youngsters are now reasonably confident about their future.

Striving not Resigned: A Nation of the Self-Employed

One of the comments frequently heard in the India vs. China debate is that change in India is bottom-up, while change in China is top-down. Part of this bottom-up change is the extent of the entrepreneurial energy that exists at the grass roots. India's organized sector accounts for less than 10% of the jobs in the country, and the informal sector actually drives employment. Since most of Consumer India wants to get ahead in a hurry, being self-employed is the means by which they can earn and construct a better life for themselves and their children. The epitome of the "resigned to life", low-energy, "time-serving" mindset is a government job, which used to be the coveted mainstay of employment in the era before liberalization and privatization.

The self-employed person, in contrast, is a striver. The rise of the self-employed and the service economy, requiring less capital and more sweat, has changed the mindset from one of demanding social justice to one of grabbing economic opportunity, to an attitude of "I can and I will", especially in urban India. Today 90% of rural households and 60% of urban households are headed by a self-employed person. In the highest income group of urban India, the proportion of the self-employed is the lowest, at about 45%, while in the lowest income group, it rises to almost 80% (source: NCAER).

The employed salary-earner has now been replaced by the self-employed as the new "mainstream market", especially in urban India. The self-employed, being much more strivers and strugglers, do not accept the boundaries set by birth, and use products much more to signal success. They are also fast adopters of any productivity tools that can help them earn more, such as cell phones and motorcycles.

The Morphing of Rural India Beyond Agriculture

One of the problems with rural Consumer India till recently has been its dependence on agriculture, and in turn, the dependence of agriculture on the monsoon season. This led to regular boom-and-bust cycles and fragile sentiments. Furthermore, in economic terms, agriculture has not been a great proposition for a variety of reasons, and has grown at just 1.9% over all these years. But rural India has now gone beyond its dependence on agriculture, in order to augment incomes from non-agricultural activities. Today, non-agricultural activity in the rural areas is almost equal to the agricultural activity (a little less than half of rural GDP is from the non-agricultural sector) and it is also growing faster, creating a different kind of rural market—non-agricultural households have higher incomes and spend a higher amount. NCAER occupation data shows a decline in cultivators, and there is enough evidence of dual-sector households. Add to this the exposure levels of the top end of rural India through connectivity and television and, in the matter of mindsets, the rural market will soon be closer to the urban market. This is already happening in the more developed states with higher incomes. This new rural market will be discussed in detail later.

Comfort with Technology

IT awareness, be it of IT power (here's what a computer can do in solving problems/improving living), or IT-driven employment opportunities, has sunk in and trickled down to the lowest social classes and to much of the rural population—be it through the demonstration effect of model projects of the non-governmental organization (NGO) kind, the 30 Internet kiosks set up at the Kumbh Mela religious festival, watching the rich use it and prosper, or the mushrooming of call centers and other computer-related services offering employment. Since they are located in specific geographical clusters, they get noticed and talked about. Cyber grandmas in the upper-middle and upper class, who have become e-mail-literate in order to communicate with their scattered flock at no recurring cost, are another example of this new comfort with technology. As the nascent projects of distance healthcare, as well as village kiosks offering varied services, gather scale, this phenomenon of IT awareness will accelerate even further.

Two main reasons why the vast but scattered rural consuming base has not been tapped by most companies and businesses are, first, the fact that the "can afford" consumers are like needles in haystacks and expensive to find; and, secondly, the enormous cost, given such poor infrastructure, of creating a business that can serve such a large geography. New technologies like the Internet and wireless broadband can solve both these problems, making it economically viable to offer a whole host of services to rural India, from banking to distance education to distance healthcare to other remotely-supported services with "thin" front ends on the ground. This will indeed transform the expectations and the aspirations as well as the economy of rural Consumer India.

BEYOND MARKET POTENTIAL: THE "TRIPLE WHAMMY" BENEFIT

Long-term sustainable market potential is just one part of the business case for India. There actually is a "triple whammy" benefit on offer for businesses: interesting and huge demographic-economic opportunity; global cost-cutting opportunities by off-shoring business processes and research and development (R&D) to India, as demonstrated by the IT and the business process outsourcing (BPO) industries and their outsourced businesses; and the "disruptive" innovation capability of a bunch of highly talented scientists and managers, who have cut their teeth in a low-resource environment and prove the point that "necessity is the mother of invention." Leading edge companies who have set up R&D and innovation centers in India say that they hope to learn a whole new set of "disruptive" innovation skills that a low-resource, high-talent environment like India spawns—the fruits of which can create significant competitive advantage if deployed in developed markets.

WHY CHINA AND INDIA?

A decade ago, *McKinsey Quarterly* described China and India as Asia's non-identical twins. As the years roll by, it is very clear that they are indeed so. They offer different capabilities and different sources of risk, they have different performance profiles in various sectors and they both have "disruptive" capabilities, but of different kinds. They offer different types of strategic benefit in the portfolio. Each country presents different sources of risk, as described very eloquently by Arun Maira, chairman of Boston Consulting Group, India, in his book *Remaking India:*[2] *One Country, One Destiny.* He says that both India and China are trying to cross a river, with each having slippery stones underfoot and a rope overhead for support. In the case of China the slippery stones are its polity and its institutions and the rope overhead, its economy. In India's case, the situation is the exact opposite.

Most global businesses have stopped asking the question "Should we be in China OR India?" They now think in terms of "Chindia", a phrase coined by Credit Lyonnais South Asia to describe the two markets, which complement each other and which are both "must haves" in the portfolio of any business which considers itself global.

ENDNOTES

[1] Indian Readership Survey, conducted by Hansa Research group for MRUC, Media Research Users Council, *www.hansaresearch.com*

[2] Maira, Arun, *Remaking India: One Country, One Destiny,* Sage Publications, 2005

3

Understanding Consumer India's Demand Structure

———⟫⟨———

The most startling revelation emerges from the simple data in Table 3.1. Tabulate the population rank, the gross domestic product (GDP) rank and the GDP per-capita rank of the BRIC economies (Brazil, Russia, India, China), in purchasing power parity (PPP) terms, and compare them with the data for the United States. On this basis, the USA ranks as number one and is the world's largest economy. In terms of per-capita GDP, it ranks 10th (after some small countries such as Bermuda, Guernsey, and Luxembourg), even though it has the fourth-largest population in the world. China, on the other hand, ranks third in GDP terms and number one in population; however, it ranks 108th in its per-capita GDP. The pattern for India is even more extreme; in fact, the most extreme of all BRIC economies. It is the world's fifth-largest economy, but ranks a lowly 153rd in its per capita GDP. And even if it clocks a spanking 8% rate of GDP growth over the next 10 years, this scenario is not likely to change.

Country	Population rank	GDP rank	GDP per capita rank
China	1	3	108
India	2	5	153
Brazil	7	11	97
Russia	10	10	81
USA	4	1	10

Table 3.1 Rankings of BRIC and USA

Source: The World Factbook 2007, Central Intelligence Agency (2006 data estimates)

As the BRIC Report of Goldman Sachs points out, in the future the world's largest economies may not be the world's richest economies. It is this characteristic of being individually poor but collectively rich that fundamentally differentiates emerging-market economies from developed economies, which are both individually and collectively rich.

The implication of this rather innocuous statistic is that the structure of consumer demand in an emerging market, specifically India, is totally different from that in a developed market. Consumer demand in the emerging economies is made up of many people consuming a little bit each, adding up to a lot. Marketers in developed economies, however, are used to working with an exactly opposite demand structure; namely, a few people consuming a lot each, adding up to a lot. Therefore, neither the pricing paradigms of developed economies nor the cost structures of their usual, tried and tested, global business models are appropriate for India's demand structure.

The organized retailing business is a prime example of this. In developed markets, the store design, store economics, and, indeed, the entire science of retailing, is built around the assumption that a geographically focused catchment area or a single high street will have only a few people who will consume a lot each. Their other assumption is that if there are not that many people in a given prime location to generate the required sales, per square foot, for economic viability, then a shop established further away, in a non-prime location, can be made to generate it, by persuading consumers from a wider catchment area to drive further afield, lured by an attractive discount. Part of that discount can be recovered from the lower costs of the real estate at a non-prime location and part from the increase in the number of people served.

Using this paradigm, the first organized retail forays into the Indian market were made by local retailers with global retailers as collaborators, and were a spectacular failure. The high overhead costs of designing and managing a modern store required large-sized outlets in order to generate the sales per square foot required for profitability. However, even highly populated catchment areas did not have enough per-capita consumption to generate the required sales per square foot. Low car ownership and a profusion of nearby shops with reasonable goods and services made the factory outlet or the far-away mega-supermarket model unviable, as well.

A workable solution for food and groceries finally emerged in the form of Subhiksha, a chain of small-sized (mostly around 750 sq feet) hypermarkets in all the residential localities of a city. Serving the same catchment area as the mom-and-pop store and generally having the same size too, Subhiksha's advantage was its economics of scale; as a result, it was able to generate value in purchases and customer service, which the stand-alone mom-and-pop store could not match. It questioned these taken-for-granted rules of modern retailing, and not just in terms of the prescribed "ideal" size of a store. Because its stores were so small, it had no labeled aisles for customers to walk through and select what they wanted. Customer interface was provided by a computer screen at the counter, on which they selected their purchases. The goods (significantly cheaper than at the mom-and-pop store) were home-delivered at no extra cost. Subhiksha thus succeeded in creating a successful retail model that mimicked the structure of the customer demand—a lot of little shops, selling a little bit each, collectively adding up to a lot.

THE GREAT INDIAN ROPE TRICK OF NUMBERS

India's demand structure manifests itself in counter-intuitive ways. I call it the great Indian rope trick of numbers. One of India's leading scientists once said that the advantage of having such a large population is that even if an infinitesimally small percentage of Indians are good scientists, it is still a larger number of scientists than most smaller countries with better education systems can boast. In the same vein, people are often surprised to hear that the poor Indian consumers, for some categories, consume, in value terms, far more than the rich consumers. The unwritten, unexamined assumption many of us make is that rich consumers offer higher market potential than the poor. That is not quite true.

An example of this was forcefully brought home to me when I was consulting for a two-wheeler (motorcycles, scooters, mopeds) company. Figure 3.1 shows the structure of the demand for two-wheelers in rural India; it provides the relationship between penetration or ownership of two-wheelers by income group, the number of households in each income group, and hence, the number of two-wheelers bought by each income group.

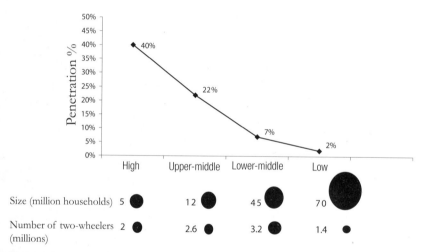

Figure 3.1: Rural India: Two-Wheeler Market

The lower-middle income group has less than one-fifth of the household penetration of two-wheelers compared to the high income group; but it has nine times the number of households. So it actually accounts for 1.6 times the sales of two-wheelers to the high income group. However, marketers are more comfortable focusing on the target market of high-income consumers, because the business model that can profitably sell to and service a 7% penetration market needs innovation.

NCAER runs a periodic large-sample survey on household consumption, called Market Information Survey of Households (MISH). The results are again counter-intuitive but plausible, if you think about them in terms of the Indian rope trick of numbers. Calculated on a basket of 28 commonly used fast-moving consumer goods (FMCGs), the findings are that the lowest income group has three times the *value* of consumption as compared to the highest income group. An even more telling statistic is that the *value* of FMCGs consumed by the lowest rural income group is double the value of the consumption of the highest income group.

MARKETING TO SUCH A DEMAND STRUCTURE

So to all those who propagate the theory that there is a magic per-capita income number at which consumption in a market "takes off," I point out that consumption has already "taken off" in India at far lower income levels. What hasn't taken off is the average marketer's ability to innovate strategies to profitably serve demand structures that are characterized by large populations with low incomes, low to moderate penetration levels, and low per-capita consumption levels.

The oft-narrated story of shampoo sachets shows one way of cleverly managing a market that has a demand structure of a lot of people consuming a little bit each, adding up to a lot—and how such a strategy can, in fact, expand the market. The traditional bottled-shampoo market had higher unit prices than most people in a poor country could afford, and hence, had low penetration as well as slow growth. Offering shampoo in 30ml quantities in sachets brought the unit price of consumer purchase down dramatically, enabling a large number of users to use the product, once in a while, and created an expanded user base, additional volume, and a value market as big as the bottled-shampoo market. Today there are two shampoo sub-markets in India—the regular-use, bottled-shampoo market and the special-occasion, infrequent-use, sachet-shampoo market. The latter comprises a large number of women who *regularly* use shampoo—not at a fixed periodicity but once in a while—for special occasions when they want their hair to look good and use cheaper traditional products or toilet soap the rest of the time. I call this the "party pack" market. It would be a mistake to think of this market merely as a small-size, trial-pack market and focus all effort on trying to "upgrade" sachet users to regular use of bottled shampoo. As a matter of fact, the "party pack" market is the mainstream for India.

The same demand structure also operates for the diapers market, where babies are made to wear diapers for special occasions when they are taken out to a formal place, or when traveling long distances, where changing them is a problem. What is inhibiting the growth of this market is the lack of a "sachet" strategy to enable a large number of parents to use them on occasion, but regularly.

The cost side of the equation for such strategies requires relentless innovation as well as cost reduction. In the case of sachets, the continuous effort is to bring down the cost of packaging while improving its efficacy. An interesting story is how Hindustan Lever had to ensure shampoo-sachet margin stability by filling exactly the right amount of shampoo into each sachet—since their conventional filling machines were not precise enough for such small quantities, they had to create attachments for them, learning from fuel-injection pumps that were used by the automobile sector to inject exactly the right amount of fuel each time.

THE PREMIUM–POPULAR–DISCOUNT CONSTRUCT OF THE INDIAN MARKET STRUCTURE

An age-old construct of market structure that is almost the Holy Grail of Indian marketers is that there are three broad segments in the Indian market, called premium, popular, and discount, which are defined by price-performance ranges and are bought by rich, middling and low income consumers respectively. Every category hitherto, be it FMCGs, durables or even industrial products, has had its rules and conventions about the boundaries of price and performance in each segment; and consumers have also "obeyed" the rules of not buying into segments above or below their station in life.

While there has been no formal definition of who a premium, popular, or discount customer is, the rule of thumb in consumer markets, based on historical data, has been that the top 10% of people by income constitutes the premium market, the next 30% the popular market, and the last 60% the discount or mass market.

An analysis of the expenditure and income for these three bands at the national level (see Table 3.2) shows that the top 10% of consumers in terms of their income accounted for, in 2006, 34% of India's income and 30% of its consumption expenditure. The next 30% account for another 36% despite being one-third as rich—if the GDP indexed to a 100 is 100 for the top 10% of consumers, then it drops to 35 for the next 30%. However, by the rope trick of numbers that we have just discussed, three times as many people with one-third of the income create a second-tier market of roughly the same size as that of the top tier. Similarly, the bottom 60% of consumers, despite being one-seventh as rich as the top 10%, have a greater share of the total consumption expenditure—because there are so many of them. Translated back into the premium–popular–discount market structure, this means that, in India, these segments are roughly equal in terms of total value, though they are vastly different in terms of the number of consumers in each and their respective income levels. Welcome to another version of the great Indian rope trick of numbers.

% of population by income percentile	National income share of each percentile	Consumption expenditure share of each percentile	GDP per capita indexed
Top 10%	34.1	30.0	100
Next 30%	36.1	36.6	35
Lowest 60%	29.7	33.4	14

Table 3.2: Consumer Stratification by Income and Expenditure

Source: Business World Marketing White Book 2006 "Solving the Income Data Puzzle", Bijapurkar and Bhandari.

In industrial or business-to-business (B2B) products, the structure of the buyer market is determined by a whole host of supply-side issues specific to an industry (not the least of which is historical regulation). In markets that have historically favored small producers, the "unorganized" small-scale buyers are far greater in number than the large-scale, organized sector buyers. And by the magic of the great Indian number trick, a lot of small buyers buying low-priced equipment or services can—and do—create a market as large in value as that created by large buyers. The former is often catered to by small suppliers and is known as the "unorganized" segment of the market, while the latter is catered to by large companies or the "organized" sector. It is not unusual to see many large companies define their target market and report their market share in terms of the organized sector alone (that is, large buyers, large suppliers), and totally miss the point that there is a market, perhaps several times more valuable, at a lower price-performance point. The relative sizes of these markets (organized/unorganized) can range from 10–90 (to as much as 50–50). It must be pointed out, however, that not all these market structures are truly reflective of the customer demand. The history of disproportionate tax subsidies and other cost advantages for certain kinds of products and manufacturing operations has created distortions in the supply segments not matching the demand segments. While this situation has changed to a large extent over the past 15 years, it has caused enough confusion in the minds of marketers, especially those from overseas, who do not always remember to make the distinction between free-market, product-market structures that are indicative of the consumer-demand structures and regulated-market, product-market structures that are quite disconnected from the consumer-demand structures.

What happens to this market structure, especially in B2B markets, when economies liberalize and the differential duty and tax structures on different kinds of products and producers are rationalized, making it no more attractive, beyond market considerations, to operate in the popular segment than the premium segment?

THE BREAKDOWN OF THE PREMIUM–POPULAR–DISCOUNT CONSTRUCT OF MARKET STRUCTURE

The initial assumption, in the early days of liberalization, was that a large part of the popular market would migrate to the premium end and the popular segment manufacturers would die a slow and natural death. However, the reality was slightly different, as is always the case with India. In categories like FMCGs, the reverse happened and the popular segment grew; with richer consumers also opting for it. In computers, the "gray market" goods of system assemblers grew; in industrial water-treatment plants, the standard systems market grew by comparison with the more-expensive, more-customized products, to name just two instances.

The reason for this is that, as unequal incentives started to be withdrawn and as small marketers were forced to come into open competition with their larger counterparts in the premium segment, "rogue" marketers emerged, especially from within the smaller manufacturers, who refused to respect the unwritten price-performance rules of the category; hence, consumers now have an explosion of price-performance combinations to choose from. Till recently, it was in everyone's interest to respect the rules of the game and (see Figure 3.2) restrict their innovation to "fill in the blank" new price-points such as mild premium and high-end popular, but respecting the "rules" of how much performance one could provide at what price.

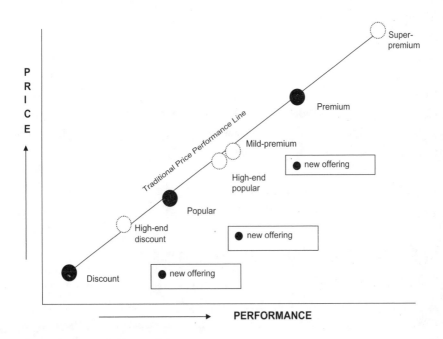

Figure 3.2: Premium–Popular–Discount Market Construct

However, now, it's a free-for-all. Rules on what is the right level of performance for a certain price segment are breaking down. As we saw earlier, this is being driven especially by the popular and discount-segment manufacturers, who have significantly upgraded their quality, now have access to cheaper imported raw material and better equipment, and are exploiting their low cost base. In the automotive sector, a 125cc motorcycle is being offered at a 100cc "popular" price (Victor from TVS). Superior styling that usually comes with a high-end popular price tag, is now available at discount-segment prices (Boxer from Bajaj). Similarly, a small car that usually belongs in the "B" or popular-product category by historical Indian market rules, is now available with all the features of the premium category (Swift from Maruti). Both Tata Motors and Maruti, India's leading automotive manufacturers have announced that they are working on a small car priced as low as US$2,230, which will be ready for commercial launch in the near future. This will dramatically lower the price threshold for cars—presently, the price of the cheapest car available in the Indian market is three times this figure. With the rigid codes of the market breaking down, consumers too are now liberated in their choices, and are beginning to choose freely across the board, oblivious of the category their station in life merits, as marketers see it in their heads.

In the FMCG sector, this has resulted in rich consumers opting to buy popular rather than premium-category products. Marketers have christened this as "down-trading" by consumers; that is, buying at price points below where they should, and have suggested that this is the nature of the Indian consumer—mean and stingy. In fact, it is not the consumer who has "down-traded" but the supplier who has "up-traded" his offer, and the popular and discount segments, in many cases, now offer a real value advantage in terms of equivalent if not better benefits at a lower price. There are also the shifts in consumer choices affected by changes in related categories, which marketers choose not to notice. For example, rich consumers who are now able to buy, at marginally higher prices, super-premium skin creams far superior in performance to those they used to buy are happy to settle for very basic toilet soaps, now that the quality of these soaps has been raised to a high level of acceptability on lather, perfume, and fat content. Equally, lower-middle-class consumers are now buying high-end, popular-priced, anti-ageing and other specific-property soaps, which are now available at a price they can stretch for and afford. And this story repeats across many categories.

In sum, if one were to be honest, the paradigm of premium–popular–discount = rich–middle–poor is now quite irrelevant. Most old India marketers and marketing-services providers, including even retail-audit companies, are resisting recognizing this, because the new paradigm that replaces this needs to be found and all thought and action frameworks changed as well.

The New Market Structure Construct: By Value Orientation[1]

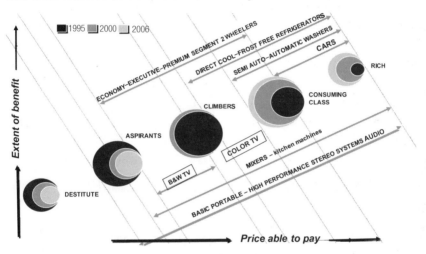

Figure 3.3: Consumer Classes : What Are They Buying?

Source: ORG-MARG

In an effort to find a more realistic way of constructing the structure of the market, NCAER has clustered Consumer India into five types of consumer groups based on what they consume and created a template called the Consumer Classes Framework[2]. This is the consumption-based model equivalent to the premium–popular–discount = rich–middle–poor income consumers construct of market structure that we have just discussed. Figure 3.3, shows that there are five consumer classes based on their consumption patterns:

The Rich: Those who have most of the "luxury" goods like cars, PCs, and air conditioners and are generally the consumers of premium products.

The Consuming Class: This class has about 70% of the "utility" durables like motorcycles, refrigerators, and washing machines and the bulk of regular FMCGs.

The Climbers: Those who have at least one major durable in their homes—either a food mixer or a sewing machine or a television—and who are the main consumers of popular segment consumer goods.

The Aspirants: Those who are just entering consumption and have the very basic goods, like a watch, a bicycle, a radio, or a table fan.

The Destitute: Those who own and consume practically nothing, living as they do from hand to mouth.

It is interesting to see that while the same durable is being consumed across the consumption classes, the performance-price points within them are many. For example, the cheaper direct-cool refrigerator and the more expensive and more modern frost-free refrigerator; the 100cc basic economy bike, the 110–125cc performance feature rich bike labeled "executive," and the premium 150cc bike which is perceived as being more of a racer and less of a roadster; or the semi-automatic and the automatic washing machine, and so on.

VALUE ORIENTATION-BASED CONSUMER MARKET STRUCTURE

In all my focus group work with these consumer classes, I have found that these consumption-based clusters also harbor a very interesting construct—that of value orientation. The different consumer classes have distinct orientations about how they perceive benefit and cost, when they consume (see Figure 3.4).

Benefit-Maximizer Class: *This is the "rich" class* oriented toward "money for value"—willing to pay more and more for better and better benefits. This group is what I would call "anywhere-in-the- world consumers who just happen to be in India." Ironically, due to a misreading of their value orientation, in the early days of liberalization, this consumer class was targeted with older (not the latest available in other parts of the world) models of Mercedes cars and mid-market brands of Scotch, which it rejected. These are people who had come out of a time warp, but rapidly caught up with the world in real-time consumption. "As good as you can get anywhere in the world" is what loosens their purse strings. Today, they are the target for the latest from all luxury brands, whether in apparel, watches or crystal ware, typically sold through very select-location retail outlets in the major cities.

Cost-Benefit Optimizers: The "consuming class" is oriented towards "value for money," in contrast to the "rich" who are oriented towards "money for value." They judiciously balance benefit and price all the time, in order to make "value-optimizing" decisions. This is the class that is not in the market for absolutely premium products, but for what we call high-end popular products. However, categories as diverse as skin care, automobiles, and footwear have seen that where there is a breakthrough in functional performance available at a much higher price, this "consumer class" does opt for it. They, however, are very hard to seduce with imagery-oriented brand benefits as the major reason to buy.

Cash-Constrained Benefit Maximizers: These are the "climbers," who say, "This is all the money I can afford; what's the best that I can have within this?" This is the target group that old India hands refer to as "price point" buyers, and who form the core and the backbone of the popular segment. Karsanbhai Patel, the legendary Indian marketer who launched Nirma, is the original targeter of this consumer class. Nirma was a brand of detergent launched in the mid-eighties at one-third the price of Surf, from Hindustan Lever. Nirma gave Hindustan Lever a run for its money by outselling it 10 to 1 in tonnage terms. Patel offered "adequate quality at affordable prices" and to customers who did not want to pay more than they were prepared to pay for a laundry soap, a detergent powder at that same price point was benefit maximization—even if the detergent had 65% soda ash, was harsh on hands and may have ruined clothes in the longer term. The consumers' answer was that they used a stick to stir the bucket of detergent so that their hands were protected; they could not say whether 10 years later their bed sheets would disintegrate or not; and they appreciated the whitening power of detergent over the gray-white of laundry soap. Eventually, Hindustan Lever also launched a popular brand called Wheel to target this customer. As the market has got more sophisticated, the benchmarks of "affordable price" and "adequate quality" may have increased significantly, but the consumer class of this value orientation still exists.

New Entrants Into Consumption: In the mid-1990s, the "aspirants" fuelled the growth of the FMCGs and durables. The "paisa" pack

(100 paise are equal to one rupee) of tea and detergent, low-price shampoo sachets, and loose glucose biscuits are some of the offerings aimed at this segment who, by virtue of being new consumers, are occasional consumers. They shampoo their hair on special occasions, and use bathing soap otherwise. They use sanitary napkins when going out. They watch television at neighbor's house, and use a pay phone when needed.

Not Yet Into Consumption: The "destitute," living as they do from hand to mouth, do not yet consume anything. This category is the wellspring that will fuel growth of the other consumer classes, as incomes increase.

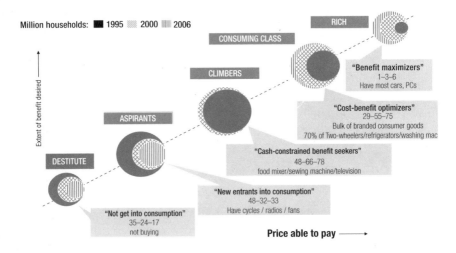

Figure 3.4: Value Orientation-Based Market Structure Model

Source: NCAER

The numbers in the table refer to the number of households, in millions, for each class in 1995, 2000, 2006

THE GENERIC MODEL OF THE INDIAN MARKET

This value orientation-based consumer-class model is a generic Indian model that works for all businesses. In office automation, there are those who are "anywhere in the world buyers who happen to be in India" who will buy the same world-standard configuration and brands that their counterparts in other parts of the world will have. Then there are the progressive Indian companies that are cost-benefit optimizers.

I used to work for a market-research company that was just that. We had state-of-the-art computers and software for our data analysis, non-branded cheaper PCs with a high-speed Intel chip for researchers, and cheap local computers for the office assistants. The many annoyances encountered as a result of this were not considered major, given the overall outcome. Then there are those organizations and shops that have a fixed automation budget and shop for the best deal from the small, one-stop shops in the electronics market providing hardware and software. And the "new entrants into consumption" aspirants are those who have one computer that is shared by everyone in the office, usually non-branded, cheaper PCs. This segmentation works for hospital-services consumers, cell-phone subscribers, education, chemicals, and every other category you can think of. Typically, cost-benefit optimizers (the "consuming class") have multiple usage between premium–popular–discount products in the same household. For example, there is a very high degree of ownership and usage of both two-wheelers and cars in a household, the idea being to optimize status signaling, comfort, and running costs.

Farmers in India can also be segmented by this construct, based on their farming "business model." There is the "return on investment"-oriented farmer who is ready to spend more money to earn more money and does not hesitate to buy an international, big-brand tractor with all the attachments. Then there is the productivity optimizer who will settle for the best local brand with the latest technology and mix and match implements and manual operations. The cash-flow minimizer is the small farmer whose farm barely supports him and he will buy an assembled tractor—the cheapest one available that does the job adequately; and there is the "just entering farm mechanization" farmer who custom-hires a tractor but does not buy one. Finally, there are all those one-with after and two-acre farmers who cannot use anything but bullocks to plough their fields.

Based on this basic generic model, a multi-pronged strategy can be devised for the Indian market for practically any category.

SIZES OF CONSUMING CLASSES

The NCAER track of consumer classes shows (Figure 3.4) that the two largest consumer classes are the "climbers" and the "consuming class," with about 75 million households each, one looking for benefit maximization at a set price point, and the other willing to optimize both benefit and cost until the outcome is satisfactory. It is interesting to see the change in the market structure from this construct, over the past ten years. In 1995, the two major chunks of the market were the "aspirants"—the new entrants into consumption—and the "climbers," who were cash-constrained benefit maximizers. Ten years later, it is the "climbers" and the "consuming class" that form the bulk of the market—a very distinct evolution of the market towards greater benefit sensitivity and less price sensitivity.

The rich, benefit-maximizer segment has grown at a fast pace, but is still a minor six million households, as against 75 million each of the other two. This six million, by virtue of being geographically concentrated and easy to access with minimal distribution, may be a very good target for luxury product and service brands. However, they represent the sideshow of the mainstay of Consumer India; namely, the "climbers" and the "consuming class." In characterizing urban-rural differences, the same pattern as with income classes is applicable.

Structurally, the rural market is about eight years behind the urban in terms of the relative sizes of these different consumption segments, although this absolutely does not mean that eight-year-old urban strategies will work for rural India. The rural consumer's expectations are totally different, since he is exposed to the rest of the world in real time. The urban rich will form a larger part of the urban market than the rural rich of the rural market. "Aspirants" (new entrants into consumption) will be far more important in number in rural Consumer India than in urban Consumer India, where "climbers" (cash-constrained benefit maximizers) and the "consuming class" (cost-benefit optimizers) will be the most important groups. This means that we can see far greater volume-driven market growth in rural India and value-driven growth in urban India.

DYNAMICS OF FUTURE GROWTH: THE VIRTUOUS SPIRAL OF DEMAND

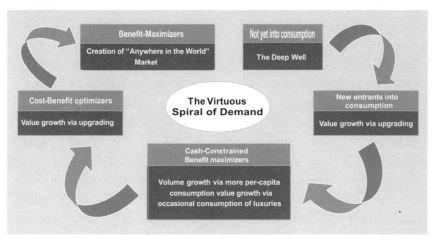

Figure 3.5: Different Growth Levels From Each Class

Different consuming classes can drive market growth in different ways (see Figure 3.5), and an appropriate mix of strategies is essential to capture the different sources of market growth. The sources of growth are:

Volume Growth Due to the "Destitute" transforming into "Aspirants": As economic growth occurs, the "destitute" will transform into "aspirants" and enter the consumption arena, creating an "automatic" volume growth for several categories. This is the "do nothing, just wait for the incomes to rise" growth. Categories like toilet soap and detergent and other basic personal-care items gained a great deal in the mid-1990s from this source of growth. Now, however, they have almost fully penetrated the market and have to look at other sources of growth.

Volume Growth Due to the "Climbers" Increasing Their Per-Capita Consumption: As the "aspirants" become "climbers," they fuel volume growth by consuming greater quantities of products than they did earlier. This is true for any category, from textiles (expanding wardrobes) to poultry (chicken twice a week and one piece for everybody in the house, not once a week and only for the men). There are more occasions for consumption and a greater quantity is consumed per occasion, of all categories.

Value Growth Due to the "Climbers" Occasionally Using "Superior" Products Instead of What They Usually Use: "Climbers" also contribute to volume and value growth through occasional use of luxury or indulgence items. These are best defined as superior-performing substitutes for what they are currently using. Two good examples of this, which have already been mentioned, are the occasional use of disposable diapers when taking children out on special occasions or on journeys; and the use of sanitary napkins by users of home-made napkins occasionally, when going on a journey, during the exam season, and so on. Another example is the use of bottled soft drinks that are served to important guests (instead of the low-priced squashes and syrups), where the dosage and the quantity of sugar can be controlled depending on how much the drinker is worth. The "regular occasional" use of shampoo sachets that we have discussed earlier is another prime example of this. Even when it comes to retailing, they make occasional visits to the supermarkets to buy their "family treat" food products such as dry fruits and special spices.

Value Growth Due to the "Consuming Class" Upgrading to Better-Quality Products/Brands: For mature categories such as toilet soaps, home-care products, refrigerators, and motorcycles, the growth of the "consuming class" and its quest for better value both drives value growth. They move from scooters to motorcycles, from direct-cool to frost-free refrigerators, from popular toilet soap to premium, and so on. Most categories of this kind will see growth in the premium segment, functionally superior products, and brands. The Indian experience has been that this growth is hard to come by unless marketers make the effort to continue to deliver "value right" products at the premium end, where the basis of value is superior functionality and user experience. In fact, when this does not happen, we see the reverse phenomenon of down-trading, which we discussed earlier, where the value optimizer decides that he is getting more optimal value from a cheaper toothpaste or soap or basic model television than the brand he is currently using.

The sudden and inexplicable stalling of revenue growth of the FMCG industry in India was due to down-trading by this consumption group, who were spending their money upgrading their cell phones, cars, and homes. There was not much penetration-driven volume growth to be had since this is now a mature, well-penetrated category.

Value Growth Through Creation of a Super-Premium Market for the Rich Benefit-Maximizer: Where the creation of appropriate "money for value" offers has occurred—notably, cars, apparel, home fittings and accessories, jewelry, and watches—there has been value growth from this market. The six-fold increase in this consuming class makes it a good market niche for international brands, offering "world-class quality at world-class prices", and many of them are already here and exploiting it in a focused way.

IMPLICATIONS FOR STRATEGY

Consumer India is a multi-tiered consumer base requiring a multi-pronged strategy. One size cannot fit all of it, and all talk of the "average" of the market is at one's own business peril.

A portfolio of offerings is essential in order to fully capture the multi-faceted market opportunity that India has to offer in the foreseeable future. The premium–popular–discount price-performance paradigm that Indian marketers have worked with all these years is here to stay for a while longer, given the income/population structure of Consumer India. However, the behavior of consumers with respect to this three-tier market paradigm is becoming increasingly complex.

These offerings should ideally span a wide bandwidth of price-performance points, ranging from "exactly the same thing that you will find in London" to "paisa packs." Obviously, each of these will need to be delivered by different business and distribution systems. While the consumer-interfacing retail outlets serving the "consuming class" and the "climbers" may be the same, the distribution system will need to be different. In the case of the one serving the "consuming class," who are value optimizers, the distribution system may need to be a relatively higher-margin, higher-service, demanding one. The system serving the "climbers" or "aspirants" should be high-reach, lower-margin and less-demanding.

As we saw earlier, Consumer India's demand structure is fundamentally different from that of the West, in that it has lots of people consuming a little each, which adds up to a lot of consumption. In fact, an analysis of where the volume estimates in the business plans of most multinationals went awry in the early days showed that it was not so much in the "penetration" or adoption numbers predicted, but in the assumption that the per-capita consumption numbers would be the same as in other countries.

We are, as I once said in an interview with the *Asian Wall Street Journal*, a nation of "underdosers": Partly because Consumer India cannot afford to consume more, yet wants to participate in consumption; and partly because there is so much scarcity and deprivation all around that careful consumption is ingrained in everyone's DNA, even in that of the better-off consumers.

The Indian marketer has learnt from watching the behavior of his consumers that when there are a lot of people consuming a little bit regularly or occasionally, a "community consumption" strategy is needed to tap into them. The success of community-use models like cyber cafés and STD/ISD (national and international long-distance calling) telephone booths is that they amortize the investment across many people and thus effectively create a pay-as-you-use model. A few telephone owners consuming a little are not as attractive as many call booths catering to a lot of people consuming a little each.

The Indian market has always embraced this—before television became affordable, the community television was its first introduction to media consumption without ownership. The high readership-to-circulation ratio reported for most magazines often makes me wonder if there are any pages left in readable condition. And the latest National Association of Software and Service Companies (NASSCOM) study shows that access to the Internet is four times the number of connections, a multiplier that can only increase given the success that we are seeing of cyber café (and the product for the lower-tier consumer—the cyber *dhaba* (a cheap, frills-free, small roadside shack to access Internet)).

Cable operators, each of whom has a dish antenna and provides cable connections at a fee of US$5–10 per month to a small catchment area of a few thousand households, will have a larger market than Direct-To-Home (DTH) operators. Just like the STD/ISD booths, job shops providing photocopying services also thrive. New tractors are bought by farmers at prices that usually are not justified by the economics of their farm, but there is enough opportunity for custom-hiring or community use, which enables pay back.

Another model to tap the large potential of occasional consumers is the small pack with low unit price, characterized by the success of the sachet. The whole idea of lower unit size and price packs of everything from shampoo to cough drops is to enable lots of people to consume a little bit each, which will ultimately add up to a lot. Thus we have large numbers of people who are occasional but regular consumers of things.

Finally, the consumption logic that drives the lower one-third or half of Consumer India is different from that which drives the rest of Consumer India—even for the same product. When gel toothpastes first came onto the market, while the marketer intended it to be a statement of modernity and new-generation toothpastes, the lower-income end of the toothpaste consumers adopted it quickly because, in the gel form, a little toothpaste went a long way and that satisfied the child's desire to have the toothbrush full of toothpaste and the mother's need for economy. We squeeze the very last drop out of everything. Housewives will tell you how they control the consumption of expensive food items like ketchup and cheese by delaying their replacement purchase.

ENDNOTES

[1] *Business Week* cover story, 22 June – 6 July, 1998 issue

[2] *Indian Market Demographics – The Consumer Classes*, by S L Rao and I Natarajan, NCAER Global Business Press, 1994.

4

Just How Much Purchasing Power Does Consumer India Actually Have?

———⟫◦⟪———

HOW NOT TO THINK ABOUT PURCHASING POWER

Perhaps the most difficult question to answer is the simplest one: "How much purchasing power does Consumer India actually have"? The answers are always varied and contradictory and the real story is pretty hard to piece together. The obvious answer in terms of a gross domestic product (GDP) per-capita number would be to conclude that there isn't very much purchasing power here to interest marketers of mainstream consumer goods. However, as always, averages about India are misleading and the reality is quite different and far more complex.

A *New York Times* report of December 10, 2005 pointed out that based on the trends of car sales of the last five years, India is "one of the world's fastest-growing car markets". It went on to say:

> Fifteen years after India began its transition from a state-run to a free-market economy, a new culture of money—making it and even more, spending it—is afoot. So intense is the advertising onslaught, so giddy the media coverage of the new affluence, that it is almost easy to forget that India is home to the world's largest number of poor, according to

the World Bank. Still, India's middle class has grown to an estimated 250 million in the past decade, and the number of super rich has grown sharply as well.

The resurgence of talk about the Indian middle class always makes me a bit nervous. The mythology of the Indian middle class has caused more heartache than happiness to business: it has no clear definition, its size has been hotly contested and it needs to be understood carefully before it is used blindly as a basis for investing in the Indian market.

THE MYTH OF INDIA'S MIDDLE CLASS

The popular mythology of the Indian middle class is that there is a large, homogeneous chunk of people at the heart of Consumer India (numbering between 200 million and 500 million, depending on whose estimate you choose to believe) who have the bulk of India's purchasing power and a great enthusiasm to consume. It is on the back of this juggernaut that many businesses planned to ride their way to mega-profits in the 1990s—and had their hopes belied, their business plans torn asunder, and their large new capacities lying unutilized.

The truth is that the "Great Indian Middle Class" was a seductive idea that was conceived, packaged and sold to the world by India as part of its sales pitch for foreign direct investment (FDI) in the early-to-mid-1990s—when all it had to offer was a GDP per capita of less than US$20 per month, and a lot of hype and hope for the future. The story put out was that there was a sleeping beauty called Middle Class India, comprising 250–300 million people, who had money and a burning desire to consume, and nothing decent to buy. And with just one kiss from Prince Charming, that is to say, with the mere availability of previously unseen goods and services, there would be a huge release of demand pent up for decades.

Of course, this did not happen and, by early 2000, the talk of the existence of the "Great Indian Middle Class" had considerably subsided. However, after lying dormant for a while, the idea is resurfacing— it always does whenever there is an upswing in the demand cycle or when we have a shortfall in supply, leading to the illusion of runaway consumerism.

The confusion continues. Pavan Varma, the sociologist bureaucrat and author of *The Great Indian Middle Class,* has declared recently that the number of people in the middle class has now swelled to 500 million. But there are others who describe it as "the fabled beast", "the unicorn" or, in the inimitable words of Shashi Tharoor, "something that is perhaps more sociological than logical."

As someone who was part of the creation of the myth, I would like to be part of its clarification too. Here are the things to think about when the theory of the "Great Indian Middle Class" is presented as the basis for a business case or a strategic plan:

There Is No Unique or Universally Accepted Definition: In the book *Guide to Indian Markets 2006*, Hansa Research (a leading market-research agency that conducts the mammoth 200,000+ sample size survey, the Indian Readership Survey) makes the following observation:

> The size of the middle class in India has been debated for the last 10 years. There are diverse estimates ranging from 100 million (20 million households) all the way to 400 million (80 million households) that have been floated by various individuals and institutions. In the last couple of months we have met a number of senior marketing professionals to understand what, in their opinion, is the real middle class. Every one of them had a unique definition. Some used parameters such as income and socioeconomic class, while others defined it in terms of ownership of durables such as cars and televisions. A few held that the middle class are those who are participants in the consumer economy.

This sounds exactly like what they say about pornography, "I can't define it, but I will know it when I see it!"

Its Beauty (Size) Lies in the Eyes of the Beholder: Hansa Research was forced to conclude that "It soon became obvious that there is no common definition for the middle class. Nor is it something that has been accurately sized. In fact no one really has a fix on this nebulous entity called the middle class."

Any statement about the size of India's middle class, no matter how authoritative a source it emanates from, therefore, is a totally subjective number. One definition often used by multinationals is, "those at the top end of the population [by income] who can afford to consume international products and brands as much as any global consumer." By this definition, through the lens of the US$50 branded jeans, the US$100 sports shoes, or the US$60 Scotch whisky, the size of the

Indian middle class is no more than 100 million at the most. People talk a lot about the cell-phone revolution in India as an indicator of the swelling middle class. Actually, there are currently 13 million cell phones in India and even if this doubles in the next year, that is still only 26 million owners of cell phones—a far cry from a 500 million middle class. Even at one cell phone being used by the entire family, that's still only 100 million users, at the outside. However, through the lens of an fast-moving consumer goods (FMCG) marketer, the size of the middle class, defined as those who can afford to consume mid-priced or popular-segment toothpaste, soap, or skincare products, is about 250–300 million.

However, under the National Council of Applied Economic Research (NCAER) definitions that we examined in the previous chapter, the "consuming class" of 375 million (75 million households), defined as cost-benefit optimizers who account for the bulk of branded consumer-goods purchases, would qualify to be called the middle class.

By the logical definition that the middle class is the middle majority of the market, the top 10% of the population who account for 34% of national income would not be "middle class"; nor would be the bottom 60% who account for another 30% of the national income. The 30% in the middle, who contribute 36% of the national income, could qualify for the "middle class" label. Therefore, they would be 300 million in number.[1]

Compared to the Middle Class in Developed Countries, This is Much Poorer: What is hardly ever articulated, and perhaps not quite recognized, is that the Indian middle class, whichever way you define it, is still far less affluent than the middle class in other countries. Hence, the surprise that people often have at how little the Indian middle class consumes compared to the European, American, or even Chinese middle classes.

The criterion the NCAER used in 2005–06 for the middle class was "an annual household income of between US$1,900 and US$2,900 (approximately)." On that basis, it estimated the size of the middle class to be 34 million households or 170 million people. By international standards, this does not really qualify as middle class.

If, however, we were to say that the label "middle class" should stand for a certain amount of consuming power and that based on the data from other countries we believe this should be at least US$5,000 per household, then the size of the middle class in 2005–06, according to NCAER data, was 21 million households or 105 million people. These people, whom we would like to term middle class, actually represent the top 10% of India's population in income terms.

Beware! It is Dangerously Limiting for Business Planning: Worse still, despite being notional and subjective, if treated as gospel, it leads to non-exploitation of opportunity and lazy strategy. Dr A S Ganguli, a former chairman of Hindustan Lever, director of Unilever, and later, Chairman of ICI India, had this rather sharp comment to make about the mythology of the middle class on which multinational entrants into India so deeply based their strategy:

> One of the more prominent topics preoccupying corporate India as well as foreign investors is the real size and promise of the Indian consumer market. The most widely quoted estimates have put this number between 150 and 200 million consumers. Following some marketing disappointments, downward estimates have gained prominence and the view is that it could be as small as 20–25 million consumers.
>
> This shrinkage in estimates based on consumption and purchase of a certain class of goods represents a severely restricted sample. Such arbitrary downward estimates of numbers do not truly reflect a state of restricted opportunity, but rather non-exploration of opportunities that the rest represent, whose needs for purchase and consumption continue to remain unsatisfied...

...and, I might add, who harbor purchasing power and may or may not qualify for an ambiguous label called the middle class.

HOW TO THINK ABOUT THE PURCHASING POWER OF CONSUMER INDIA: FROM A MONOLITH TO A MULTI-TIERED CAKE

My suggestion is that we abandon this fruitless debate about the size and the affluence of the Indian middle class and change the mental model that most marketers have of Consumer India. Replace the model of a monolithic middle class of large numbers of people who have approximately equal purchasing power with a model of many layers of people (a multi-tiered cake, perhaps) of uneven size and with different levels of affluence in each layer.

To quote from Hansa Research again, "a good understanding of these layers would be more pertinent [to understand the purchasing power of India] than trying to determine the size of the middle class."

The rest of this chapter is devoted to doing precisely that. It describes different ways of slicing or stratifying Consumer India based on different definitions of affluence, and sizing and profiling these layers or strata in different ways. Why confuse the issue further with different definitions of affluence? Isn't there one "best" way to work with? The answer, regrettably, is no. All sources of data do not provide exactly the same kind of information, and in order for a comprehensive picture to emerge, several of them need to be pieced together. To complicate matters further, there is (and will continue to be) a lot of opinion based on partial facts, using some favorite databases and ignoring others that tell a different story. These debates on purchasing power bring to mind a popular Indian story about an elephant and six blind men of Hindoostan. Each was asked to touch the elephant and then describe his impression on it. "It is like wall," said one, having touched the side of the elephant. Another said it was like a rope, having felt its tail. A third insisted that it was like many pillars, based on the legs, and between them they came to blows. The truth was that the elephant was indeed like all of those. So too, the answer to the question of India's purchasing power will constantly be the subject of confusion, because many of the answers will be contradictory, but they will all, most likely, be true.

The endeavor in the rest of this chapter is to enable strategy developers to do a one-time examination of all the facts, piece them all together to visualize the whole beast, and then come to their own judgments about whether it is attractive or not. Furthermore, since different people are comfortable thinking about market opportunity using different criteria (the classic "glass is half full–half empty" debate), what follows would also enable them to develop their own point of view. Finally, since pluralism always prevails in India, and different (though equally respected) data sources will always be prevalent and there's no knowing which one will be quoted, it makes sense to see for yourself the extent to which they all converge and diverge.

Stratifying Consumer India Based on Income: The most obvious metric to use to define layers or strata of affluence is income. However, income data in India has always been a contentious issue. Income data needs to be obtained from household surveys and there are some unique problems with getting people to report their income truthfully. Income is almost always under-reported, especially at the higher end of the income spectrum. This has nothing to do with weak survey design methodology, but more with cultural issues. I have had years of discomfort trying to explain to understandably puzzled overseas business people when they pose the question, "How can someone who earns so little afford to buy so much, and still manage living expenses for a family of five? What's not adding up?" The fact is that there is some logic to the illogic of survey income data, some consistency in the under-reporting.[2] For now, here is a simple survival guide for using household-income distribution data in India intelligently.

• Do not use it literally. Income is always under-reported. The most rigorous survey, the National Data Survey on Savings Pattern of India (NDSSP), conducted in 2004-5 for the Ministry of Finance by India Economic Foundation and AC Nielsen, accounts for only 59.6% of the total disposable personal income in the country, as put out by the National Accounting Statistics of the Government of India.

• Do not try to reconcile in order to compare across different surveys—it is frustrating and fruitless, because they all report differently defined income classes, elicit income data using different questions, index current survey income, for comparison, to different base years and, all things considered, it's a Tower of Babel out there.

• Income data has proved over the years to be what statisticians would call reliable but not valid—each reports a certain kind of income construct—and if you repeat the survey again and again using the same questions, you do get exactly the same answers. So while income is understated and does not measure the real thing, it is perfectly useable for grading the population based on its relative purchasing power and for comparing the growths and declines of various income groups over time. Therefore, a household earning US$1,240 according to survey data will definitely be earning much more; however, it will be twice as rich as households earning US$620 from the same survey. Furthermore, comparing the number of households that earn a certain amount today compared to ten years ago (after adjusting for inflation) is accurate.

Consumption Data vs. Income Data: I had a call one day from the CEO of one of India's big business houses. He was on a trip abroad and was giving a talk on business opportunities in India for the automotive sector. The supply-side facts about the industry looked great—turnover, growth in sales, margins, Deming prizes, cost positions, technology, and so on. Then came the demand analysis. He needed a few slides on the demand environment/market-potential side to complete his talk. "What is the definition of the High Income Household in NCAER reports?" he asked. I gave him the answer—this was in 2002, and the high-income band was defined as a stated income of Rs.180,000 and above per year (about US$3,830 per year). The estimated number of households having that income was about 14 million only. He gagged. Even on a purchasing power parity (PPP) basis, it was less than US$2,000 per month for a family of five, with education, healthcare, food, and rent all having to be met from this amount, not to mention buying cars. Yet, around that time, about 600,000 new cars per year were being sold in the country. And if you removed all corporate and commercial purchases from that figure, that was still a lot of cars for such few people, with so little income, to buy.

However, when you look at the consumption levels revealed from the same survey, it did show a lot of cars owned. Even at one level below the highest income group (that is, at the level of households earning between Rs.135,000 and Rs.180,000 a year) as many as 60% had motorcycles and about 30% had cars. And if you calculated the total number of cars bought in the previous year based on the household survey data number, it tallied reasonably well with sales data from car manufacturers.

Consumption data from surveys is accurate and tallies well with supply-side information. Here's the mantra to remember: Consumption is like maternity, a certainty. Income is like paternity, merely a matter of inference.

UNDERSTANDING THE AFFLUENCE OF THE INCOME STRATA: CALIBRATING INCOME NUMBERS IN TERMS OF CONSUMPTION

My advice to most people is not to worry about exactly what the right level of income should be to justify labels like high, medium, or low income. Anything is fine; labels are labels. Also, since survey income is understated, labels like "US$620 to US$1,240" ought not to be taken literally. The best way to make sense of the income layers and of what affluence they actually harbor is to work with income percentiles; and to get a concrete fix on the purchasing power that goes with stated income labels and study what people in each income bracket actually consume.

To illustrate, NCAER data (2002) describes the different layers of consumers, labeled by income and by words such as "seekers" and "strivers," and calibrates their purchasing power in terms of what durables they consume (see Table 4.1). For example, they describe a layer called "seekers," about 10 million in number, who have a stated income between Rs.200,000 and Rs.500,000 a year per household. On this income, 70% of them have basic durables such as televisions and refrigerators, a little less than one-third have entry-level cars and 13% have air conditioners. They also describe a layer called "deprived," comprising 70% of India's population, who own virtually none of the items that are considered basic necessities for consumers around the world—personal motorized transport, a color television or a refrigerator.

I use a stratification scheme (a special analysis done by Hansa Research using Indian Readership Survey (IRS) data), where affluence tiers are constructed based on income percentiles and calibrated in terms of their purchasing power (defined as what durables they own and what FMCG products they use regularly). This needs to be done separately for rural and urban India, since they are two different worlds, about ten years apart in their consumption behavior. This gives a far better fix on purchasing power than an income number in isolation. From this analysis (see Table 4.2), it is clear that 85% of rural India does not have the power to consume very much at the prices that currently prevail in the market. This does not, however, mean that they, (a) collectively have no money, or (b) have no desire to consume. It just means that no one has managed to innovate a "value right" (that is, "benefit right–price right") set of products for them.

Income classes	Annual household income (000s rupees)	% of Indian households in each income class	Number of durables per 100 households in each income class				
			Motorcycles	Color Television	Refrigerator	Air conditioner	Car
Sheer Rich	5,000–10,000	0.02	91	117	100	38	77
Clear Rich	2,000–5,000	0.11	77	113	81	40	69
Near Rich	1,000–2,000	0.29	66	89	68	32	66
Strivers	500–1,000	0.91	75	69	64	28	54
Seekers	200–500	4.8	70	74	62	13	29
Aspirers	90–200	21.9	47	40	34	2	4
Deprived	<90	71.9	7	5	4	0	0

Table 4.1 Affluence Layers Based on Income
Source: NCAER

URBAN - INDIA

	Tier 1	Tier 2	Tier 3	Tier 4	Tier 5
	Top 10%	Next 14%	Next 24%	Next 33%	Last 19%
Estimated households (in millions)	6	8	15	20	11
Durables owned (percentage of Tier)					
Color television	91.1	78.2	60.9	32.5	14.6
Refrigerator	82.6	59	35.3	11	3.3
Motorcycles	66.3	50.2	31.5	11.3	3.6
Car	22.4	5	1.2	0.2	0
Telephone	76.4	47.8	24.8	8.1	2.6
Washing Machine	47.7	21.6	8.8	1.7	0.5
PC	18.3	5	1.3	0.2	0

RURAL - INDIA

	Tier 1	Tier 2	Tier 3	Tier 4
	Top 4%	Next 10%	Next 35%	Last 51%
Estimated households (in millions)	6	15	51	74
Durables owned (percentage of Tier)				
Motorcycles	43.1	24.6	8.3	2.2
Car	3.5	0.8	0.1	0
Color television	40.1	27.7	12.3	4.5
Telephone	33.3	19.4	6.6	1.7
Refrigerator	24.9	14.3	3.6	0.9.
Washing Machine	3.8	1.7	0.3	0
PC	1.2	0.3	0	0

Table 4.2: Affluence Layers based on Income Percentiles
Source: (IRS)

In Table 4.3, the rows describe the strata or layers, the columns profile each layer in terms of size, the relative consumption intensity index of the layer based on the penetration of 50 consumer durables and FMCG products, the urban-rural profile of the layer, and finally the consumption intensity index of the layer multiplied by the population size or thickness of the layer, which is the total consumption weight of the layer.

The last column provides yet another startling view of the structure of purchasing power, thanks to the Indian rope trick of numbers that we have already discussed. The lowest consumption stratum has less than 1% of the consumption intensity of the top consumption stratum; however, by virtue of being *83 times* its population size, it accounts for 62% of its total consumption (and hence purchasing power). Similarly, the consumption layer of the "strivers", which accounts for 35% of Consumer India's population, has a greater total consumption than the highest-consuming layer of the rich, which is a miniscule 0.5% of the population despite having 60 times higher consumption intensity.

Layer name	% of population	House holds	Relative consumption intensity index	Profile % urban–rural	Consumption intensity index x population**
Samriddha 1 (prosperous)	0.5%	1/5	1,997 = 100	96–4	100
Samriddha 2 (prosperous)	0.5%	1/5	1,997 = 100	93–7	100
Sampanna (well off; not wealthy)	2%	4/20	484 = 24	89–11	96
Siddha (achieving; just entering upper classes)	3%	6/30	235 = 11	76–24	70
Unmukha (aspiring; moving beyond the average)	9%	19/95	119 = 6	60–40	113
Saamaanya (average/ordinary)	10%	21/105	65 = 3.2	45–55	68
Sangharshi (strivers)	35%	71/355	32 = 1.6	30–70	113
Nirdhana (poor)	40%	83/415	15 = 0.75	11–89	62

Table 4.3: Affluence Layers Based on Consumption Intensity (IRS Consumption Pyramid)

** (Consumption index x population) is the basis on which total purchasing power index of the strata has been computed

Table 4.4 provides some of the base data on which the consumption index has been computed. For each consumption-intensity stratum, it provides the penetration of different durables. Therefore it is easy to see that even for the miniscule top two layers, accounting for 1% of Consumer India, the penetration of cars, air conditioners, PCs, and even modern packaged food is limited to 26–71% and far from universal.

The top six layers of consumers, who account for 25%, of Consumer India are consumption-enabled to varying degrees. However, even the lowest of these, the *Saamaanya* or average layer, representing 10% of the population, are firmly on the road to consumption—70% use shampoo, 54% have bank accounts, and 30% have motorcycles.

Layer Name	Households /Population (millions)	% of households consuming...								
		Televisions	Cars	PCs (Internet)	Air conditioner	Washing machines	Motorcycles	Modern foods**	Shampoo	Bank account
Samriddha 1 (prosperous)	1/5	100	71	59 (42)	48	81	65	55	93	94
Samriddha 2 (prosperous)	1/5	100	44	42 (24)	26	76	72	39	91	93
Sampanna (well off; not wealthy)	4/20	98	24	18 (3)	5	53	69	25	89	87
Siddha (achieving; just entering upper classes)	6/30	94	10	4	-	30	62	9	85	80
Unmukha (aspiring; moving beyond the average)	19/95	92	2	-	-	8	50	1	79	69
Saamaanya (average/ ordinary)	21/105	79	-	-	-	-	30	-	70	54
Sangharshi (strivers)	71/355	51	-	-	-	-	6	-	69	33
Nirdhana (poor)	83/415	6	-	-	-	-	-	-	38	8

Table 4.4: Consumption Profile of Layers in Consumption Pyramid (IRS)

** 3 out of 5 of the following products consumed = jams, cheese, ketchup, instant noodles, soups

There are no U-turns on the road to consumption, and as consumption confidence grows and more and more people in a given layer acquire things, consumption growth happens very quickly. Therefore, despite current consumption indices being low, I would count all of this 25% of Consumer India as offering the potential for a vibrant, growing consumer market.

A whopping 40% of Consumer India, the lowest consumer layer of the "poor," has no purchasing power for any consumer durables at all and only 8% of them even have a bank account. The next best layer, the "strivers", which covers another 35% of the population, has over 50% television ownership and about one-third having bank accounts. It is easy to see what a step jump this is, as a springboard to consumption. Television provides the informational resources to aspire to a better life, and banking sows the seeds of financial planning in the areas of earning, spending, borrowing and saving.

However, even though the lowest consumption layer has no durable ownership to speak of, its FMCG use is quite impressive according to the IRS data. If any proof were needed that purchasing power is a function of the supplier's drive to value-innovate and not of intrinsic consumer wealth, this is it. Thanks to Hindustan Lever's efforts at lowering the price per unit, 75% of this layer has purchasing power for shampoo, detergent, and tea (available in sachets) and edible oil (available loose). About half of this layer has the purchasing power for dentifrices, but only 16% use toothpaste. Penetration of pain-relieving rubs and balms is also pretty impressive in this layer.

However, if we were to go strictly by the conventional, globally understood mental picture of a middle-class consumer and what his consumption ought to be, then, based on current consumption behavior, the top four layers of Consumer India (Table 4.3) comprising 60 million consumers would qualify. And that number would increase to 95–100 million by the reckoning of a low- to mid-priced FMCG marketer.

SUMMING UP ACROSS SURVEYS: THE VERDICT ON PURCHASING POWER

The judgment across all surveys and data is that 70–75% of Consumer India cannot be counted as healthy consumers. NCAER puts the figure at 70%. The IRS consumption pyramid puts this figure at 75% and the income–consumption calibration puts this consumer group at 70% too (Tier 5 of urban India and Tier 3 and 4 of rural India—see Table 4.2).

The top 30% of Consumer India can be divided into a 50–60 million people with high purchasing power, a 100-million layer below it, who are well on the road to consumption, and another layer below that, of 100–150 million consumers, who have just begun the consumption journey.

However, we have learnt that consumption growth happens very quickly thanks to consumption confidence that grows with every unit increase of penetration in a given layer, accelerating consumption further (more "people like me are buying this or that…if they can, maybe so can I"). Table 4.5 gives an idea of consumption increase in a five-year period in rural India, 85% of which (see Table 4.2) we have written off as not having consumption power.

Item	% of rural households owning / consuming	
	2000	**2005**
Color television	3.7	11.1
Refrigerator	3.2	4.2**
Packaged biscuits	39.1	54.2
Soft drinks	9.8	12.2
Shampoo	13.3	31.9 ***

Table 4.5: Penetration of Consumer Goods in Rural India

** While a 1% increase does not appear to be much, on the massive base of rural India, about 140 million households, this accounts for 1.4 million refrigerators, which is actually quite a lot. The color television penetration increase amounts to 10 million households, which is the size of Sweden's population or half of Australia's population.
*** This massive increase in shampoo consumption is the effect of packaging innovation, lowering price points, and unit sizes enabling regular occasional consumption.

TRANSLATING THIS INTO GDP PER CAPITA

Using the methodology described in *Solving the Income Data Puzzle* income distributions from survey data have been used to create a GDP figure for each tenth of the Indian population and, consequently, to generate a per-capita GDP distribution as shown in Table 4.6.

If we were to link Table 4.6 back to the earlier discussion (see p.72) of purchasing power based on income + consumption or based on consumption alone, the picture would be as shown in Table 4.7.

Deciles in terms of income	GDP (US$ billions)	Population (millions)	GDP per capita (US$)
1 (highest)	204.3	108.8	1,876.0
2	94.6	108.8	868.7
3	71.3	108.8	654.7
4	50.3	108.8	461.7
5	47.9	108.8	439.9
6	37.1	108.8	340.7
7	32.3	108.8	296.6
8	24.8	108.8	225.8
9	19.2	108.8	176.3
10 (lowest)	12	108.8	110.2
Total	**599.0**	**1,088.0**	**550**

Table 4.6: Affluence Layers Based on GDP and GDP Per Capita (2003–04)

Percentage of population	Population (millions)	GDP (US$ billions)	GDP per capita (US$)	GDP per capita of other BRIC countries (US$)
Top 1%	10.9	51.5	4,733	Brazil 2,700
Top 5%	54.4	136	2,500	Russia 2,610
Top 10%	108.8	204.3	1,876	
Top 20%	217.6	298.9	1,374	China 1,100
Top 30%	326.4	370.2	1,136	
Bottom 70%	761.6	228.8	300	

Table 4.7: Summary of GDP Distribution (2003-04)

To put it in an international perspective:

• The top 10% of India by income, is a little more than 100 million people, who account for about 35% of India's overall income, 45% of its household savings, and 30% of its expenditure. The figure of 100 million makes them three times the size of Canada, five times the size of Australia, a bit less than the double that of France, and about 60% of the population of Brazil. They have a per-capita income of about 60% of Malaysia's level and about 80% of Brazil's level (see Figure 4.7).

• The top 30% of India by income, is a quarter of the size of China's population and has an equivalent GDP per capita.

IS THERE A MAGIC NUMBER ABOVE WHICH CONSUMPTION TAKES OFF?

It is correct that the top 30% of India by income, who have been classified as those with consuming power based on their proven consumption behavior, do have a per-capita GDP of US$1,136 (2003–04); so perhaps there is some credibility to the number of US$1,000 per capita that is often touted as the consumption take-off point.

However, at the category level, the consumption data for certain FMCG items with a history of aggressive value innovation (detergents, tea, shampoo) shows that consumption can take off well below the US$1,000 mark.

IS THERE A FORTUNE AT THE BOTTOM OF THE PYRAMID?

The simplest way to think about Consumer India's purchasing power is to split it into three layers of approximately equal *aggregate* purchasing power, as shown in Table 4.8.

Percentile of income	Population (millions)	% of national income	GDP per capita (US$)	GDP (US$ billions)
Class India Top 10%	109	34.1%	1,878	204.6
Mass India Next 30%	326	36.1%	662	216.6
Pyramid India Last 60%	653	29.7%	265	178.2

Table 4.8: GDP Distribution in Class, Mass, and Bottom of Pyramid India (2003–04)

Clearly, at the bottom of the pyramid, there are 650 million people who earn less than a dollar a day. However, collectively, they account for a market opportunity of GDP US$173.3 billion (in 2003–04), which is approximately double that of Singapore or Malaysia. By 2005–06, this number has grown to US$226 billion.

Can this fortune be profitably retrieved? Yes, if innovative, low cost-benefit, value-right business models can be created for tapping it. No, if cost structures from richer country business models are mechanically transplanted.

POSTSCRIPT

Was such a detailed, academic, exhausting tour of methodology and numbers from various sources really necessary? What's the point of data that will be outdated even before this book is published? Yes, such a tour of methodology and sources was necessary, because I have seen far too many CEOs and strategists picking any income number a consultant puts in front of them, without any idea of what that really means, and making investment decisions based on it. Just as worryingly, I have seen misleading presentations from big-name consulting firms, based on erroneously analyzed figures (one of whom arbitrarily moved the income data slab upwards by 30%), stating "team analysis" as the source, alongside NCAER.

The purpose of this chapter was also to provide a framework (illustrated with 2003–04 data) for thinking conceptually and analytically about Consumer India's purchasing power and about how to massage the available data sources into more customized pointers for different businesses, as well as to enable interpretation and integration of all the numbers that exist aplenty in India.

PROGNOSIS: WHAT WILL HAPPEN TO EACH PURCHASING-POWER LAYER IN THE FUTURE?

It is a no-brainer that as India's economy continues to post +6% real GDP growth each year, the purchasing power will increase. At the aggregate level, the BRIC Report of Goldman Sachs forecasts that in 2010, India's GDP per capita will be over US$800 and in 2015 it will be US$1,149; that is, equal to the per-capita income of the top 30% of Consumer India today, the layer that we have examined and classified as healthy consumers or those who will soon be consumers.

Technopak, an Indian retail consultancy, says that by 2011 an additional US$122 billion will be added to consumer spending.

However, as we have seen from all the data analysis above, the layers of purchasing power reflect the true worth of Consumer India more than an average number.

At different points of India's economic growth, different layers of income grow or decline, resulting in periods of strong growth for certain kinds of products.

The period 1995–96 to 2001–02 saw the high-income layers growing the most (see Table 4.9). The highest income group grew the most, followed by the upper middle in both urban and rural India. The lowest income group declined, more sharply in urban India, while the middle group grew modestly everywhere. It was therefore not surprising that the expected middle class boom did not happen.

Annual Household Income*	% average annual growth rate 1995–96 to 2001–02			% average annual growth rate 2001–02 to 2005–06		
	Urban	Rural	Total	Urban	Rural	Total
High	17.3	12.1	15.3	12.5	11.5	12.2
Upper middle	8.4	7.0	7.8	5.7	6.8	6.2
Middle	4.8	4.9	4.9	3.1	9.7	6.6
Lower middle	0.7	7.6	5.6	0.2	4.1	3.2
Low	-8.5	-2.7	-3.5	-5.8	-5.1	-5.2

Table 4.9: Growth in number of households in each income group

* NCAER at constant prices.

In the period 2001–02 to 2005–06, the uppermost income layers continued to grow the most, but there also was a sharp increase in the middle layer of rural India.

The prognosis for the period 2005–06 to 2009–10 is shown in Table 4.10.

Annual Household Income	% average annual growth rate for 2005–06 to 2009–10		
	Urban	Rural	Total
High	14.7	13.4	14.2
Upper middle	5.5	8.4	6.8
Middle	1.4	14.8	9.7
Lower middle	-3.6	1.0	0
Low	-14.3	-9.4	-9.9

Table 4.10: Projected growth in number of households in each income group

Source: NCAER constant prices.

In the next four years, the rich households will continue to grow—both urban and rural equally—but a rural middle-income boom is also forecast. This "middle income" is really between Tiers 2 and 3 of rural

India—modest consumption, and about 20–25% penetration of most durables.

Simultaneous with this predicted rise in economic growth is a predicted fall in population growth rate—and one that will be seen more sharply in rich households than in poor ones, making the rich even richer in terms of disposable income.

Finally, if this increase in income is accompanied by a substantial drop in price thresholds, then there will be strong market growth for a variety of products and services. We have already seen this is categories like cell phones and color televisions.

ENDNOTES

[1] Bijapurkar, Rama and Bhandari, Laveesh Business World Marketing White Book, 2005, *Solving the Income Data Puzzle*

[2] Bijapurkar, Rama and Bhandari, Laveesh Business World Marketing White Book, 2005, *Solving the Income Data Puzzle*

5

Schizophrenic India

<hr>

MANY INDIAS, EVOLVING DIFFERENTLY

For years, businesses have been trying to come up with a singular and definitive view of India and the Indian market. Lately, however, most of them are beginning to realize that finding the Holy Grail of success in the Indian market lies in understanding its plurality; and that in order to extract the maximum value from the Indian market, they need to develop the mindset, the strategy, and the competencies to manage that plurality. India's plurality goes far beyond the heterogeneity of a consumer base of 62 sociocultural regions, 23 languages, totally diverse food habits, climatic conditions, cultural orientations, and so on. Neither is managing plurality about operational marketing practice executing programs and policies, tweaking products and pack sizes, and communication for sociocultural diversity.

Understanding plurality in the context of the Indian market is about recognizing that the "monolith" mental model we have of *one* India and *one* Indian market should actually be replaced by a "schizophrenic India" mental model, which thinks of India as actually being a collection of many discrete islands of smaller Indias—each of which has its distinctive economy, distinctive consumer character, and demography, as well as distinctive demand drivers and consumption patterns. It is also about recognizing that the many discrete islands will evolve in different ways, depending on where they are and what forces affect them, creating many more discrete islands or little Indias for the future.

THE LOGIC OF THE DEMAND SEGMENTS

Market analysts and businesses operating in India have all too often been defeated by what they describe as the fickle and capricious behavior of consumer demand in India. For no apparent reason, sales patterns suddenly shift and sales volumes start zooming upwards or slowing to a crawl. It is not unusual for several quarters of steady growth in the premium segment of the market to be abruptly followed by equally healthy growth in the discount segment of the market. The usual familiar factors, such as a slowdown in gross domestic product (GDP) growth, environmental shocks that shake consumer confidence, or new entrants into the market, cannot explain this behavior in the Indian market. It is not unusual for poor monsoon seasons to be followed by a spurt in motorcycle sales but a decline in toilet-soap sales.

However, when all this is viewed through the lens of the "many Indias," which are, in effect, many distinctive demand segments, it becomes clear that there is a logic behind all the apparent illogic and capriciousness of consumer demand in India. The key to understanding and forecasting the behavior of the Indian market is to recognize its schizophrenic nature and accept that the overall demand patterns that we see are actually the aggregate of these individual demand segments. And each of these individual demand segments is subjected to a different combination of forces; each one also responds differently to the same environmental forces and hence has its own pace of demand growth and consumer evolution.

IT India and Agricultural India are examples of two totally different small Indias or demand segments. The first is rich, relatively small, very young, and well educated. It has a little over 1.5 million people directly employed in it. Counting all their dependants, IT India would have about 10 million people and about 5% of India's GDP. In sharp contrast, Agricultural India has 50 times more people but only five times the share of India's GDP. It is older and is very low on education. One is global in outlook and benefiting hugely from the forces of globalization that are flattening the world, while the other is extremely local in outlook and very vulnerable to the forces of globalization and World Trade Organization (WTO) directives. IT India's consumer confidence hinges on the behavior of the US economy, while Agricultural India's consumer confidence depends largely on the behavior of the local rain god. However, to see the two as being on a continuum of modernity to age-old inertia would be too simplistic. Interestingly, IT India has many young people from very small towns who are experiencing the bright city lights for the first time and are struggling with culture shock, while Agricultural India embraces cell phones, the Internet, technological magic, and television with ease.

Rural India has two distinctive demand segments within it, of which Agricultural India is just one. Non-Agricultural rural India is half the population size of Agricultural rural India, but it is an equivalent-sized economy. They are the Non-Agricultural entrepreneurs of rural India and this explains why motorcycle sales in rural India are not well correlated with the usual agricultural cycles. Motorcycles are the basic business enablers for these entrepreneurs, enabling them to widen their footprint of operation and transact between the rural hinterland and the nearby towns.

A bad monsoon season, which has the power to swing India's GDP growth rate by over one percentage point, does not affect IT India at all. And US immigration law has no effect on Agricultural India though it can make or break IT India.

Government employees form another interesting mini-India or demand segment. The government economy comprises about 20 million people employed in government and quasi-government jobs—taking families and direct dependants, I would estimate that this economy harbors 150–200 million people. They account for more than two-thirds of organized sector employment, although they are just 20% of the total population of the country. They are, however, mercifully, not a growing segment but a shrinking one. The hallmark of this entire group is cautious, regular, and planned spending and surges in spending when the entire group receives special bonuses with arrears of pay all at once.

In the 1990s, the durables market in India suddenly boomed. Some unfortunate companies assumed it was the beginning of the rise of the middle class. Then the growth died out and the market returned to its original levels. The reason for the one-time starburst of demand was this interesting demand segment called government employees—well paid and with a high degree of bargaining power over their employers. They had been accorded a retrospective pay hike and suddenly at least US$4 billion was pumped into the disposable income of this demand segment. This is just one of the many illustrations of how environmental factors can affect just one demand segment and create significant distortions in the overall market. Today, as the government contemplates privatization of some of the larger, government-owned businesses, a large part of this demand segment, which stands to lose its jobs, has become savings-oriented and cautious, and there is an impending boom for mutual funds and pension schemes.

In sharp contrast to government-employee India is the self-employed India, whose growth is matched by the decrease in formal employment in the government sector and the transition of the manufacturing sector from the old, small-scale, labor-intensive factories to modern, large-scale, capital-intensive ones. On the other hand, since labor laws in India have not been liberalized and the threat of politicized trade unions still looms large, almost all of the organized sector, including the government have moved to outsourcing services to small-sized satellite vendors who tend to have far lower overheads when compared to the organized sector. This set of forces has provided lots of opportunities for self employment. Today, almost half of the urban India male workforce is self-employed. Rural India has always been self-employed, in the sense that they have been agriculturists or freelance agricultural labor. However, as discussed in Chapter 2, with over half of rural India's GDP coming from non-agriculture, over one-third of rural families are engaged in some form of non-agricultural activity and are either self-employed or work in micro-scale enterprises. Since the services sector requires virtually no capital, especially if done on a very small scale, it is the logical activity for most self-employed people. The consumption behavior and the drivers of the self-employed are very different from those of the employed and, as yet, most businesses have not geared themselves to serve this kind of customer.

The dependence of the self-employed, mostly on the services sector, where there is intense competition and low customer loyalty, gives them exceptionally fragile consumer confidence. The business people among them (as contrasted with the professionals) have a fair amount of black money or undeclared income and will spend on "invisible" or hidden assets and, at a time when the economy is booming and confidence is high, they spend freely. Equally at the first signs of interest-rate hikes or stock market hiccups they go into a non-spending shell.

LIBERALIZATION'S IMPACT ON INDIA'S SCHIZOPHRENIA

When India began its journey into consumerism, Consumer India was relatively simple. There were two Indias, one rich and urban; the other, poor, rural, and agrarian. We called them India and *Bharat*, the ancient historical name for India, which is still used in Indian languages and is also constitutionally recognized. We thought that with liberalization and the resultant economic growth, we would see the arrival of a huge and homogeneous mass of the "have somes," the so-called middle class. The belief was that with this rapidly evolving, homogeneous, consuming mass, the rural–urban divide would be blurred and a uniform "western" cultural outlook would emerge. As far as marketers were concerned, one mainstream size ought to have fitted most of the market.

In actual fact, of course, this did not happen. It was almost as if the laser beam of liberalization fell with varying intensity and varying characteristics on different parts of Consumer India, which were at different points of socioeconomic development. The result was many different patterns of change resulting in many Indias—an even more schizophrenic India than when the journey began (see Table 5.1).

Before liberalization, there was the miniscule rich India and the poor India: the "haves " and the "have nots." With liberalization came the "have somes," the "have some mores," and the "poor but not as poor," as the national income growth trickled down in varying degrees to different segments of people.

Urban and rural India were two distinct Indias, called India and *Bharat*. Urban was rich, rural was poor. Urban was industrialized, rural was agrarian. Urban had modernity, rural did not. Since liberalization, different states in India have grown at varying speeds. Given more freedom to operate, different private companies and banks, by themselves or in partnership with governments, began to have an impact on pockets of rural India. The result? Not two uniform blocks of India and Bharat, but many oases of development in a desert.

From	To
Two Indias	Many Indias
Rich and Poor India	Many shades of rich, not so rich, not so poor, and poor Indias (five consuming classes)
Urban India and Rural *Bharat*	Many oases and deserts within India as well as *Bharat*
Two age cohorts with uniform consumption ideology—all brought up in a socialist ethos	Four age cohorts with distinct consumption ideologies
Three economies—agriculture, manufacturing, government	Five economies—agriculture, manufacturing, government, services, IT

Table 5.1: The Changing Face of Consumer India Through Liberalization

At the start of liberalization, there were two age cohorts in the country —the pre-Independence generation and the first post-Independence generation. While there were the usual generational differences between them, they were still very similar due to the socialistic and xenophobic ideology that they were brought up on, and they saw only a crawling change in their lives. Following liberalization, we now have two new age cohorts; the first ever capitalist generation of liberalization children and the next generation who will grow up in an India that is confident about its new path and has found its moorings.

At the time of liberalization, India had three broad occupational groups—it was the heyday of government jobs and the government was the most sought-after employer. If you weren't lucky enough to get a secure and safe government job with healthcare and pension guaranteed, even for your widow, then you looked for a factory job. Or you were a farmer. Since liberalization, several new occupation economies are emerging—the most prominent and transforming of these being the IT economy. Referring to the impressive increase in Indian women winning international beauty pageants and to the equally impressive increase in Indian IT companies winning large overseas contracts, a wag famously commented that the reason why they bloomed so soon and so well was that India had neither a Ministry of Beauty nor (at that time) a Ministry of IT.

IT was India's first export-oriented economy—uncontrolled, manned by professionals, enormously accretive, and one that shared its wealth with its employees. It created a totally new mini-India, a far cry from the days of stringent foreign-exchange controls, when going abroad was the preserve of the rich and the sophisticated. It enabled lots of unsophisticated, middle-class engineers to go abroad and bring back stories of the world beyond to folks back home. With the advent of call centers, this new India is going to get even larger and spread its tentacles even deeper into the average Indian home.

The service economy is another occupational segment that was born after liberalization, and is the mainstay of the self-employed individual and the micro-entrepreneur. As discussed earlier in this chapter, it has a unique character, and though the fastest-growing sector of the Indian economy, it will remain largely a collection of individuals and very small firms who work for themselves.

Newer and newer occupation-led economic sectors will continue to emerge, driving even greater plurality, and they will create more interesting demand segments and mini-Indias, different in character from what we have known so far.

FUTURE VIEW

In the future, this pattern of many Indias becoming many more Indias will continue. Since the starting points of each of these Indias are so different, since the composition of people in each is so different and since the economic, political, and social forces at work are also so different, the resulting positions of each of these Indias will not converge to make for a homogeneous, singular, Consumer India in the foreseeable future. State-level diversity continues to grow, with regional parties in power in most states and pursuing different kinds of economics and politics.

Sunil Khilnani, the Oxford historian, in his brilliant book *The Idea of India,* tells the story of an Irishman who was asked if trousers were singular or plural. His reply was that they were singular at the top and plural underneath. Khilnani goes on to say that India is like its national dress, the *dhoti*—plural at the top with endless folds underneath. I call this plurality "schizophrenia" because there is no saying which of these many Indias nestled within the overall India is the real one; and there is also no saying how many more personalities will emerge over time.

RE-EXPLORING THE IDEA OF "MY TARGET INDIA" AND ITS IMPLICATIONS FOR BUSINESS STRATEGY

In the first chapter, we endorsed the notion that India is an idea, not a geographical entity, and suggested that every business needs to define its own "target India" and not expend too much energy on trying to find the Holy Grail of *the* India.

Hindustan Lever (now Hindustan Unilever India) has decided that growth for its utensil and fabric-care business will come from the "least-developed India"—deeply rural, media-dark, low on literacy, poor, using traditional products like ash and mud for cleaning. The company has a unique capability, born out of its history of creating new markets, and has the infrastructure and operational capability to undertake a genuinely pioneering market-creation effort, at a reasonable cost, by leveraging its existing, geographically well-spread infrastructure and dealer network. This pioneering effort starts even with the locating and listing villages all over India, pinpointing them on a map, reaching them in the absence of good roads, carrying out promotional activity, gathering crowds, and organizing product and education demonstrations through village fairs, and so on. In the last year, they did this for 30,000 villages, purely contacting 13.6 million women personally, in eight states of India.

ICICI Bank, on the other hand, has decided that the developed and well-off rural India is their India to focus on for the next round of growth—an India which has the aspiration, the exposure, and the need, but not enough supply of sophisticated, urban, top-end services such as wealth management for high-net-worth individuals.

Many a Fortune 500 multinational company (MNC) defines, narrowly and usually by default, its target India as the rich, urban, educated "anywhere in the world consumer who happens to be in India." The size of this India is miniscule in population, maybe the top 5%, which collectively represents an India that has about 20%

of the country's total GDP. It is easy to serve, but there is too much competition for it. The size of ICICI Bank's new target India is the top 1% of rural India, which probably has 5% of the GDP; it is easy to serve for someone who is already a big, urban winner since it represents a quick way to mop up a pool of ready and waiting demand at far lower incremental costs than the benefits received. Hindustan Lever's next target India is the 20% band at the bottom, which has about 5% of the GDP and is upwardly mobile, creating a guaranteed, loyal, new consumer pool, with virtually no competitor wanting to target them.

So "my target India" could be the self-employed India, who might be offered a whole slew of specially tailored products and services with innovative pricing and delivery systems. An aggregator model could offer financial services, sell real estate, and organize broad-based, preventive healthcare (since staying well and earning a living are so closely correlated for people who have no regular pay checks coming in at the end of the month), as well as offer a whole range of a productivity tools and services. In fact, offering grid-computing-based, pay-as-you-use services and simple, ready-to-use software as business solutions for the self-employed sector is a very interesting proposition: it automatically creates the backbone of infrastructure for a growing community that has none of the traditional support systems. However, as pointed out earlier, this group has an exceptionally fragile consumer confidence and is likely to overreact to sudden shifts or temporary downturns, consequently creating "bubble" markets that marketers have to watch out for.

Different "target Indias" have different levels of pain and gain, attractiveness, and competitiveness. The interesting thing, though, is that you can actually do a lot of customization in defining "my target India," and do not need to use cookie-cutter templates of the many Indias available (though if you want to choose that too, there are many pre-defined mini-Indias available to choose from). It is a bit like a kaleidoscope. There are many individual pieces that can come together in a multitude of ways to make a myriad of patterns—you just have to manipulate them until you find a combination that works for you, given your strategic objectives, your pain-gain profile, and your competencies. As India evolves further, more pieces will be added to the kaleidoscope, enabling the definition of even more customized "target Indias."

VARIABLES FOR DEFINING "MY TARGET INDIA"

The rest of this chapter describes the individual pieces in this kaleidoscope—the variables around which the demand segments or the small Indias can be built, so that strategists can piece them together to define "my India." At the more operational level, this will help business managers and market analysts construct forecasting and analytical models to throw light on the apparently illogical demand patterns that they see. Figure 5.1 provides a picture of the main drivers of the "schizophrenia" of Consumer India.

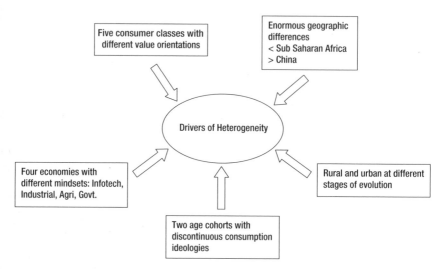

Figure 5.1: Schizophrenic (getting worse)

Consumer Classes: Consumer India has five consumer classes with different value orientations, as we discussed earlier—benefit maximizers who are willing to pay money for the desired level of value; cost-benefit optimizers, who balance value and money to find the appropriate level of value for money; cash-constrained benefit maximizers, who have a fixed price point they are willing to pay and shop for the maximum benefit available; new entrants into consumption; and the destitute, who form the fund of future consumers.

Urban–Rural: Urban and rural India are different worlds and are evolving at different speeds. While it is generally correct to say that, on average, rural India is ten years behind urban India in assets and amenities and has half the per-capita income of urban India, it isn't universally true. Some parts of rural India could end up becoming even more developed and advanced than urban India as they leapfrog towns with new and better infrastructure, technology, and a superior retail environment. An observant chief executive once made the comment that rural India shops the way urban America does at factory outlets— it travels long distances to a very large, one-stop, "stocks everything" shop and buys in large quantities. However, the US of is far more fertile ground for a viable range of megastores than urban India will ever be. Within rural India there are about 150 districts which are similar to urban India in assets and amenities and have a mindset that someone once described as "ural"—urban and rural. And as discussed earlier, there are the Non-Agricultural rural and the Agricultural rural India as well, with different relative sizes in different states.

States: The 28 states are totally different from one another—some growing at the pace of China and others growing at the pace of sub-Saharan Africa; some with progressive, modern governments that encourage private enterprise and others with repressive, old-fashioned ideologies and inefficient state systems. The term *Bimaru*, Hindustani for "sick," is used to describe a contiguous belt of north Indian states that perform poorly on all economic and human-development indicators.

Literacy in states varies from 91% in the southern state of Kerala, to 75–80% in the large western and southern states of Maharashtra and Tamil Nadu, to less than 50% in the northern state of Bihar. Given that the starting point of most states in terms of per-capita income and level of economic and social development is so varied, and given that their economic growth rates are, and will continue to be, so varied, it is to be expected that state-level disparities will only grow. Furthermore, additional powers are devolving to the states as more state-level political parties are emerging and it is not unusual to see a party in power at the center that controls very few states. Some states are business-and-investment friendly; others are not and that is also reflected in how much foreign direct investment (FDI) they attract and whether they receive large World Bank or Asian Development Bank (ADB) loans for projects. There is a story, hopefully apocryphal, about how a large, prestigious business school, promoted by prominent members of India's diaspora and Indian industry in partnership with two Ivy League American schools, eventually found its home. The story goes that they first decided to set up in Mumbai, since that city is India's business capital. The government of Maharashtra state (of which Mumbai is the state capital), known for its parochial ideology, immediately demanded reservation of seats for students from the state. The delegation then went to Bangalore, India's Silicon Valley, where the government of Karnataka invited them to meet the chief minister, who did everything that Indian politicians are wont to do—he was late for the meeting, distracted, said "yes, yes, yes, of course," but did not offer free land or any other benefit that should normally accompany such an initiative. They then moved on to Chennai to meet the regional party governing the state of Tamil Nadu. They were met at the airport by people with garlands and then told that these garlands were for them to give to the chief minister of the state, whom they were to meet for breakfast. The delegation then moved on to Andhra Pradesh, to the city of Hyderabad. They were met at the airport with garlands— meant for them—and, hold your breath, received by the chief minister himself, who came with offers of free land and an agreement which would insulate them from all forms of bureaucratic interference from the ministry of education.

The communist government of West Bengal has been aggressive in its wooing of investment, besides being the only state in India to have implemented land reforms whereby the small farmer gets to own the land he tills. The result? An interesting amalgam of urban and rural development.

Age Cohorts: As described earlier in this chapter, India has two distinctive age cohorts who have been raised with totally different worldviews and ideologies, not the least of which is their consumption ideology. Children born after liberalization are India's first, free-market, capitalist generation and their parents are India's first, post-Independence generation, brought up with a socialistic, xenophobic outlook. With liberalization children now coming of age and entering the workforce, and soon going on to set up their own homes, we are seeing distinctive new patterns emerging in the mosaic of Consumer India.

Four Economies: We have discussed this at length earlier in this chapter. It is interesting to see how the combination of the service economy and the Non-Agricultural rural in advanced and progressive states is an example of a newly emerging "target India." Such a definition reveals the opportunity for a whole new generation of businesses which can offer a whole set of new solutions to new needs ranging from low-cost grid-computing and mobile, wi-fi-based Internet access for small rural entrepreneurs, to digital pathology and x-ray labs with appropriate technology to enable the data to be digitally transmitted to doctors in cities, to hub-and-spoke models of micro banks linked to larger banks, and so on.

POPULATION STRATUM-BASED DEFINITION OF "MY TARGET INDIA"

Conventional wisdom had it that market potential and consumption sophistication were correlated with population strata. Metro India, small-town India, semi-urban India, and rural India are some of the phrases that are often heard to define "my target India." However, as explained earlier, with so many forces at work, the predictable order of things has changed. Smaller-population towns have been a source of significant growth that consumer-durable manufacturers and retailers are recognizing and nurturing and rural India has several segments of varying quality within it; and, as explained earlier, the many forces of development at work have created oases that no longer follow the logic of population strata or town size. Hence, blanket, definitions of "my target India," by population stratum or state or any combinations of these, are no longer wise. This will be discussed further in a later chapter.

THE PAIN OF STRATEGIC BUSINESS SEGMENTATION

It is true that doing business in India demands a complexity of strategy that is way ahead of its present market worth. There are several markets, including China, where the complexity needed is far less for a market that is worth a lot more. The best articulation of this I heard was from an exasperated American CEO who was attending a business strategy presentation and demanded to know "Why do we need a Rolls-Royce approach to segmentation for a market so small?"

His business manufactured and marketed polyurethane, which was used in several industries for varied applications (example as the basic raw material in footwear and mattresses, as insulation in refrigerators, as roofing spray for sealing and water proofing in the construction sector, for seats and door lining in cars and so on). He was told that in the Indian market, each end-user industry could not be considered a single homogeneous segment for the purposes of strategy development. It needed to be further sub-divided into three or four sub-segments with diverse quality requirements, cost structures, and hence polyurethane purchase behavior. So, for instance, "footwear manufacturers" could not be treated as a single homogeneous segment. There were two roughly equal sized segments–numerous small footwear manufacturers who used recycled old tires to make low cost rubber footwear for poor Indian consumers, and fewer, larger, top-of the line footwear exporters who manufactured for demanding western market brands. The former were ready to switch to using low-grade polyurethane instead of rubber, provided the price was low enough; the latter often bagged export orders without having the expertise to fulfill those orders, and chose their polyurethane vendor based on what technical expertise and innovative cost saving manufacturing methods he could suggest. Clearly, no single strategy could work for the entire footwear end-use segment. Similarly, the construction end-use segment required more than one strategy since it comprised a sub segment of fly-by-night small contractors doing shoddy local jobs, and another of international construction companies, with world class practices and standards.

Therefore, to fully exploit the Indian market opportunity, the business needed to pursue plural strategies, through multiple strategic business units (SBU), organized appropriately in terms of systems, structure, skills, costs and investment-return profiles. One SBU for example would be targeted towards the belly of the market, needing to offer appropriate quality at low prices, gradually upgrading in price and quality as the market evolved, A second one could be a nicely profitable "jewel in the crown" business, targeted entirely at international companies operating in India, desiring global suppliers offering world class standards of quality at global prices. In the first case, the company would be getting in on the ground floor of a major long-term opportunity, but also one which would not be profitable in a hurry, and which needed patient and steady investment in marketing and R&D in products, processes, and the overall business system, in order to get the costs right. In the second case, the company would be playing the comfortable global game for the limited scope and size of global India—a few LNG pipeline projects, small volume top-end models and brands being offered in India by global car, appliance, and footwear companies where indigenization of specifications was not being contemplated. This would be a profitable, slow-burn approach, which, taken by itself, would miss the evolving opportunities of the Indian market altogether.

However, there is, regrettably, no way out of this. India is plural (schizophrenic) to a degree that makes the European Union look totally homogeneous by comparison. Many mini-Indias make up the larger India. The kaleidoscope keeps having new pieces added and, with every turn, creates a new picture to deal with. The good news, however, is that there is plenty of choice for creating competitive advantage by defining "my target India" innovatively.

6

Demographic, Psychographic, and Social Determinants of Consumption

——⊱•◦•⊰——

"What do we need to know about the caste system in order to do business in India?" I was recently asked while addressing a group of CEOs of US companies who wanted to understand India and China better. My answer was "nothing." One of them persisted. "And in order to understand Indian consumers?" My answer again was a flat "nothing"; and I added that caste influenced voting behavior but not consumption behavior and that it was often very hard to tell a person's caste from a person's brand-buying behavior or his or her home. However, you would need to know a lot about other factors that influence consumption, like social class (as opposed to caste), ethnic diversity that influences just about every aspect of consumption from world-views to food habits, and about psychographic diversity. Style clans and tribes are increasingly being created with the forces of liberalization affecting different people in different ways and allowing for different ways of self-expression through the products and services that they consume.

As discussed in the previous chapter, India is not one entity but actually a kalaeidescopic collection of many different Indias. There are many mini-Indias, each of them a mini country in its own right, with distinctive forces acting on each. Each lives in its own era and, hence, as writer Arundhati Roy puts it, "India lives simultaneously across 400 years."

However, there is a further twist to this tale. Within the confines (and the broad consumption paradigms) of each of these mini-Indias live many different segments of Indians, defined in terms of sociocultural—ethnic—"life mindset" variables, which cause them to consume in different ways. Therefore, "my target India" needs to be defined one level further, keeping some segments of people in each of the mini-Indias, discarding others, to carve out a final "target India." This chapter discusses some of the variables that could be used for this next-level definition of "my target India."

DEMOGRAPHIC DETERMINANTS OF CONSUMPTION

Socio Economic Classification (SEC) of Consumer India

The Socio Economic Classification (SEC) system is perhaps the most widely used, consumer classification system, since it combines social and economic factors through intelligent use of the demographics of occupation and education, both of which exert a major influence on consumption patterns in India.

The SEC is a special favorite because through it we are able to identify consumer segments, not just in terms of how much they consume but also in terms of what they will and will not prefer to consume. Moreover, as it is closely correlated to income as well, SEC is intuitively easy to understand—just as income is—yet, in terms of its predictive power, it goes well beyond income.

The SEC system was developed in the early 1980s by the Market Research Society of India, which was looking for an alternative measure of income that was easier to collect, but was closely correlated to income and based on data which would allow Consumer India to be segmented into different potential consumption segments. This search led to the Social Economic Classification system for urban India based on the occupation and education of the head of the household, defined as the Chief Wage Earner (CWE).

It is a fact that in India, occupation and education shape not just an individual's earning capacity but also their family self-image and social status and set the tone of how they live. The "people like us" or "people not like us" differentiation is very strong in everybody's mind and governs behavior. Perhaps the position that occupation occupies in defining how people live has its roots in the caste system, and it continues to be a big definer of lifestyle even today.

Thus, a junior executive with a professional qualification working in a firm will live differently from a shopkeeper with similar income levels. What each of them considers worth spending money on will also vary greatly. The former may think that the soft, gentle, Johnson's baby powder, costing three times as much as normal talcum powder, is worth spending on, while the shopkeeper may prefer to put that money into dry fruits. The former may think that fancy bed linen is a necessity; the latter may think that it is a total waste and that fancy tiles at the entrance of the home make more sense.

This difference is more marked when it comes to adoption of products and services that require a certain social and cultural capital and not just economic capital; for example, newspapers, laptops or computers at home, travel on holidays abroad, and so on. Television adoption is more income-driven, but the programs watched are SEC-driven.

The marketing director of one of India's largest hotel chains narrates what happened when he offered a discounted package at one of his luxury hotels, where the room charge was discounted and food from the hotel was optional. The kind of people who came, he said, did not know how to use a shower and a western toilet properly and were far more down-market than he would have liked for his brand. He concluded, after some thought and investigation, that the willingness to pay for food at five-star hotel rates (even though discounted) was a function of social class and had he bundled food into the package as well, he would have got the right profile of clientele.

Spending on books, computers, and other knowledge tools, especially for children, is also social class-sensitive. A family from a lower social class, even with income comparable to that of a family from an upper social class, may spend a lot of money on clothes and shoes and more visible accessories for their kids rather than on computers. Cell phones have transcended class distinctions, and are driven almost totally by income, as they have moved from being an indulgence, or an option, to a necessary productivity tool.

The rural SEC system is based on two variables; education of the CWE and the type of dwelling (permanent or not permanent) that the household lives in. These two variables have been found to be most closely correlated with income, and to be the best determinants of what people consume or are likely to consume.

This SEC system is now a standard industry framework used for all consumer goods and services, including financial services. I personally prefer SEC to income, because its framework is more akin to the mental models, in marketers' heads, of the consumers they are targeting. It often happens that marketers assign an income label to the target consumer they are developing strategy for; and when they come face-to-face with a randomly selected sample of members of that income group at a focus group, they find there is absolutely no resemblance between their mental model and the reality. This does not happen much with SEC classification.

The Urban SEC System

The Urban SEC System is an ordinal scale that goes down from A (the highest social class) to E, with shades in between of A1, A2, B1, B2, E1, and E2. There is a miniscule top end called SEC A1+, but it is usually used to refer to "not in our orbit"—as in, "Well, I think this will work only with A1+." The grid in Table 6.1 provides details of the classification.

In urban India, SEC A are households where the head is very well educated—a college graduate or postgraduate in a middle or senior-level position if employed, or has his own business.

SEC A: This group represents the top 10% of the urban population, and under 5% of all of Consumer India. It comprises about six million households or 30 million people, of which SEC A1, a subset of SEC A, is just two million households or 10 million people. This is the miniscule group that all foreign lifestyle and luxury brands target. They mostly live in the large cities.

EDUCATION		Illiterate	Literate but no formal schooling/School upto 4th grade	School 5th grade- 9th grade	Secondary school certificate/ Higher school certificate	Some college but not a Graduate/Professional	Graduate/ Post-Graduate General	Graduate/ Post-Graduate Professional
OCCUPATION		**1**	**(2/3)**	**4**	**5**	**6**	**(7/9)**	**(8/10)**
1. Unskilled workers		E2	E2	E1	D	D	D	D
2. Skilled workers		E2	E1	D	C	C	B2	B2
3. Petty traders		E2	D	D	C	C	B2	B2
4. Shopowners		D	D	C	B2	B1	A2	A2
5. Business-men/Indus-trialists with employees	None	D	C	B2	B1	A2	A2	A1
	1 – 9	C	B2	B2	B1	A2	A1	A1
	10 +	B1	B1	A2	A2	A1	A1	A1
6. Self-employed professionals		D	D	D	B2	B1	A2	A1
7. Clerical/ Salesmen		D	D	D	C	B2	B1	B1
8. Supervisory level		D	D	C	C	B2	B1	A2
9. Junior officers/ executives Senior/Middle		C	C	C	B2	B1	A2	A2
10. Senior/ Middle officers/ executives		B1	B1	B1	B1	A2	A1	A1

Table 6.1: The Urban SEC System

SEC B: This group represents those who have a high level of one or the other factor—education or occupation—but not both. In SEC B1, for example, the CWE could be a college graduate but in a lower-level job than SEC A, or could have the same high-level job as SEC A, but not the same education.

SEC B is double the size of SEC A, having about 11 million households. It exists between the 11th and 30th income percentile of urban India. SEC B is what people usually mean when they talk of the "middle class" that is desirous of consuming more and more. They are the social class that comprises the "wannabes," struggling very hard to arrive and conspicuous consumers of everything they can afford. If you get SEC B on your side, then you pretty much have your future growth insured. They are geographically a little more widespread than SEC A.

I would be SEC A1; my realtor would be SEC A2 (he is a graduate and has his own business). My contractor, who has two or three employees and no college education, would be SEC B1. He recently bought my Honda City car for his family (he couldn't afford a new one); he also has a Maruti van, which he uses for all his work-related errands.

SEC C: This group has modest education: typically, the CWE will have finished school and maybe some college. They are shop owners or have low-level jobs as skilled or unskilled workers. Or they have less than five years of schooling and have their own minor businesses— shop owners of small corner stores or businessmen with no more than five employees.

SEC C comprises 12 million households, about 60 million people— double the size of SEC A, and slightly larger than SEC B. It is the core consumer of products in the price band that is at the border of popular and discount segments. Some 80% have televisions, 70% of them being color; 40% have refrigerators and an equal number have personal transportation.

SEC D: This group are those households where the CWE has not finished school, though he/she has had between five and nine years of schooling, and is typically self-employed or works as a clerk or a supervisor in a small store or factory—a classic, lower-end, blue-collar worker. SEC D households are about 14 million in number, roughly equivalent to those in SEC C. They are the aspiring urban poor, who experience great upward mobility in and through their children, who make do with necessities and unbranded products, but aspire to more. Some 70% have televisions, half of them color; 20% have refrigerators; 20% have motorized transportation.

Neeta, a masseuse who works at a health club and earns Rs.5000 per month, is typical SEC D. She spends Rs.2,500 on food, owns a small one-room tenement in a *chawl*, which is a housing community with common toilets and very basic facilities. She sends her children to study in English-medium schools and spends Rs.1,500 on that. She cooks with LPG gas, pays Rs.150 to the cable-television operator so that the family can have cheap entertainment, and owns a second-hand cell phone with a pre-paid card for her customers to call her and schedule appointments. Her lifestyle has lots of paradoxes. She has a refrigerator, her clothes are hip, but there are open gutters in front of her house; and when rats enter her house and family members get bitten, they are rushed off to the local doctor for tetanus shots. Her children speak English and will definitely become at least SEC C when they start out in life.

SEC E: This group is the ultra poor of urban India. SECs C, D and E are spread all over urban India, in the big cities as well as the small towns.

The Rural SEC System

The Rural SEC System is on a scale of R1 to R4. It is based on the education level of the CWE and the dwelling lived in (*kuchcha* or not permanent, semi-*pucca* or *pucca*, which means permanent). For details see Table 6.2.

R1 and R2 are the major consuming classes in rural India, R3 and R4 still being very poor. Just under 5% of all rural households are R1 (college-educated CWE and living in a permanent structure) and a little over 10% are R2. Together they account for about 22 million households or about 110 million people. In sheer comparable scale, they are equivalent to one-third the population of urban India, despite being only 15% of rural India. Close to half of rural India is R4; and R3 and R4 together are a whopping 85% of rural India. However, rural India is very different in different states, and even within certain states, where R4 is actually far smaller than R3 and upward mobility has set in.

About 60% of R1 and R2 would have a television, admittedly half of them would be black-and-white, compared with 25% of R4 households. Television is a major source of exposure to the world and also the source of aspiration. Therefore, the fact that 30 million R3 and R4 households have television is, in itself, a significant pointer to the awareness and desire to consume of this group—should the right supply come along.

The fact that 80–90% of R3 and R4 use detergents in some form or another is a tribute to the pioneering efforts of Hindustan Lever, and demonstrates how value-right products and a marketing juggernaut can work in creating markets out of the poor. In contrast, only 12% use mosquito repellants, for which there is a definite desire but not the same level of marketing effort. The difference between R1 and R2 and R3 and R4 is best illustrated by the fact that almost 70% of R1 and R2 rural households use toothpaste, while only a little over 30% of R3 and R4 use it. The gradual and inevitable rise of R3 and R4 incomes is the real massive growth story of the future.

TYPE OF HOUSE

EDUCATION	Pucca	Semi-Pucca	Kuchcha
Illiterate	R4	R4	R4
Literate but no formal school	R3	R4	R4
Up to 4th std.	R3	R3	R4
5th to 9th std.	R3	R3	R4
S.S.C / H.S.C	R2	R3	R3
Some College but not Graduate	R1	R2	R3
Graduate/ Postgraduate (General)	R1	R2	R3
Graduate/Postgraduate (Professional)	R1	R2	R3

Table 6.2: The Rural SEC System

Relative Purchasing Power Across SECs

The SEC groups are very well correlated with income, in that the mean or modal value of income in SEC A1 will be greater than A2, which will be greater than B, and so on. There will, of course, be individuals in SEC B, especially, who could have more income than those in SEC A, more so nowadays, as entrepreneurial opportunities abound and skills get rewarded. So the invaluable plumber-cum-electrician, with a few years of schooling and five assistants, could earn more than an executive in a public-sector bank. However, the purpose of the SEC classification is to catch the fact that he will spend less on the curtains or the newspapers in his home, and non-stick cookware may not be found in his kitchen, even if he goes on a package tour of Europe. In order to arrive at an objective measure of the relative purchasing power of each SEC, Hansa Research, using Indian Readership Survey (IRS) data, has computed a measure for each social class, based on consumption, not income (IRS 2005 data of 242,118 households). They call it the "household premiumness index," or HPI. This measure is based on the penetration in each social class of 50 variables: 18 consumer durables, 22 fast-moving consumer goods (FMCGs), four services and six demographic variables.

The graphic representation of Consumption Intensity Index based on these variables is shown in Figure 6.1.

The steep drop in consuming power between social classes is self-evident and often the increase in the number of households does not make up for it. Even between SEC A1 and A2 the purchasing power, or, to be more precise, the consumption power, falls to half. SEC C has double the number of households compared to SEC A and one-fifth the consuming power. SEC A, which is just 1% of all households, clearly has disproportionately high consumption potential. The best rural social class, R1, which is just six million households, has consumption potential somewhere between urban SEC C and B2.

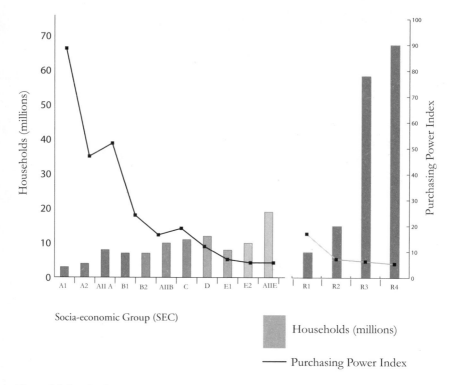

Figure 6.1: Purchasing power comparison across socio-economic groups.

Source: IRS 2005

Defining "My Target India" in Terms of SEC

SEC A1: The frequently used definitions of "my target India" by luxury brands, which want to target people who are "anywhere-in-the-world consumers who happen to be in India", with their lower-end offerings, would be SEC A1, numbering 10 million people, the tip of the India iceberg.

SECs A and B: These form a greatly favored "target India" definition and refer to the "prospering and spending" India, comprising the A and B social classes, about 17 million households or around 85 million consumers. High-end Indian brands and upper-end international brands, which can locally manufacture and reduce costs, define their "target India" as A and B, and their game is to get increased per-capita consumption from these two classes, rather than to drive large volumes.

SECs C and R1: These form a nice continuum of the "middle India" market based on their consumption patterns, numbering about 18 million households or over 90 million people. Some 70–80% of this group have televisions, 30–40% have refrigerators, and 40% have motorcycles. This is where urban and rural meet, and this would be the "target India" for budget brands and value stores.

SECs D, E1 and R2: These are similar in terms of consumption power and together form "mass market" India, comprising about 37 million households or 185 million people. Some 60–70% of these households have televisions, though about half of these are black-and-white; 15–20% have refrigerators; as many as 30% of R2 have personal transport, as compared to less than 20% of SECs D and E. Given the poor state of public transport in rural India, a two-wheeler is a very coveted and high-priority purchase because it substantially increases mobility and hence earning capacity.

SEC E2 and R3: Finally, there is the "poor but consuming" India, which has been discovered by committed FMCG companies and is catered to with micro-pack offerings for consumption. This is the SEC E2 and R3 market of about 70 million households and about 300 million consumers. Of these, 37% have televisions, more than one-third of those being color, and 10% have motorized motorcycles. About 80% use a bazaar-bought, dental-hygiene product, either toothpowder or toothpaste; there is near-universal penetration of toilet soap and detergent in some form or other; and about 19% of these households use some bazaar-bought, skin-care product. (All data for this section has been drawn from the IRS study of Hansa Research, done for Media Research Users Council (MRUC), 2005 data).

The Self-Employed as a Distinctive Consumer Class

Self-employed people in India have distinctive needs that drive their consumption behavior. This is more so than self-employed people anywhere else in the world, because in India most formal support systems, such as healthcare or pensions, or even easy access to rented apartments, have been typically built around employers and the self-employed have no access to them. In a strongly confident economic environment they provide a demand kicker for popular FMCGs and durables. They are a major source of demand for a range of "work partner" durables. Cell phones, workhorse-sturdy motorcycles (especially in rural India) and low-end vans are special favorites with them, puzzling many a market observer as to why otherwise-low socioeconomic class folk like plumbers, carpenters, and auto-rickshaw drivers are so heavily driving the growth of these items. The answer is that these are seen by them as "work-partner productivity tools," and are valued by them as worth spending money on, in order to increase incomes significantly.

However, their consumption is not all about pragmatism and good sense. Ego plays a big part too.

I once did some work on a motorcycle brand. It had an ugly design by conventional standards; bulky, showy, and visually startling. Though it had a core constituency of buyers, it did not appeal to a wider audience. The explanation for this was found in its buyer profile—almost totally self-made businessmen, mainly small traders and shopkeepers.

Growing up as they did in an environment where either you were from a business family or you had to be employed in a proper government or private-company job, they keenly wanted to signal arrival and having "made it." Hence their preference for this motorcycle design. A follow-up benefit segmentation study on the motorcycle category showed that 23% of the two-wheeler buyers were "dominators"—big ego, have money but are in search of social approval, and wanting power, impact and visual dominance in a motorcycle. They were mainly traders. In fact, cell phones, sturdy motorcycles and low-end vans are part of the "work-partner productivity tools" value space that the self-employed spend money on, especially in rural India—to the surprise of many an observer.

In fact, offering grid-computing-based pay-as-you-use services for the self-employed sector is a very interesting proposition in that it automatically creates the backbone of infrastructure for a community that has none of the traditional support systems but is growing.

PSYCHOGRAPHIC DETERMINANTS OF CONSUMPTION

Psychographic Consumer India

Kishore Biyani, the founder of India's most interesting retailing business, Future Group, defines his company's "target India" as the "aspirational class." According to his definition, anyone who does not feel the yearning for a better life, despite living in these present heady times, is not worth losing too much sleep over. To explore his target group further, we once did some market research in Dharavi, a large, impoverished neighborhood in the middle of Mumbai, which houses people all the way from SEC B to E, with a smattering of SEC A households also. We interviewed young, educated people with good jobs and enough money to be able to move to better localities in the suburbs but who continued to live in Dharavi despite the numerous inconveniences and the lower status it signaled to the outside world.

Despite their protestations that they were saving up to move, eventually, to their dream house near the heart of the city, Kishore Biyani defines them as "dreamers" but not "aspirers." The "aspirational class" definitely demonstrates upward mobility even if in small stages.

Himachal, a 27-year-old driver who works for a limousine service in Mumbai, has bought one small Indica car that he runs as a taxi in his village in Orissa, employing his distant cousin to drive it. He prides himself on having used a cell phone since 1998, talks of his ATM card and wonders how to set up an "electronics showroom" in his village, since someone else has already beaten him in setting up a petrol pump on the highway near his village. He is typical of the aspirer that the new India will see more and more of.

Several years ago, Rediffusion DYR the Indian affiliates of Young and Rubicam (Y&R), showcased a cross-cultural classification system developed by the former, which resonates well with the Consumer India of today. Applying that system, Consumer India can be divided into the "resigned," the "strivers," the "mainstreamers," the "aspirers," and the "successful."

The "resigned": These are the really poor who are struggling for survival and have pretty much given up on life, living at a subsistence level.

The "strivers": These are people those whose goal is to improve and escape from hardship. Like Neeta, whom we discussed earlier, they value hope and luck and try to offer their children an escape into a better orbit of life. Micro credit-based retail models and discount brands of FMCGs are aimed at this segment. Often you find that they do not have enough money for food but will pay for basic FMCGs and send their children to an English-medium school.

The "mainstreamers": These people are the middle majority who seek security, value social acceptance, and whose motivation is family responsibility and conformity. The young here are typically the children of the "strivers." To this group, brands are about signaling belonging to a group, not about self-expression. Blending in is fine. Sticking out is not. This is the target group for whom brands like Hero Honda's *Splendor*, the market leader among motorcycles in India, have been built. In both product and brand value, *Splendor* defies all western conventional wisdom of how flamboyant a motorcycle should be.

The "aspirers": The wannabes, are those who want to be perceived as successful, and for whom status and envy are important. A leading brand of television with the tag line "neighbor's envy, owner's pride" and a mid-priced detergent bar that portrays envy-inspiring success with the tag line "wonder how his shirt is whiter than mine?" are examples of targeting this segment.

The "successful": This group wants material success and control, achievement and recognition. The "aspirers" eventually evolve into the "successful." Most modern retail and high-functionality premium brands are targeted here.

It is not just people that have mindsets; cities do too. Consumer researchers say that each town has its own mindset, of which they can identify three types: "arrived," "striving," and "escapist." Bangalore, India's Silicon Valley, and home of the IT revolution, typifies the "arrived" mindset, which displays the assurance of guaranteed progress, and the balance and harmony between cultural capital and economic capital. Hyderabad, though equivalent in size, is not yet there but is well on its way to becoming a version of Silicon Valley too. Nagpur, Ludhiana, Madurai, Surat—all Tier 2 towns—are examples of the "striving"— totally focused on not getting left behind, on bettering lifestyle, on maximizing earning and maximizing fun, displaying the impatience of those who have heard the epiphany, and have much catching up to do. Varanasi, the ancient holy city, and to a lesser extent Bareilly, in the poor-performing state of Uttar Pradesh in the north, and perhaps Vijayawada in the south, are examples of the "escapist" mindset— wanting to do better but still feeling weighted down with problems, aware of opportunities that could be had, but not knowledgeable or energetic enough to work towards getting there. Consumer-goods sales and acceptance of modern retailing and entertainment venues correlate well with these mindsets.

Age Cohorts

Virginia Valentine, founding partner of Semiotic Solutions, a UK-based cultural-analysis and market-research firm, describes an age cohort as follows:

> It comprises a group of people born at roughly the same time in the same place or country. Consequently, they have experienced the same major economic, political, and social upheavals at about the same age. Their lives are punctuated by the same crises. They share the same nation—memories of music, film, entertainers, public figures, fashions, and fads. And they encounter every new decade, each with its own particular flavor, at similar stages in their lives.

In the chapter on Schizophrenic India we discussed the age cohorts that exist in India today, and what ethos each of them comes from. First, there is my parents' generation, namely the pre-Independence generation born before 1947. Then there is the post-Independence genaration, who can be called "midnight's children," a term borrowed from the author, Salman Rushdie. This actually encompasses two sets of people. The first set comprises those who were born between 1940 and 1970 and who are today between 35–65 years of age. The second set comprises those who were born between 1970 and 1985 (specifically, this set can be called "midway children"). They are today about 20–35 years old. Lastly, there are the young, those who are under 25-years-of-age today, whom I call "liberalization children"—the oldest of them were just about eight or nine years old when liberalization happened at the beginning of the 1990s.

The pre-independence generation accounts for a little less than 10% of India's population, and the "liberalization" generation for 35%. "Midnight's children" born in the 1950s and 1960s account for 26% of the population, the balance of 30% being those "midway children" born in the sunlight years of the 1970s and 1980s, between Indira Gandhi's heyday and liberalization.

These age cohorts are particularly relevant to a discussion on consumption, because each of them has been raised with totally different worldviews that have naturally influenced and shaped their consumption ideology and hence their consumption behavior.

The pre-Independence generation's worldview, maybe its very consciousness, was shaped by the Gandhian values of simple living and high thinking, of abstemiousness and self-reliance, of reducing one's wants and so forth.

"Midnight's children" and "midway children", the latter perhaps to a lesser extent, bore the brunt of post-Independence nation building. They saw wars, famine, and food rationing and coped with an identity that was either a badge of sufferance or a cross to bear. (Many from this generation fled to the USA and the UK, and later to the Middle East, swearing never to come back to penury.) While both these generations are products of the same post-Independence socialistic ethos, only the "midway children" were young enough at the time of liberalization to be able to adopt a new worldview.

I call this generation, particularly the "midway children," the "Rajiv Gandhi age cohort", because it was he who first fired their imagination with his clarion call, " Let's take India into the 21ˢᵗ century." His persona and policies epitomized the changing face of India in the latter half of the 1980s, as did his attire—home-spun *khadi pyjama-kurta*, teamed up with Gucci shoes and expensive imported dark glasses.

If those from the pre-Independence generation are unhappy consumers, "midnight's children" are guilty consumers. My mother, who is 75, bemoans the fact that she needs to use air conditioning to survive the 45°C summer heat. "I have become soft," she says with genuine pain. "Midnight's children" and "midway children" consume, but are always justifying and rationalizing their consumption, saying that they can walk away from all this at any time.

Each of the age cohorts has a different set of attitudes to "foreign-ness"; for instance, in their response to foreign big brands. The pre-Independence generation, of course, was told to boycott foreign goods during Mahatma Gandhi's "Quit India" movement and was made to feel quite guilty about using anything "foreign." "Midnight's children," as well as "midway children," grew up in splendid isolation, listening to the discourse on self-reliance and the constant admonition that the country's precious foreign-exchange resources were not to be frittered away. Yet they could not help but see the difference in quality between the shoddy *swadeshi* (domestic) products that the inefficient domestic industry produced and the few smuggled foreign goods, of far better quality and design, that made their way into the country. Furthermore, because so few people traveled abroad, a pair of Levi's jeans was a very proud possession indeed for any teenager then. Today, like liberalization, things foreign are a sensible, pragmatic choice, but primarily if their purchase can be justified on the grounds of their functionality rather their brand or badge value. This is because with liberalization, one of the important things that happened to this age cohort was an enormous surge of the slogan "proud to be Indian—India is as important for the world as vice versa."

This age cohort, of "midnight and midway children," which is today's mainstream "ruling" cohort, has experienced life both before and after liberalization and has seen the enormous progress after liberalization. Thus, they enthusiastically push their children to avail themselves of all the opportunities "we never had." The higher social classes amongst them are at the peak of their earning careers and consume, almost in a childlike manner, by themselves and through their children, to make up for all the years of childhood deprivation. I often say that the youth market in India is found amongst the adults in their 40s and 50s. Yet, this cohort is still very value-conscious, does not like to waste money, is perennially guilty about consuming, and needs a rational and function-based reason to part with the big bucks.

For the liberalization generation, of course, having been born, or at least brought up, in a consumption-friendly environment, consumption is a positive thing. Growing up as they do in a getting-richer ethos, they are a materialistic cohort. Having or getting all the goodies that life has to offer at such an early age is obviously and naturally very important for them. And it almost goes without saying that for them the labels "foreign" or "Indian" or even the cultural overtones of "imported" do not exist.

Today, most of the heads of households and housewives are "midnight's children" or "midway children." The early liberalization generation is just beginning to enter adulthood and we are at the point where liberalization children are about to begin setting up their own homes. Whether this will change things dramatically or marginally is yet to be seen. However, the numbers show that even in 2025, about half the households will still be run by "midway children," making the coexistence of various shades and grades of consumption ideologies a fact of life in contemporary Consumer India.

ETHNICITY

Consumer India is a federation of different cultures that just happen to be sharing the same geography and to some extent, the same history. The situation is analogous to the European Union, where constituent countries are actually very different from each other. And yet, just as there is a shared and clear European ethnicity that is different from say, African ethnicity, there is a shared Indian ethnicity. Is there such a thing as "pan-Indian?" Or is that also merely a "geographic expression like the equator," as Churchill said? The answer, as always in India, is yes and no, depending on the category, and the proposition.

There are many levels at which businesses in India have dealt with ethnicity and made it work for them.

In the area of media and entertainment, there is no single channel, film producer, or film star that enjoys "pan-Indian" popularity. Even Bollywood, the Hindi film industry, is not popular in south India where regional language films prevail. It isn't just an issue of language but of cultural identification. Ekta Kapoor is a very successful producer of television soap operas and her programs command the highest viewer ratings across the country, much to the envy and bafflement of her competitors. Her story lines are seen to be regressive and ordinary by many critics, yet she amasses a loyal viewership. Her formula lies in creating programs around different ethnic groups, because she knows the depth to which ethnic identity influences consumer preferences. Anyone else would have chosen to go with a "pan-Indian" set of characters and dub the content in different languages. But that would not have released the full potential that identification with roots could provide.

Several companies have chosen to consider ethnicity as one of the many variables in their operational marketing strategy, but not as a major decider of their business-market strategy. Product formulations are suitably changed to suit ethnic preferences, while keeping the brand proposition the same. For example, a brand of tea called "Taaza," popular in the 1990s, was positioned across India on the same platform of "freshness" (the literal meaning of the name in Hindi), but contained high-flavor Darjeeling or strong Assam tea, depending on which part of the country it was available in. The cooking-oil category also tends to maintain the same brand across India with the same consumer proposition, but the contents vary in different parts of the country using different types of oil (mustard, sesame, coconut) to cater to different culinary requirements. Advertising often has a singular concept, but is subtly designed for different cultures, in exactly the way global advertising is; an enormous amount of original effort is needed to ensure that the communication retains its flavor in all languages and is not translated literally. Market research, especially qualitative research, is another area which needs an enormous amount of process and skill to synthesize findings drawn from culturally and linguistically diverse groups. Distribution strategies have also been altered by region. A tap-attached, drinking-water purifier discovered to its chagrin that a singular distribution strategy across the country did not work because in hygiene-conscious south India, consumers expected to find the product in modern chemist stores, while in the gadget-collecting north Indian market, it needed to be distributed through mom-and-pop household-utensil shops. Of course in regions of the country where water was short, the product itself was not suitable and had to be modified to a tablet that could be added to a bin of stored water.

The popular notion was that as the Indian market evolved, it would get more homogeneous and "pan-Indian" brands and products would work; in fact, even global products and brands directly transplanted would work. Now we know that exactly the opposite is true. With modern retailing chains making it easier to tweak merchandizing to suit a locality, the big, national, "pan-Indian" brand is now being given a run for its money. The big, national FMCG brands from large companies are increasingly under attack from small but sharply targeted brands who operate in narrow, localized geographies. Addressing the highest common factor of the market has been the way to play for big consumer companies so far. Until about a decade ago, they had the big advantage of being national—most of the media was national too, making it suboptimal and wastefully expensive to use national media for a regional brand. The media, especially television, has become much more strongly localized, these days. Regional language, ethnic, state-level television has firmly entrenched itself, regional political parties are here to rule and national political parties perforce have to ally themselves with a whole host of regional satrap parties in order to be able to form a government at the center. With localized television comes a whole host of localized identities now able to explore themselves, and perhaps it is time to think about the ethnic factor as a strategic variable.

Kishore Biyani from The Future Group, believes that every community in India has a cultural DNA and it is possible to configure business propositions around these. He is certainly right about the cultural DNA. The Gujarati community, for example, is the one that owns most of the motels in the USA. They have a strong entrepreneurial gene, the women are au fait with the stock market, despite having very little formal education, and they will travel all over the world with their own cooks so that they get their own vegetarian food, exactly the way they like it. Food is very important to them, and the queues outside many a Gujarati restaurant bear testimony to this. They continue to buy and store, in bulk, commodities such as oil and rice and while they will spend in the kitchen, they are not so ready to spend on house beautification! The north Indian, on the other hand, is the showy one, where the family food and family living quarters are Spartan, but food served to guests and the drawing room décor always makes a statement. Yet they are adept at achieving high show-off value at minimal cost. After one particularly difficult market research assignment, for a paint company, we discovered that the reason our user and volume estimates were not tallying was that the drawing room walls were painted with plastic emulsion, while the ceilings, where guests did not often gaze, were painted with distemper. Similarly, even if drawing rooms were painted with plastic emulsion, the bedrooms, where guests do not go, were painted with cheap distemper.

North Indian weddings are opportunities for an extreme display of wealth, where even the bridal trousseau is displayed for all to see. I remember a study done on how different ethnic groups were responding to a generally inflationary environment. It was called "tightrope walking on a shoestring budget," and the findings showed that certain communities had cut out the high-priced Johnson's baby soap and were bathing the child with cheaper soap but ensuring that guests were served cashew-nut biscuits. Others were keeping the children's portfolio of products unchanged but were moving to home-made pickles and jams and saving money there.

THE EMERGENCE OF NEW CULTURE CLASSES AND CONSUMPTION TRIBES

In a recent interview with *The Times of India*, VS Naipaul, the famous writer of Indian origin, said that he did not believe that future strife in India would be between the rich and the poor. He said that it would be a "clash of civilizations" within India. And maybe we are beginning to see that. He refers to a particular emerging group as "green card wallahs," saying that they aspire to and emulate an American lifestyle even if they don't live there. I have a friend who calls them RNIs or Resident Non-Indians (a twist on the word NRI or Non-Resident Indian, which is used for the Indian diaspora). In contrast to this is another group that is "proud to be Indian." Ethnic men's wear, ethnic homes and minimalist living are fast emerging as trends. The Indian trader or *bania* community is an interesting mix of the old and the new —he will take his wife to Bangkok for an expensive holiday and buy his children an expensive video game, but his shop will be dusty and run down by modern standards, exactly the way his grandfather ran it.

The uninitiated westerner may be tempted to dismiss all this as a whole lot of stereotypes peddled by story tellers, but those familiar with marketing to Consumer India know that this diversity is for real, and can be ignored only at their own peril.

While it may be too early to say that "my target India" can be defined as a collection of tribes or culture classes or ethnic communities, this space definitely needs to be watched, especially if you are a retailer, a financial services provider or a food company.

7

Understanding the
Process of Change

———◆———

HOW TO READ AND PREDICT CHANGE IN CONSUMER INDIA

The Force of Change

India changes in very insidious ways which are hard to see. Sometimes, it appears like everything is changing; yet, at others, it seems like nothing ever changes. Executives who work on that annual ritual called the "strat plan" confess that year after year they watch with an eagle eye and a wide-angle lens for signs of changes that will reshape their markets and usher in new threats and opportunities for their business—and report not having found any changes worth mentioning. Yet, five years later, they invariably discover that their market is starting to look distinctly different, causing them to ask in bewilderment, "When did we blink and not see this happening?" The answer lies in understanding the process of change in India.

To most developed-market watchers, change is about acceleration. As we were taught in high school physics, Force = Mass x Acceleration. However, we automatically assume that the only way to generate a significant force of change is to have a large acceleration. But in India it works the other way around. Conventional wisdom, that "doesn't everybody know" authoritative piece of knowledge, tends to forget that if Force = Mass x Acceleration, then a small acceleration (small changes over long periods of time) can also unleash a large force of change, if the mass that is changing is very large. That's how change comes about in Consumer India—a large mass of people moving with a very small acceleration unleashes a large force of change. It is a bit like an enormous iceberg. Even if the center of gravity shifts marginally, a whole lot of water is displaced. A slight change in the income of rural India brings in its wake a huge new market; a slight inclusion of western food or western clothes in the wardrobe creates a quick-growing market and, of course, an illusion that everyone is changing—except that the change is not visible through surveys.

The language of high acceleration change is about megatrends and discontinuities and key drivers of change, all very testosterone-laden statements. The language of low acceleration change is more feminine. It is about almost invisible, below-the-surface change caused by change confluences (a collection of small changes that occur simultaneously) that lead to slowly swelling change waves, creeping trends, and resultant ripple effects. This chapter provides a framework for how to read and recognize change in Consumer India.

Change Confluences

The reason change confluences are easy to miss is because of their very nature. They are caused by the coming together of several little changes, each of which, individually, appears insignificant; but when they occur together, they cause a change confluence or a change wave, unleashing significant changes in markets. Consumer India excels at this, changing a little bit on several dimensions at the same time, thus collectively resulting in a changed market and consumer landscape over the medium term. These changes occur not only to the consumer-intrinsic world (economic, demographic, resultant lifestyle, and worldview), but also on the supply side, where any given market space can be affected significantly, even by small increases in sophistication and the evolution of apparently unconnected market spaces, each moving at a different speed.

An example of such a change confluence is what adversely affected the fast-moving consumer goods (FMCG) industry in 2000, leading to a puzzling decline in demand and consumer "down-trading" (that is, switching to options in a lower price–performance band), despite incomes going up and an overall increase in consumer confidence. Most of the early attempts to understand what was going on were confined to the FMCG category itself and the conclusion was that nothing within the FMCG industry had changed dramatically. It was only a broader investigation that revealed that there was a change confluence outside the FMCG world that was to blame. There was a sudden boom in housing finance and consumer credit caused by a fall in interest rates and the simultaneous blossoming of several categories of consumer durables, tempting consumers to buy their own homes and stock them with white and brown goods, all payable in equal monthly installments. Because consumers had borrowed so much for these, they had committed a large part of their future income towards paying off loans and the residual amount had to be kept for food and FMCGs. Obviously, down-trading and careful spending resulted. As one consumer put it, if status-signaling was to be done, then spending on a brand new car did it far better than spending on a premium brand of shampoo or aftershave.

Another example is the premium hotel industry that was hit by a change confluence in the first decade after liberalization. Changes feeding into the confluence were travel-related, communication-related, and social. Air travel had just been privatized and after decades of suffering an indifferent government airline monopoly, consumers at least had choice in the form of the many new private airlines. Suddenly, from two flights a day from Mumbai to Delhi, there were now 14. There not being enough traffic to sustain all of them, they vied with one another to pamper the business traveler. The car industry also came into its own at exactly that time, and the bumpy pieces of non-air-conditioned metal that had previously passed for cars were replaced by modern cars. The business traveler could do a comfortable day trip and avoid overnight stays altogether. At the same time, cell phones had started to grow rapidly, changing the norms of business communication by reducing the need to travel at all. Thanks to the aggressive growth in the economy and the rise of service businesses, especially financial services, there was a shortage of staff and senior management got younger, had younger kids at home, and wanted to spend as many nights as they could at home. Suddenly, the basis of competition and perceptions of what constituted features and price value delivered by hotel rooms changed quite dramatically.

Till then, hotel economics was based on the assumption that one day's work for an out-of-town visitor resulted in two nights stay and since travel was expensive and cumbersome, people also tended to stay longer on each trip, and spend more on services like laundry. These assumptions led to the creation of appropriate services, and a pricing and checkout system was configured for longer stays, but was not as profitable for shorter stays. Moreover, premium hotels spent a lot of effort and money in developing facilities and fine dining experiences for older clientele who were almost one generation behind the power men and women.

A further example shows the effects of change confluence on a less affluent market. I once did some work for a bicycle company whose market share was beginning to decline. Nobody paid much attention to it, dismissing it as statistical aberrations in market share measurement. However, when it was clear that it was a downward trend, albeit slow, a detailed market analysis was done. Historically, buyers of bicycles were generally poor villagers who wanted the cheapest piece of metal with two tires, and were not willing to pay more for something better. There were no obvious visible signs of change in the market and each year, at strategy review time, no change were recommended. However, when we finally looked more closely, we noticed that over the past five years, several small changes had been taking place, which collectively had reshaped the market. We noticed that although bicycle buyers still comprised the lower-income villagers, the average income had risen, equivalent to what would have been classified as lower-middle income five years earlier. Also, the age profile had got younger and the school- and college-going proportion had increased. The mindset was not about the cheapest possible bike to buy, but about getting better quality for a slightly higher price with greater functionality in brakes and stability. The startled CEO suddenly said, "You mean we are youth marketers?" He also said in a worried tone, "We have to overhaul our entire R&D department. They can do value engineering and provide less or the same benefit for less money. But now we need to look at value addition." The fact is that the entire market had been reshaped by a combination of little demographic, economic, and supply-side forces. First, thanks to liberalization and the pattern of economic growth in that period, the lowest income group in rural India had declined sharply, leaving only the ultra poor, who could not afford anything much. The erstwhile lowest income group had moved one rung up the income ladder, but since the price gap between motorcycles and bicycles was so large, they remained bicycle buyers, but with higher standards of living and higher expectations. Schools had been established nearby and more young people were going to these more local institutions. At the same time, some of the older folk chose to opt out of the bicycle market and switch to public transport, which had marginally improved. Thanks to better communication, the area of activity or the geographic footprint of the average skilled worker in a village—the carpenter, tile workers, and small, door-to-door salesmen—had also widened, making the present bicycle far too humble both in style and functionality for the new consumer.

A whole new category of bicycles had to be invented, which were not quite the sports or mountain bikes popular in the rest of the world, but were roadsters with higher functionality and sporty looks that are priced affordably low. Several attempts have been made but with limited success so far, and it appears that the traditional bicycle has had its day, and the new one has not yet been innovated to everyone's satisfaction.

Morphing Change vs. Molting Change

There are two ways in which change can happen. First, there is molting change; like the snake which, overnight, sheds its old skin to reveal a brand new skin. But that is not the way change happens in India. Change in India is of the morphing kind—a slow but definite transformation from within, like an amoeba which, with every tiny particle it ingests, changes shape infinitesimally; and over a period of time, almost without us noticing, we end up having a totally different-looking amoeba.

Many people look for evidence of molting change in India and almost inevitably end up being frustrated by two common phenomena called "mixed verdicts" and "continuity with change," both of which are typical of morphing change. India launches space shuttles and satellites by breaking a coconut, for good luck, at the launch site, just before countdown begins; and new computers are welcomed into offices by anointing them with a red dot of vermillion powder used during usual Hindu prayers. If that is a picture of old-fashioned modernity, then the other side of it is poor, illiterate fishermen in the coastal state of Kerala who check market prices on their cell phones to determine at which jetty to land their catch. And young people continue to want to have weddings with all the traditional rituals; yet the henna that was traditionally applied on palms of hands now, since wedding outfits have got more revealing, also graces the small of the back and goes around the arm as an amulet; and the traditional song and dance now has a distinct Bollywood movie flavor to it.

Mixed Verdicts

Anyone wanting to read change in India must be prepared for mixed verdicts, which are the hallmark of everything Indian, be it India's economy or polity or markets and consumers. The best illustration of this can be seen in India's voting behaviour and nuances of government-formation based on a "first past the post" system. After a general election, it is not unusual to find that the party qualified to form a central government has a majority of the seats but a minority share of the vote. Does this reflect the nuances of electoral arithmetic or the people's preference in a democracy? Increasingly, no party at the center is getting the clear majority of seats needed form a government and must enter into pre- or post-poll alliances with popular regional parties. Depending on the choice of the regional partners, even the smallest party can wield influence over the economic policy of central government. The questions that cannot be unambiguously answered are: "Is such a parliament reflective of the people's mandate or is it the result of someone's genius in understanding the electoral arithmetic?" and "Does this indicate the maturing of India's democracy (multiple-party alliances to truly reflect its plurality) or the creation of a banana-republic-style fractious alliance between several strange bedfellows?"

Here's another example of mixed verdicts. Between 1996 and 2006, India had the highest continuous growth in national income ever, yet less than 20% of Indian households will have enough spending power to qualify as mainstream consumers of normally priced consumer goods. However, there are sharp reductions in poverty levels, bringing large numbers into the consuming fold for the first time, with limited consumption of low-priced goods. The question is "Does India qualify in the world foreign direct investment (FDI) sweepstakes of 'attractive markets of the new millennium'?"

Even in the top eight cities in India we see that ownership of cars is only 25%, and air conditioners 10%, among the topmost socioeconomic class (SEC A). Yet in the top 23 urban centers, half of the lowest SEC (SEC E) households has a television, one-third an audio system, and one-fifth has cooking gas and satellite TV access. Is this a vibrant consumer market, or is it not?

Continuity with Change

And if confused verdicts leading to difficult judgments are one hallmark of morphing change, "continuity with change" is the other. For example, young people tell me that they no longer want to have the traditional arranged marriages, but, they don't want to move to love marriages either, with all the effort of finding their own partner. They want engineered marriages, where the arranged-marriage process still works, only in a more modern way. The boy's side descending with a vast retinue on to the girl's home is now modernized to just the boy and his immediate family visiting a mutually arranged hotel, club or friend's house; and then, instead of the expected instant answer after just one meeting, it is now OK to meet alone, or loosely chaperoned, a few times before making a decision. As Santosh Desai, then president of McCann-Erickson India and one of India's best-known cultural analysts opines, the dating market isn't here, but the mating market has just been decontrolled.

Modernity in India has often been likened to a tight fist loosening. Women are not moving en masse to western apparel, but the *salwar kameez* is giving the sari a run for its money, even in the smallest towns; The traditional *salwar kameez* is getting more fusion in its look, and has spawned a new genre called "east-west" outfits. The tunic on top is getting shorter and shorter and the *salwar* at the bottom getting more like trousers; the *dupattas,* or large stoles, that are mandatory for modesty in the traditional design, have not been dispensed with, but they have been reduced to thin wisps of chiffon. At the same time, tops worn over jeans are getting longer and longer, so that even girls from conservative families can wear trouser bottoms or jeans without raising parental eyebrows.

I always wondered how the sari would morph, given that it has been an unchanging six yards of unstitched fabric, draped in just one way with infinite minor variations. And of course while we were busy looking at how slowly the sari was changing, the traditional sari blouse has changed much more: daring, halter-necked, off-the-shoulder, sequined, and much more, giving the garment a new lease of life for young women.

Extended families still exist, but they have loosened in some significant ways to accommodate individuality. The defining space of an extended family is usually a common kitchen, and modern extended families still have a main common kitchen. However, modern extended families also now permit a kitchenette for the younger generation, so that even non-vegetarian food can be stored, heated, and consumed in orthodox vegetarian households—as long as it is brought in from the outside and not cooked at home.

In the cargo-carrying truck market, it was automatically assumed that as the market evolved, it would consolidate and develop into a typical market structure. The current market structure of lots of small truck owners owning one or two small trucks each would give way to larger and larger trucks, and the small trucker would eventually get swallowed up by larger fleet owners. However, consolidation is happening, but in a morphing, "continuity with change" way. Several small truck owners are aligning as a constellation around a bigger trucker, forming a fleet that is controlled, though not owned by, the big trucker, who has the market access. The bigger trucker ensures that they all buy the same brand of truck in order to form a buying group that can get preferential treatment with suppliers, and encourages them to add new trucks gradually, sell off the very old ones, and effect small net increases in the number of trucks each of the smaller truckers owns. For the truck manufacturers, the market share risks are the same as if classical consolidation were occurring in the market, but the benefit of market consolidation in terms of having fewer, larger customers to serve does not accrue. Any truck manufacturer who looks for change in this market through molting lenses, and through the lens of international analogies, will end up betting heavily, at his own peril, on large trucks.

Large international market leaders like Volvo who came in with only the large trucks are now hastily adding smaller trucks to their portfolio.

Rural India is a classic case of morphing change. We will discuss its changing contours in detail in a later chapter but here is a brief outline of how it morphs. Even as people continued to argue that over 70% of the Indian population is being supported by 26% of the gross domestic product (GDP) (that is, the agriculture sector) rural India had diversified beyond agriculture and had added another equivalent-sized, non-agricultural economy to itself. How did this happen? It happened in a hard to notice, creeping kind of way. Children of rural households went to nearby large towns for their education and realized that the farm was not large enough to support their aspirations or even occupy their time when they came back. Since government jobs were no longer easily available because of downsizing, they typically started doing some extra non-farm business to stay gainfully occupied. Initially, this was a small part of the household income but, over time, it grew, and the tone of the household changed from that of a farmer's house (and lifestyle) to that of a small businessman or service provider. With this came a new self-image and new consumption behavior.

Creeping Trends and Ripple Effects

Looking for the megatrends or huge waves that come and sweep society in their wake is a bit of a futile exercise in Consumer India. The things to look out for are the creeping trends. The creeping rise in income is one clear trend. On an average, the growth in national income doesn't look like it has enough acceleration to cause much of an impact; however, over the years, the change in income levels and self-perception and, hence aspiration, become evident in less than one generation. The thought that "one day, my children and their children will have a better life," has changed to, "soon I myself will begin to live differently." The mindset then also shifts from *dreaming about* a better future to *planning for* a better future.

The change in employment patterns is another example of creeping trends. Occupation shifts have crept slowly and changed the face of Consumer India, without any fanfare. From a consumer base of predominantly farmers and government servants, Consumer India now has a large chunk of the self-employed, especially in service businesses, both urban and rural. This is happening, bringing with it a whole new set of opportunities, mostly untapped.

The blurring of boundaries between India and *Bharat* (urban–rural), the "ural" mindset that we talked about earlier, is yet another morphing change, caused by the exposure to television and decreasing power distance.[1] The changing attitude of the poor from demanding social justice to grabbing economic opportunity is yet another creeping trend, best portrayed in the electoral defeat of Laloo Yadav, the former chief minister of Bihar, who asked his people why they wanted roads—did they have cars to drive on them? No? Well, then, if they still wanted roads, the rich man would drive by in a car and spit on them. So it was better not to have roads, he explained to his largely illiterate electorate. His recent and sudden electoral defeat after several victories, was caused by a hitherto subservient electorate deciding to cast its vote, instead of voting its caste. This is indicative of another creeping trend which certain sections of the media have labeled as a preference for "development over dignity" (as in, voting for a person of your own lower caste).

The increase in literacy in each succeeding generation is one more example of a creeping trend. Again, while the percentage of the population who have finished school or achieved a college degree does not increase at a rapid rate, the total number of years of formal education is slowly increasing, and when aggregated over a large mass of people, the impact is quite significant. This is one of the factors that is driving another creeping trend—the rise of "womanism." Womanism is not the more overt and aggressive feminism, but a milder creeping version of it that negotiates for more space and power within the broad framework of traditional gender equations; and something we will discuss further in the subsequent chapter on women.

Predicting Future Change: The Analogy Trap

During my brief stint with one of the "Big 5" consulting firms, we would undertake copious team analyses that would plot multi-country data with GDP per capita on one axis and the per-capita consumption of anything we were studying on the other. The conclusion always was that on the basis of empirical evidence, as GDP per capita increased, the people of India would consume a certain volume of cola, beer, or toilet soap, wet wipes, Viagra, or whatever. This was a representative example of the thinking of the analogy school, a great favorite of many, especially the consulting fraternity, which assumes that all emerging markets will follow the same path as developed markets and that the world will, in its fully developed state, look exactly like the USA. (As far as colas are concerned, I have always found the assumption that cola consumption is an inevitability that comes with GDP per capita growth hard to swallow. First of all, it is a bit of a shame to link the state of development of a society to how much colored water it consumes per capita. Maybe Indian kidneys are different, or maybe we do not have enough clean public toilets, and that why we hesitate to give our kids a drink of cola away from home!)

The truth is that analogies need to be thought through carefully. Information on global warming, health hazards from fast food, the latest research into causes of cancer, and so on are all available in real time and in as much graphic detail to nascent market consumers as they are to developed market consumers. Should then the former simply follow the same beaten path that the latter have traversed? And as the former managing director of Unilever India, Arun Adhikari, once said to me, the very purpose of studying history is to learn from it and try to see if you can escape that fate; a lesson that a large Indian retailer I work with has taken to heart. If Wal-Mart-style hypermarkets are what modern western society is all about, then the consumer will go in that direction, as long as no one creates a modern Indian version of the same. "We are chaotic people," he points out. "We do not like shopping in straight and neatly labeled aisles, or operate with checklists that are linear." So he designs his hypermarkets the way traditional Indian bazaar shopping is done—with islands rather than aisles.

Actually, this lack of relevance of analogous markets is not so difficult to comprehend, if one were to ignore the issue of corporate imperialism for a while. Friends of mine who live in the US do not text message or are not as cell phone-friendly as the average small-town Indian. They are well served by the extensive landline network and are far more Internet-penetrated, using a variety of handheld devices. It is exactly the reverse for several poor Indians, for whom the landline is inaccessible and the Internet not widespread, but the cell rates are affordable, text messaging is cheap, and available in Hindi too.

How then does one predict the cultural future of Consumer India? The only way to do it is to painstakingly construct it from first principles, by studying age cohorts, by looking at cultural drivers of change (see next chapter), and by understanding the process of change and the DNA of the society which is changing.

The DNA of Indian Society: "This As Well As That"

In retrospect, the expectation in the early years of liberalization of market analysts, me included, that we would see an India overrun with the western way of living, eating, and thinking, was naïve. The mental model that all of us had was that there would be a short, sharp battle between tradition and modernity and the winner would be modernity, with traditional ways of doing things falling by the wayside, buried in the archives of history. The dominant logic was that it was a zero-sum game and that there could be only one winner. This OR that! But Consumer India surprised us yet again, by adopting a "this AS WELL AS that" approach.

Engineered marriages, computerized horoscope-casting, and cyber *aarati* (screen savers featuring pictures of favorite Gods) abounded. In fact, even as the traditional fundamentalists loudly voiced their disapproval of the celebration of Valentine's Day and the "westernization" of Indian culture, in just a couple of years, aided by television soaps, *Karwa Chauth*, has become the new home-grown Valentine's Day. *Karwa Chauth* is a romantic old north Indian ritual, where the wife fasts all day for the well-being of her husband, then when the moon rises, she looks at the moon and her husband's face and he feeds her the first morsel of food that breaks her fast.

Another example is from the chocolate market. Ever since I can remember, chocolate companies have been asking how they can get a share of the traditional Indian sweets market, especially during festival time. How could they get chocolates into the traditional exchange of sweets during *Diwali*, the Festival of Lights, when people send each other boxes of Indian sweets? They tried advertising but with no success; they tried special chocolate flavors and special gift boxes printed with traditional Indian motifs, but that didn't work too well either. Eventually, the small players of the market innovated the right "this as well as that" combination, which took off—a set of individually wrapped chocolate mounds of uneven shape, packed in traditional decorated clay lamps used for the traditional lighting up of the house that is done by everyone for *Diwali*.

The food market evolution is another example of the "this as well as that" hybrid solutions that Consumer India revels in. The batter for making *idli* and *dosa*, the staple rice cakes and pancakes of south Indian homes, became available in plastic packets, made everyday by a host of housewives and distributed through local grocers. Such solutions, applied to other foods as well, have succeeded in pre-empting the entry of ready-to-eat processed food. For example, as lives get busier and more and more women have less and less time to cook, cooking at home is bound to decline. However, the solution has not been the adoption of packaged food or a change of food habits, as the analogy school would have thought or imagined, but the rise of a cottage-sector "kitchen outsourcing" industry. An increasing number of women are supplying "tiffin boxes" of home-made food in each of the big cities, their consumers being not just the bachelors and hostel dwellers but homes as well. So the cook who cooked in your kitchen has been replaced by the cook who cooks in her own kitchen and supplies the food to you; and by the cook at the professional kitchen (the mental model here is that of a community kitchen, not a restaurant).

If home-made food is warm, wonderful, and fresh, and its factory-made alternative is cold, clinical, and not fresh, then such solutions are actually the best of both worlds. Made on a micro scale, as if at home, by other housewives, they are ready to cook (all negative labor outsourced) but allow for the cooking to be done at home (the positive labor retained).

And McDonald's now offers varieties for the vegetarian and the Indian palate, enabling the impeccable fast-food experience of McDonald's to come in the comfortingly familiar form of the *aloo tikki*. Not to be outdone, the local Jumbo King chain takes an Indian street dish called *vada pav* (an Indian burger) and offers it the McDonald's way.

Generally, we find that outer-directed change or change outside the precincts of the home is quite revolutionary, while change within the home is evolutionary. As a marketer, you deal with the same individual living in two different and sometimes contradictory worlds. The western mind is conditioned to think in terms of "this OR that." It gives rise to a split personality, causing great dissonance. The Indian mind can happily cope with these real contradictions, and not feel hypocritical or misaligned. Oriental societies generally have far less dissonance than occidental ones, and they do not find too much tension between the different facets of their living—the westernized version of them in the world outside, and the Indianised version in the world at home. Some call it hypocritical and two-faced; but actually it is just a high tolerance level of ambiguity. I know of young wives who are virtually unrecognizable when they get changed at airports as they fly away from in-law country, and do the reverse when they come back. Far from feeling pressured, they pride themselves on their adaptability, and their husbands admire them all the more for it.

Anyone familiar with the history of India would actually have known that this is the way India would respond to the new influences brought by liberalization. It would bear repetition to say that societies change around their DNA. And plurality, or "this as well as that," is the DNA of Indian society, and is the essence of the Hindu way of life. Think of the stories about the Hindu pantheon that every child in India grows up with, irrespective of religion. The concept of the *avatars* (incarnations) creates many dramatically different versions of the same God and says that all are but different facets of the same person. So Ram, the ever-good, ever-dutiful, ever-obedient, insipid god who deferred to public opinion and made his wife publicly undergo tests to prove her chastity—and finally abandoned her when she was pregnant—is actually the same person as Krishna, the playboy cowherd sharpshooter around whose deeds some of the best romantic poetry and music has been written. He is a brilliant manipulator, had many women in his life, and maneuvered his way out of trouble often. Equally, most Indian men have no trouble believing that the bloodthirsty Kali, the ever-patient devotee of her husband Parvati, and the strong, eight-armed, multi-skilled and tough Durga or Shakti are all different versions of the same goddess.

The moral relativism of the Hindu way of life is often startling to those encountering it for the first time. You can cross the seven seas and eat and drink forbidden foods but you can come back home, take a dip in the Ganges and be morally purified and as good as new. In the days of the British Raj it was not unusual to see clerks in government offices wearing shirts and ties on top and *dhotis* and sandals below, because as they sat at their desks, the top part of their bodies was all that the British officer saw. On a similar note, Brahmins all over India are forbidden from eating non-vegetarian food but Brahmins in Bengal are allowed to eat fish, because, in Bengal, fish is considered a vegetable of the sea.

The economy also is clearly a hybrid model of "this as well as that" —socialism in some form, free-market economics in some form, all coexisting. The future of Consumer India, therefore, must not be thought of in terms of "ring out the old, ring in the new," but more as a coexistence, fusion, loosening of rigid structures, new ways of doing old things, and so on. Maggi noodles (instant noodles), whole wheat with *sambaar* (south Indian spicy lentils) flavoring, Punjabi Chinese food, ready-to-wear, pre-stitched saris, and herbal cosmetics coexisting with glycolic facial peels, and the *Gayatri mantra* (a highly revered Hindu chant from the Vedas) available for download as a ring tone, if you are hip enough for that!

The Contradictory Indian

At an MTV conference many years ago, a youth-market observer called the younger generation of India the "dual passport" generation, to signify how they were a contradictory blend of western modernity and Indian tradition. Pavan K Varma, a well-known author on India, in a media interview about his book *Being Indian: Why the 21st Century Will Be India's,* says that we Indians are a bundle of contradictions: "We are focused and will work towards a goal despite formidable obstacles. So we are resilient, ingenious, ever hopeful." Anyone who sees the epic proportions to which we take the saga of high school and college admission exams, with an entire nation, rich and poor, coming to a standstill, will not doubt our single-mindedness or sense of purpose.

Yet Indians are very relaxed in their acceptance of dug up roads, mounds of uncleared garbage, eternal traffic jams, and abysmal services from public utilities for which they pay good money, or the way they litter, spit, and relieve themselves in public spaces. The poor will borrow to go to a rural private practitioner for their child's illness, but not demand better from a government clinic.

The increase in the number of women working outside the home was widely expected to trigger large-scale changes in the way the home was managed and a surge in the use of convenience products. However, the neglected detail was that Indian women are just as contradictory as men, just as much "this as well as that." Outside the home, she is her own person, the confident, "in control" working woman, but inside the home, she is the role-bound wife and mother. So while there is an increase in personal-products purchases, there is no surge in the use of convenience foods or disposable diapers within the home.

ENDNOTE

[1] Social psychologist Geert Hofestede's construct referring to the extent to which less powerful members of a society accept and expect that power is distributed unequally.

8

Cultural Foundations of Consumer India's Behavior

———⊱·0·⊰———

Of the three foundations of consumer behavior—psychological, social, and cultural—the last one is the hardest to see and to decode, because it is deep and changes slowly; yet it wields considerable power. As Virginia Valentine, the founding partner of Semiotic Solutions, often says, "Culture isn't inert. Its pretty ert. If it isn't working for you, then it is probably working against you."

The complexity of understanding the cultural foundations of consumer behavior increases significantly in markets where age-old cultures are ruptured by sudden and sharp events that cause ideological, political, economic and even technological discontinuity. Since cultures are embedded to varying degrees and slow to change, the events are forceful (for example, the fall of the Berlin Wall, the collapse of the Soviet Union, the opening up of China, the liberalization of India) and inevitably result in a redrawing of the cultural map of the market, bringing some unusual opportunities and unforeseen threats in their wake. An understanding of the cultural future of such markets in transition is critical for CEOs and strategists who need to gear up their organizations to compete in the future.

The contours of India's cultural future are still unclear, partly because as new evidence of the surprising ways in which India is changing continues to come to light, the old theories about inevitable westernization sound a bit simplistic. As we can easily see from the various ways in which India changes, there seems to be a new Indian culture which is an amalgam of old and new, and on which the traditional labels of "western" or "oriental" do not sit very comfortably. To attempt a forecast in matters as complicated as this would be hazardous—as they say, if you want to gaze into a crystal ball, then you have to be prepared to eat ground glass! So, instead, this chapter will provide a description of the forces that are driving cultural change in India and what we know about how they work. This snapshot of a work in progress will also provide some pretty good hypotheses about the new culture of Consumer India, and what it could mean for consumer markets.

THE FORCE OF LIBERALIZATION AND ITS CULTURAL MEANINGS

All major events in a nation's life are loaded with cultural meaning and have an impact on popular and consumer culture. So too has been the case with the liberalization in India.

The cultural meaning of liberalization and the consequent cultural shifts are best described in Table 8.1.

THE END OF CONTENTMENT AND ABSTEMIOUSNESS

The most important cultural shift is the discontent with living in genteel poverty forever. As a country, we now have an obsession with China comparisons (which includes the chief minister of Maharashtra coining a slogan about wanting to make Mumbai another Shanghai, and an Indian soldier on duty, high up in the Himalayas, who said that I should not be impressed with the good quality of Indian border roads, because the Chinese had built a double road to the border). Indians are completely preoccupied with the gross domestic product (GDP) growth rate each year, and the extreme competitiveness of the society is now shown in the epidemic of awards that have cropped up in every aspect of life. It would be an understatement to say that both the rich and the poor in post-liberalization India are in a crazy scramble

FROM		TOWARDS
1.a Genteel poverty	to	Learning to earn more
1.b Contentment and stability (for example, Hindu rate of growth)	to	Striving to keep up with others (for example, if China/South Korea/ Indonesia can, why can't we?)
2. *Swadeshi* (the name of the movement launched by Mahatma Gandhi, literally meaning "of (one's) own country"	to	International (for example, striving to make world-class goods, which can find export markets)
3. Self-reliance (no matter what the price to be paid)	to	Efficiency (if it's cheaper to buy, don't make it)
4. Isolation/aloofness	to	Exposure to/interaction with the rest of the world
5. Ideology/emotion	to	Pragmatism/rationality
6. Soft options (doing the popular thing)	to	Biting the bullet (doing what has to be done)
7. Obeying authority (for example, government dictates)	to	Freedom of choice (for example, a free-market economy)
8. Punishment/guilt/control (for example, curbing consumption through massive taxes on luxury goods)	to	Motivation/positive incentivization (for example, stimulating demand by cutting duties and lowering taxes)
9. Aiming for the lowest common denominator (for example, *Garibi Hatao*–Indira Gandhi's signature tune, meaning "banish poverty")	to	Aiming for the highest factor (for example, "Take India to the 21st century"–Rajiv Gandhi's signature tune)
10. Protection (of the weak)	to	Enabling people to become more competitive
11. Skepticism about technology ("may not be suitable to our conditions")	to	Seeking and embracing technology ("We can lead the world")

Table 8.1: Cultural Shifts Attending India's Liberalization

to maximize their earnings. Liberalization has certainly meant the death of the Gandhian discourse of living in genteel poverty, being content with the "Hindu rate of growth." It is this shift that now drives consumerism at national, institutional and individual levels.

Even the different states of the country are becoming increasingly competitive about attracting investment. A bright, young executive said to me that I didn't appreciate how stressed his generation was, because they had so many options, so few constraints, and they were all constantly worried that there was a better deal somewhere around the corner that they were not seeing or not going after.

Clearly, as Santosh Desai, former president of McCann Erickson India says, there is a new view of life today: "Life is not a condition, but a product. It is a blank that WE need to fill with achievement, enjoyment and meaning. Time is a real constraint. Therefore it is a canvas that needs to be filled."

PRAGMATISM REPLACES NATIONALISM

Ideology is dead and it is pragmatism that now rules. The student activism and trade union activity that marked the 1970s are virtually unheard of today. Political parties also have very little ideology; most of them hold centrist positions—some leaning a bit to the left, others a bit to the right. As the commerce minister said in a recent speech, since 1991, India has had five governments and six prime ministers but only one policy and point of view on liberalization. The communists practice some form of ideological protest in their role as minority coalition partner in the central government; but in their home state of West Bengal, which is the seat and source of their power, they are unabashedly capitalist.

Independent India was built on the Gandhian and Nehruvian values of *swadeshi* and self-reliance ("Be Indian, buy Indian," as the popular old slogan went). Out of this philosophy came a lot of excellent homegrown stuff, whether elite educational institutions that can hold their own in the world—such as the Indian Institutes of Technology (IITs) and the Indian Institute of Management (IIM), or the capability to build nuclear reactors, cars, computers, and more. But also came an era of splendid isolation, and an attitude of "making do." Interestingly, even as liberalization has replaced *swadeshi* and self-reliance with international standards and efficiency, India has been able to compete in the international arena by leveraging the very same capabilities developed as a result of the self-sufficiency ideology, that it now dismisses as unfashionable.

This change in values from self-reliance to efficiency has started transforming the way women in all social classes think about how they run their homes. Equally, and ironically, the abolition of *swadeshi* has also decreased the lure of the opposite pole, *videshi,* or foreign goods. Nowadays, "international" merely refers to products that match up to world standards. There are no other values attached to the label. "Made in America" has no more lure than "made in China" and the country of origin that people accept as the best could well be India.

The best view of the changing cultural mores emerges by contrasting the younger generation with their parents. As early as 1994, an article in *India Today*, based on an opinion poll of over one thousand 18–22-year-olds, pointed out presciently, that the new generation is playing by a fresh set of rules:

Rule 1: It's a war out there. Choose your weapons and make sure you are fast on the draw.

Rule 2: You've got only yourself to bank on, so watch your back.

Rule 3: Idealism is a drag. Rebellion (and non-conformity) is a bum trip, and no one has time for a loser.

Rule 4: If you've got it, flaunt it.

There has rarely been a generation so competitive (68% have set their eyes on zooming careers and outrageous wealth). Pragmatism, that once shameful word, is more than just a slogan; it's a conviction. (63% will play the game and network to get ahead; 65% would not change their religion even if it came in the way of marrying someone they loved).

In fact, marriage is seen to be a pragmatic partnership, an event that brings economies of scale, and living with parents is not such a bad deal either. It saves on the rent. There is not much talk of changing the system—the majority focuses on coping better and working the system better. The need for the goodies that life almost assures, at this point in the country's growth, overcomes any desire to rebel.

THE FORCE OF THE "ICE" WAVE: TECHNOLOGY-DRIVEN CULTURAL CHANGE

In the 1960s and 1970s all talk of technology used to be around the idea of "relevant technology." The notion was that poor countries need low-cost technology, that they must trade off things like efficiency and speed, and even certain levels of quality, in order to be able to offer "right price" products. The discourse was that high technology was for the rich, and low for the poor, and we must peg our technology levels somewhere in between. Exactly the opposite discourse is now taking place. The clamor and the conviction is for world class and world standard; the rush is on to catch up with the rest of the world and make up for lost time and lost money. High technology is seen to be the solution to create low-cost, wide-scale products and services for India, and quality that will enable it to get a share of the world's markets. Technology is perceived to be the new money-spinner, the new democratizer, the new solution to a lot of our evils, and the new definer of Indian identity—both as perceived by Indians themselves and by others in the outside world.

Information technology, communication and entertainment (ICE) are converging to create products and services that will slowly, yet definitively, shape a new India and the lives of the average Indian, whether rich or poor. This is perhaps the most potent and most important force that distinguishes emerging markets. As I have often said in this book, never before in the history of humanity have we had so many poor people subjected to so much technology, being exposed in real time to issues that affect the rest of the world.

Another, though less-informed, view of ICE is that it is about the **I**nternet, **C**ell phone ownership and conventional **E**ducation, and hence limited to the top of the Consumer India iceberg. However, the actual ICE wave that has swept the country, and continues to do so with ever-increasing force, is something that I call the $IC^2=E^2$ wave.

I stands for IT power: the power of job opportunities that are available to any qualified person, where qualification is all you need to get the job, given the huge demand and the short supply of such people; the power of services that were not available earlier and which significantly improve the quality of life or reduce the pain of everyday living—whether it is computerized railway information and booking or distance healthcare.

C^2 stands for the Communication revolution and the Connectivity leap, thanks to television and the telephone, which are touching remote villages as well. Often people look at the metric of ownership and penetration, and are deceived by, and dismissive of, the low numbers. As discussed earlier, Consumer India is about community consumption, which is a number several times larger than penetration; also the benefits of access go well beyond the individuals who have physical access to a television or a phone. There is a lot of virtual benefit that comes by hearsay or osmosis when someone in one's extended family or circle of friends has access.

E^2 represents the result of the connectivity leap and the communication revolution—an explosion of Exposure to the world, and a rising demand for Education of the practical, vocational and, preferably, of the computer kind. Private-consumption data points to an increase in the share of communication and education expenditure.

Appreciating the ubiquitousness of $I C^2 = E^2$

A taxi driver told me that his daughter, who lives in a village, paid US$100 for a computer course, which he said was "something called Windows, after which she would have to something called Words; and, while I don't know what all this is, once she does both, she would have a job." The National Association for Computer Training is looking at a US$1.1 billion market size in the next few years. The demand for education is very high, because it is now well established in the new Indian psyche that education enables greater access to information and knowledge, which, in turn, enables people to make more money. Computer education is seen to be "manna from heaven" because it enables people to participate in the big wealth-creation and growth opportunity that the country is seeing. IT parks, even in communist-run states, have become symbols of the new wealth that the new India can create, where all are welcome as long as they are educated enough.

IT awareness, be it of IT power (here's what a computer can do in solving problems/improving living) or IT-driven employment opportunities, has sunk in and trickled down to the lowest social classes and to much of the rural population in a variety of ways. There are just so many instruments of the trickle-down effect that there is quite a symphony in the offing, rising to a crescendo, albeit slowly. There is the demonstration effect of model projects of Internet kiosks set up by non-governmental organizations (NGOs) or commercial organizations; or the 50 Internet kiosks set up at the *Kumbh Mela*, a major religious festival on the banks of the River Ganges, that attracts hundreds of thousands of people; or of watching the rich use it and prosper; or the mushrooming of call centers, medical-transcription services, and other computer-related services offering employment. Since they are located in geographical clusters, they get noticed and talked about. IT is actually seen as the *Brahmaastra*, or the most powerful weapon of the gods, that can overcome almost any evil.

Television and the telephone are clearly the most ubiquitous drivers of change and their enormous reach and impact make the e-revolution feel like a minor ripple in a large pond. Television viewership studies show that 75% of urban India watches television and a majority of them watch satellite and cable channels. In developed states, half of rural people watch television; in developing states the number is still one-third. Even using the most conservative arithmetic, we are talking about over 500 million people whose lives are being reached by television. Television, as a medium, was state-controlled, (my favorite cartoon is one by the great Indian cartoonist, R K Laxman, which had two television screens, with Indira Gandhi on one and her son Rajiv on the other). Today, however, there are over a hundred channels available really cheaply, and this has created a new dimension of liberalization— liberalization of the mind. It has widened points of reference and provided windows to other worlds and, in the process, created the informational resources for people to be able to imagine and script a better life for themselves and their children.

The reason why television is the fountainhead of aspiration is lucidly explained by well-known anthropologist, Arjun Appadurai, of The New School in New York: "Imagination is not about individual escape. It is a collective social activity. Informational resources are needed for people to even imagine a possible life, weave a story and a script around themselves and place products in emerging sequences. Imagination may not always lead to action, but it is a prelude to action."

Furthermore, the per-capita consumption of television is 100 minutes on weekdays and 150 minutes on weekends; that is, around 10% of waking hours. The viewership is skewed towards women and children and is greater in the lower social classes. While purists might insist that television is not an interactive medium, all research points to the fact that it is indeed interacting deeply with the brain of Indian viewers, influencing their worldview, shaping their identity, enabling expression, affirming rights, and providing hope. The most interesting aspect of television is that it can gain access to the mind, regardless of educational status. A fascinating research study, *Satellite in South Asia* by the Institute of Development Studies, in the UK, has this to say:

> Far from passive viewing of television, people have tended to take up messages of self-improvement, self-confidence, egalitarianism, participation... It has shattered the myth of the "good Indian woman," replacing it with a bolder version and led to the unbottling of women's feelings [even though many are too conservative to approve of the changed image]... It has produced a perceptible modernization in the usage of language among middle and lower middle income [groups and] created a popular culture of western style consumerism with that of Bollywood [and] reinforces regional culture.

The connectivity leap is quite significant, too. Most of India's 640,000 villages have telephone connectivity, and it is only a matter of time before everyone has access to one. The issue isn't about telephone density, it is about the ability of connectivity to transform a person's capability to get things done and broaden the scope of his or her activity. Qualitative research has often picked up the villagers' view that with telephones, they can now leverage their contacts in cities to get help and resources to get their work done. It is about widening spheres of influence and widening areas of action.

RESULTANT CULTURAL CHANGES IN CONSUMER INDIA

In a nutshell, the cultural changes that have resulted from this include increased social mobility, a reduction in "power distance," a hunger for information, and an even greater move away from demanding social justice to grabbing economic opportunity. The old "messiah of the masses" is passé. The new "messiah with the Midas touch" is in!

Tech-Led Democracy, Reducing Power Distance

Perhaps the most powerful impact of IT has been the breaking down of the power distance: between the rich and the poor, the educated and the uneducated, and those in positions of power and those out of it. Narayana Murthy, the Infosys founder and chairman, tells a wonderful story of how he was surprised when he found a low-income colleague, the junior office boy in his office, going to an ATM rather than a teller to withdraw money. The automatic assumption that most of us make is that high technology is for the better educated to use while low technology or manual methods are for the less educated. When he asked the junior office boy why he chose the ATM over the teller, he replied that the ATM did not care if he withdrew 20 or 2,000 rupees, or whether he was well dressed or not. The teller, on the other hand, did care. A little after I heard this story, I happened to be at a vegetable vendor's, taking a long time to make up my mind about what I wanted, when a scruffy little child from the neighboring slum said to the shopkeeper that he wanted one rupee's worth of tomatoes, and quickly. The vendor mocked him—one whole rupee's worth of tomatoes?—and quickly told him to get lost. I remember thinking that had we had vegetable kiosks and automatic vending, this would not have happened. Men discriminate, machines don't.

The Government of Karnataka's *Bhoomi* project is another example of tech-led democracy. This involved computerizing all the land-ownership records in the state and, for a small fee of two rupees, allowed anyone access to them, thus liberating the illiterate or the powerless from corrupt government officialdom. In the railways, too, there is now no way that booking clerks or agents can use their position to extract black-market rate for tickets.

With the arrival of the Internet, even poor people understand that there is a way to get their ideas seen and heard, even if they do not have connections, and that there are opportunities that do come into the public domain.

The cultural impact of this is an increase in bargaining power within various sections of society, and a general move away from "this is my fate" to "I can too/why not me?" The opportunities for services that continue to reduce this power distance are indeed amazing.

The cultural labels and mythology of the social mobility of IT and IT-relevant education are dramatic. *Outlook* magazine refers to it as "silicon *moksha*" (the word that Hindus use for the welcome liberation from the eternal and painful cycle of birth and death). If you know computers, you can create the escape velocity to break free and get to the US; or at least to the nearest big city. IT education is "the ceiling breaker" and cultural labels of technology all relate to the power it has for ideas and to the manner in which it provides access to information that can lead to more money.

Thus, it is not at all surprising that the poor embrace technology and have a greater hunger for education and access to information than the rich.

Empowerment and Enablement

There are two major themes or threads that are running through India today. The first of these is the "good life"—rising incomes, easy credit, significant increases in consumption, rising aspirations, rising respect from the world outside, and so on. Coupled with this is a minimal concern or empathy for the rest of society or any desire to improve social structures—as is typical of middle-class selfishness the world over. This is the theme on which large sections of the popular press and television media ride. Even serious social issues are presented in a totally sensationalized manner, which makes them suitable for entertaining the upper and upper-middle class viewers and customers, rather than really attempting to address those issues. This theme was well captured by the slogan used by the Bharatiya Janata Party (BJP) in the last election: "India Shining." Clearly, all of India was not shining, however, because the BJP was defeated. As a newspaper article pointed out, even the semiotics of "India Shining" were very interesting. Both the words, "India" and "Shining" were in a modern western idiom that would resonate with only the urban educated.

The much more populous heartland of India, *Bharat* as it is called, did not respond to the line or the sentiment, which where exclusive in nature. Wags added another line to the slogan: "India Shining, Bharat whining." Is Bharat whining? Undoubtedly, and over *bijli sadak pani* (Hindi for electricity, roads, and water, respectively). As people see the general improvement around them, their impatience levels rise. As someone pointed out in a focus group, if you are in a ditch, you see nothing, know nothing. But as you start getting hauled upwards, you can see around you and you cannot wait to get out. And this leads us to the second major cultural theme running through India today, and gradually gathering strength: the growing demand for empowerment to get a fair share of the growth in prosperity that is sweeping through the country.

Foreigners often ask me if there is not a real risk of severe social unrest in a country where the gap between the haves and have-nots is so wide. My answer has always been evasive, because on the one hand the Hindu way of life is accepting of God's script and, hence, of the fact that someone can have a better script; yet on the other hand, the rise of rampant aspiration has always made me wonder how long it will take for aspiration to overcome acceptance. Yet again, India has shown that it has a unique way of resolving issues.

There is a new wave of demand for empowerment rising through the country. It is different from the earlier, socialist discourse of protecting the weak, and offering hand-outs to the poor by taxing the rich. It is a demand for empowerment through strengthening the poor to compete effectively for opportunities, by giving them education, institutional interventions, and so on. The theme is empowerment through enabling, and is seen in the changed discourse of NGOs, who are no longer in search of philanthropy but in search of partnerships that will enable them to have financially self-sustaining business models. The theme is also seen through the recent phenomenon of election victories of leaders of the "backward" castes (Dalits as they are called); whose constituents want them to carry the Dalit voice into parliament and into shaping legislation.

Negotiation

The theme of negotiation is very dominant in India's culture. Modernity, as we discussed in an earlier chapter, is nothing but negotiated tradition. A senior civil servant friend of mine pointed out that if we just step back and look at the country, we will see that it has become a massive negotiating table with every institution and every group of people negotiating with every other. Maybe this is the appropriate answer to the questions about the anatomy of social tension, as wealth gets more visible and the have-nots become more aspirational. The left and the non-left political parties are negotiating hard with each other; the under-privileged classes are negotiating via the politicians for a reservation policy in education that is fair; the Supreme Court and Parliament have been locked in an unhappy battle on several counts; the profit and not-for-profit sectors are painfully learning to negotiate partnerships with each other, as are the government and the private sectors for infrastructure partnerships. Within a home, gender negotiation is furiously under way, as is negotiation across generations with disparate ideologies. Themes related to negotiation are adjustability, adaptability, "this as well as that", synthesis, and hybrid models.

Hybrid Models

These themes are reflected in the way life works for an average Indian business or an average Indian home. Make do, cobble together, manage somehow, to create the appropriate solution at the affordable price. Buy a scooter and a car: use them according to the need of the hour and optimize on petrol costs and status signals. Buy an expensive detergent and a cheap detergent; one for your husband's office shirt and your child's school uniform, and the other for bed sheets and home-wear clothes. And while you're at it, buy a liquid detergent to wash silk saris at home to save money on dry-cleaning. Buy a mix of branded and non-branded apparel: buy low-cost, low-quality goods from the street to bulk up your wardrobe; visit malls to know what's in fashion and hunt for cheaper knock-offs on the high street; and buy some branded apparel as status signals and expressions of your identity. It always reminds me of Ogden Nash's rhyme "Tell me, Octopus, I begs is those things arms, or is they legs?" The theories of marketing that require people to be categorized in one way or another are far too restrictive, and even dangerous, to use for developing marketing strategy in such a market.

Contextual Morality and Ideology

When the negotiation theme plays out, the solutions are all-round accommodation, adjustment, and collusion with detachment. It is not unusual for political parties to be partners in the central government and electoral enemies at the state level, nor is it unusual for a state political party to ally with one party for one election, and a polar opposite party in the next. The electorate understands that ideology is about electoral arithmetic and pragmatism and, each time, gamely evaluates the new combination depending on the demands of the new situation. Therefore adoption of new ideas is not a problem at all, but not allowing room for negotiated solutions is a problem.

Social Legitimacy of Aspiration

Santosh Desai, former president of McCann-Erickson India, talks about the "unlocking of the social and economic fixedness of life." He says that the earlier thinking of "know your place, this is our place in the world, this is who we are not," which was something we took great care to teach our children, is now no longer valid. The idea of following your dreams and taking a chance, or aiming for a station way beyond where anyone you know has gone, are entirely legitimized. Stories of rags-to-riches entrepreneurs are celebrated, even if some of them have used doubtful methods to get there. Earlier, education alone was a legitimate aspiration. Today, a whole range of aspirations are socially legitimized, whether it is about becoming Miss Universe, a movie star, wanting your child to win a "boogie woogie" dancing show on television, or anything else that can make you rich and/or famous.

Child-Centricity

India and China are totally child-centric cultures. While in the latter this may have been driven by the one-child policy that has operated for so many years, in India child-centricity revolves around the hope and expectation that children need to be indulged today so that they can take care of their parents later. Also driving this obsessive child focus is the fact that there are far more kids than ready-made opportunities, including school and college seats, and aspiration levels of parents for their children have jumped.

FAQs ABOUT CONSUMER INDIA'S CULTURE

No discussion on the cultural aspects of Consumer India is complete without answering the following questions: (a) "Are Indian values and western values really different and, if so, where and how?" (b) "How much of the ancient past of Indian culture will flow into modern India and how much will be shed?" (c) "What exactly is the Indian cultural discourse on money, and is it changing?"

Is There a Real Value Divide?

For a long time I could not figure the answer to this question, partly because of the morphing manner in which India changes, the hybrid mix of western and Indian behaviour that we have been seeing, and the "this as well as that" negotiated settlement that Indians have had with modernity and with western influences.

However, if we were to go beyond behavior to values, which are either general guiding principles that govern behavior or broad tendencies to prefer certain states of affairs or feelings, then I think there are real differences between India and the West, as illustrated in Table 8.2.

Indian Values	Western Values
•Patriarchy	•Egalitarianism
•Ambiguity, Adaptability, Low dissonance	•Clarity, Linearity, Need for resolution of contradictions, of choosing between opposite positions
•Socially defined roles, *dharma* (translated in today's age as "know what your DNA is and what type you are and play accordingly, or you will be unhappy")	•Individually chosen roles (you can become anything you want to be)
•Patience, Passivity (*vairagya*—Sanskrit word for renunciation—especially of sexual pleasure, being the ultimate prescription for happiness)	•Impatience, Assertion (Viagra-the celebrated new drug to treat impotence and enable enjoyment of sexual pleasures)
•Continuing with tradition (in some hybrid or morphed form or other)	•Seeking novelty
•Happiness = Self harmony	•Happiness = Wealth accumulation
•Respect for Age	•Respect for Youth

Table 8.2: Value Differences

How Much of the Past and How Much of the Present?

Having taken into account all the hybrid and fusion solutions which abound and are at the core of Consumer India, we realize that there are some aspects where the past is being shed actively. Perhaps the most important aspect is in the personal construction of identity. Santosh Desai, says that the earlier Indian identity was rooted in the collective past and was about "where we came from." Even Hindu prayer and ritual demand that you give the names of the past seven generations of your family so that the Lord knows who exactly it is that is praying to him. The modern Indian identity is determined by the personal present and by the promise of the future.

However, the more interesting question that has been arising of late is how much of modern India's culture is a return to its pre-British roots. Were the Victorian era, and the equally prudish Gandhian era, which were contiguous, actually an aberration? Will we understand consumer and people culture a lot more if we go back to the pre-British days? Perhaps yes. At Sarnath, one of the seats of Buddhism, one can see Buddhist *stupas* from the sixth and seventh century BC with Mughal minarets built on top of them to welcome the Mughal emperors Babur and Humayun: another classic case of adaptability and adjustment, another "this as well as that" solution.

Cultural Discourse on Money

In the past, abstemiousness was a much lauded virtue. To have money but not to spend it, to indulge in "simple living and high thinking," were part of Gandhian ideology. Businessmen were frowned upon and the accumulation of wealth was seen as going against the very grain of what a good Indian should be doing. Now, of course, things are different: 65% of the nation's incremental GDP growth is driven by private consumption, and many ministers have told businessmen in many forums, "You have been legitimized. Please use your new-found power for the greater good." All speeches laud the growth of consumer markets and we celebrate each new cell phone, each new car, and each new television that is sold.

The idea of an ascetic, abstemious culture which eschews personal pleasure or the creation of wealth is actually a product perhaps of the Gandhian and then the Nehruvian way of life. Hindu India is probably the only culture in the world that prays so blatantly and fervently for prosperity. *Diwali,* the big Festival of Lights, is all about lighting up the home so that it is inviting enough for Lakshmi, the goddess of wealth, to step in. Nowhere in the Hindu scriptures is it written that enjoyment is not good. It always says "enjoy but do not get attached." Mythology is replete with stories around money, of money bringing sorrow but also money bringing a great deal of joy to the virtuous.

As Santosh Desai says, money is about energy (and I add that it was always so in pre-Gandhian days). There is a far more liberated view of money, from something that has to be static and held in a bank vault to something that is integrated into the flow of life.

I am often asked why, then, Indians are so value-conscious? Will they be willing to pay more for brands? Why will they not spend more to get more "feel-good" benefits? The answer partly lies in the fact that the Indian consumer is far from satiated with the "do-good" products that he owns and his wish list on this count is long. Hence feel-good products will always be second in terms of purchase priorities in the foreseeable future and badge brands will always be perceived as worse value for money than the "do-good" brands offering tangible, visible, sensible benefits.

9

Young India, Woman India: A Closer Look

P opular theories about the Indian market say that there are three things that will drive the growth and transform the character of the Indian consumer market: the coming of age of liberalization children; the changing attitudes of the Indian woman; and the rising income and consumption sophistication of rural India which will transform it into a mega market, several times the size of urban India.

The rise of "generation next" has been written about with unbridled optimism and enthusiasm, based on the coming of age of liberalization children—the almost 250 million-strong contingent of young people between the ages of 15 and 25; India's first non-socialistic generation, globally exposed to, among other things, enormous information and, unlike their parents, raised amidst a consumption-oriented and social discourse. They are expected to be at the forefront in creating a new, modern, western-oriented consumer society, as well as yield the demographic dividend that will drive economic growth.

The second growth and transformation lever is slightly less dramatic, and is based on the expected changes in homes as a result of the supposedly new, emerging Indian woman that the media in India frequently talk about. The assumption here is that more and more Indian women are now beginning to work outside the home, are becoming increasingly independent and assertive, and that they will bring about widespread changes in the old-fashioned, labor-intensive ways in which homes are managed and children are raised.

The third lever that is also frequently discussed, but with a much greater degree of skepticism, is the increased consumption and sophistication of rural India as its income and exposure to the world increase.

If the first two levers are hyped more than they should be, this one is discounted more than it should be. There is no consensus on whether rural India is a big pot of gold available to companies who have the ability to craft appropriate market strategies to unlock its potential, or a declining economy, overly dependent on the monsoon season, and similar to quicksand in that it sucks in unsuspecting businesses and destroys their profitability.

Like everything else about Consumer India, there is some truth in every point of view and every piece of conflicting data, on these three levers of growth. While, each of these does contribute to the change confluence that is happening today, the devil is in the detail, and in order to understand the big picture, looking at the detailed stories is very necessary. This chapter takes the first two of these levers of growth and change and provides data, discussion, health warnings, little-noticed changes, and points of inflection.

YOUNG CONSUMER INDIA

A Youth Market Still Waiting to Happen

One would imagine that a country with about 500 million people below the age of 25, and its first non-socialistic generation just coming of age, would have a very vibrant youth market and a youth culture shaped by a whole host of youth brands. One would also imagine that given such a huge, virgin opportunity to shape a new market space, most youth brand marketers, old and new, would be here in very high gear and with lots of visible success.

Alas, yet again, Consumer India has not responded in the way one might have expected given the experience of other emerging markets. The magic of America is very much there, but only as a place for migrating to, studying in, or working in, rather than aspiring for American brands. Coca-Cola, Pepsi, Levi's and Wrangler, to name a few, have not had the success they thought they would.

Part of the reason for this was their incorrect assumption that they had a lot of brand awareness and desire to consume awaiting them, based on the premise that the magic of America is all-pervading, everywhere in the world. The fact is that some countries are more influenced by American culture than others. India never was, in the way that the Philippines, Russia, or even China were—the first because it was a US military base for a long time, and the others because they defined their own power and influence in the world in relation to America.

There was another error of judgment on the part of overseas youth marketers when they assumed that the world's youth held similar values, desires, hopes, and dreams, without realizing that different generations in different countries might be subjected to different forces that shape their view of the world. Young India can never be like young US—because it has different forces at work. Gross domestic product (GDP) growth and per-capita income do not define exactly how a section of humanity will behave.

And, finally, because the mental model was not one of market creation, there has been no critical mass of youth marketers spending significant amounts of money, reinforcing one another, in defining a modern Indian youth culture with appropriate rituals, symbols, and role models. Those that did spend the money tried to project an alien youth culture that did not resonate in this India.

Why did such a youth culture not evolve on its own, given that the two most important ingredients were already here—large numbers of young people and tumultuous change in the environment? Because, I suspect, of the nature of Indian society, which is more about affiliation and family and less about individualism. So the young do assert themselves, but within the framework of the family, and, hence, with certain constraints on their freedom. As discussed in Chapter 7, there is still a huge opportunity to shape a space for young people which is their own, and quite different from what they do within their families. In the upper income groups, we now see a definitive trend in that direction.

UNDERSTANDING YOUTH DEMOGRAPHICS

Teenage Market Structure : Income/SEC

The most important warning that needs to accompany Young Consumer India is the fact that its demographics are disappointing.

Of the 187 million or so 12–19-year-olds, 110 million, or close to 60%, are rural and poor. They belong equally to the Socio-Economic Classification (SEC) categories of R3 and R4. R3 indicates that they come from homes that are typically semi-*pucca* (semi-permanent) and in which the father has usually studied between standard 4 and 9; at best, he has finished high school. R4 indicates homes that are typically *kuchcha* (non-permanent) structures, and where the chief wage earner has had limited or no education. An almost-identical pattern exists for the 20–25-year-olds. Of the 121 million of these, close to 60% are rural R3 and R4, and about 3% are urban social class SEC A.

Frequently, these days, magazines run stories on "the youth of India," talking of their runaway consumption of everything from wine to iPods and their attitudes to the workplace, to voting, to family, and so on. These stories are based on sample survey of the highest social classes in just four or five big cities. Such surveys represent, about 3% of India's youth at best, making any talk of how consumption will explode and attitudes will change with the passing of the baton to the new generation, a bit far-fetched. To the editors of such magazines, I send Table 9.1.

Label of attractiveness to marketers	Socio-Economic Classification (SEC)	Size of town/city lived in	Number in millions/ % of total
Rich Brats	SEC A1	Top 23 cities	0.9/0.5%
Creamy Layer	SEC A	Top 23 cities	2.2/1%
Consuming Class	SEC A, B	Top 23 cities	5.1/3%
"Stretch-a-bit"	SEC A, B	All urban	12/7%
Urban Lower-Middle	SEC C	All urban	11/6%
Urban Poor	SEC D, E	All urban	33/18%
Rural Consuming Class	R1	Rural	4.5/3%
Rural Marginal Consumers	R2 to R4	Rural	132/70%

Table 9.1: 12–19-year-olds in India
Source: IRS 2006

Rich Brats: These are the very rich, beautiful people, who are featured constantly in the media, with their ultra-western clothes and behavior, with the suggestion that they are typical of what India's next generation will be like. Projecting market sizes based on this supposedly leading-edge segment would be suicidal, however, even though they are the fastest-growing in number. Nevertheless, they are a disconnected minority, only about one million strong, having grown by 80% in the past eight years.

Creamy Layer (which includes the Rich Brats): This is the segment that premium youth brand marketers target with a fair degree of hype. This would be the heartland for Levi's or Wrangler. Their limited numbers—in all, a little over two million—explains the limited success of these brands in the Indian market. This group is also growing fast—50% in the past eight years.

Consuming Class: This group consists of some five million "big-city, well-off kids." SECs A and B are both high-desire consumers, and the big city exposes them to all the things that fuel teenage consumption—hang-out places, tempting shop displays, fashion trends (from overseas as well as locally created), the influence of richer peer groups, and their own intensely consuming parents. This would be the core target group for a youth market that conforms to the mental model of youth consumption in other parts of the world—the MTV generation, so to speak. They have high aspirations, and knowledge of the brands they want to possess. However, from a marketing standpoint, though there is a fairly high penetration, there is a less-than-desirable quantum of consumption, whether it is jeans or music or gadgets.

"Stretch-a-Bit" Consumers: Refers to a market more than double the size of the Consuming Class—12 million more young people—which is available to the marketers of premium-priced goods who have the patience to "stretch-a-bit," sustain an all-urban-India distribution network across 50 cities, and spend on the development of this market. While development may be gradual, it is certain to happen.

The Rest of the Urban Teens: A staggering 44 million in number, these are served mostly by the unorganized sector, be it in pirated music or low-priced clothes. They are a high-effort segment because they know what is available from the movies, from television, and from watching their richer peers, but they want cheaper versions of the same. They are not willing to settle for worse design and worse styles at a lower price—it has to look the same, though it could be of lower-quality fabric and trims, or have fewer frills.

Rural Teens: These are an under-served market; in fact, several marketers have yet to recognize their existence.

Such an income/exposure market structure is reflected in the jeans market—a category that epitomizes youth the world over. In India, 70% of jeans are low-priced, sold on the footpath or through small jeaneries, which are one-person, mom-and-pop, tailoring shops. They are typically priced at or under US$10 a pair. Another 25% are in the price range of US$12–20 and comprise a whole host of local labels, private labels of mom-and-pop stores or low-end department stores, who buy from small-scale manufacturers, and charge a usurious 40% mark up for distributing them. The premium end of known brands, despite being present with their cheapest models, comprises a mere 5% of the market, priced as they are at US$20–35. There is, however, joy in special high-end designer labels for the Creamy Layer, who are looking for novelty, differentiation, and "beyond the usual" jeans. And there is obviously a market waiting to happen for a high-volume, low-margin, low-priced, retailer—is this a market waiting for Wal-Mart?

I recently had one of the fund managers send me the business plan of a small, branded-apparel manufacturer-cum-retailer, with a request to spot the catch. It seemed too good to be true. The price points were very low, under Rs.500 a garment; inexpensive media such as billboards were used to build brand awareness and reassurance about quality, as well as the perception of status that comes with a label that other people recognize—even if the label has no image or badge value attached to it. The brand was retailed in the company's own and franchised single-brand stores, which were tiny, 700-square-foot spaces in residential neighborhoods, and the net margin per store was positive. The conventional wisdom about retailing, which doesn't work for the Indian market, is that large stores drive profitability, as does premium pricing. Actually, the structure of the market is quite the opposite. The key driver of continued profitable growth for this business would be energy, more than capital. Locating thousands of franchisees, who can bring the minimalist real estate needed, and managing them through low-cost processes made possible with a judicious use of technology is the real challenge. The model, however, is basically far more viable than a Gap clone or a Levi's or Wrangler exclusive-stores model.

EDUCATION, LITERACY, ENGLISH AFFINITY

Only 7% of the 121 million 20–25-year-olds are college graduates. This represents a weighted average of a much worse 4% of rural youth and a much better, though still dismal, 15% of urban youth of this age group who are college graduates.

Yet English reading is widespread—34% of urban youth read English (double the number of those with a college degree) and 13% of rural youth; that is, three times the number of those who have a college degree. The same goes for the teenagers, the 12–19-year-olds, where 37% of urban teens and 15% of rural teens read English. However, the story, as always, takes twists and turns. Even in SEC A1, the topmost social class where English-medium college education is a given, only 43% say they prefer watching English television, a number that drops to just 28% in SEC A2.

That there is rapid progress in literacy in India, even in a five-year period, is evident not just from the government statistics, but from survey data too. In the 20–25-year-old age group, 24% are illiterate. In the 12–19 age group, only 13% are illiterate. The drop is apparent both in rural India, where the percentage of illiterates drops by half between the 20–25s and the 12–19s. In urban India, it reduces even more sharply, from 16% in the older group to 7% in the teens group.

If a gender cut were taken on all the data in this section, it would perhaps look far better for the men. The young women are far worse off, and the data that we have just seen is an aggregate of both.

FAMILY ORIENTATION

While much is written about "generation next" opting to stay single, especially the women—and it is probably true of the upper social classes—on aggregate, 9% of teenagers and 65% of 20–25-year-olds are already married. In the 20–25 age group, the aggregate of 65% translates into 70% of rural youth being married, and 50% of urban youth. If 65% of this age group are already married, 40% say they have been married for four years or more. Since the majority of families in India are nuclear, especially at the middle and lower incomes, this means that there is a huge, yet untapped opportunity to shape the way the new generation lives and runs its homes.

Psychographics and Cultural Drivers of Behavior

The contexts of existence determine youth psychographics. Youth marketers of global youth brands always tell me that "teenagers are teenagers the world over." When we compare notes, we do indeed find that my teenager in Mumbai is pretty much the same as theirs in Boston or Buenos Aires: untidy rooms, rebellious natures, television and telephone obsessed, late sleepers, and so on. However, the similarity stops at such surface behavior levels. Scratch the surface and they are different—because every generation in every country is brought up in different cultural contexts, which shape their collective character, and in turn their individual behavior.

Various proprietary studies done by global marketers in BRIC (Brazil, Russia, India, China) countries show some stark differences between the youth in each country and provide some clues about the directions they are moving in. These are best expressed using the IMPSYS consumer-behavior mapping concept of Paul Heylen, as shown in Figure 9.1.

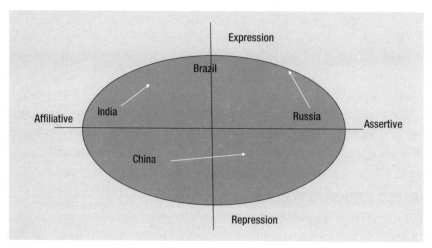

Figure 9.1: BRIC Countries: Cultural Mapping

On the "affiliative–assertive" axis (also interpretable as "we oriented–me oriented"), both Chinese and Indian young people map closer to "affiliative," while Russian youth is more "me" oriented. Brazilian youth are in between, not being family-centric but very peer group-oriented. Brazilian youth have a very strong street culture in which peer group approval is ever important. Indian youth, in contrast, are very family-centric; their cultural codes are about the kinship of an extended family, about family obligation, and the home is a shared space.

Though Chinese and Indian youth are from very affiliative cultures, there are differences in the strengths of their respective affiliative bonds. Unlike the Indian teenager who has grown up with a profusion of siblings, aunts, uncles, and cousins, the Chinese teenager has grown up in a milieu of a one-child policy and where, consequently, the larger community is the family. With the sociological changes that are accompanying the new China, the affiliative nature of society is gradually being replaced by individuality. In India, technologies like cell phones, text messaging and cheaper air travel have extended the connected family circle even more.

On the "expression–repression" axis, Russian youth are midway, but moving fast in the direction of being expressive. Highly individualistic by nature and constantly asserting individual autonomy, they cherish the ability to have an opinion at all. Indian youth are also midway along this axis, and moving towards becoming far more expressive. However, what makes them different from Russian youth is that they are very affiliative. They have socially codified norms of behaviour and even their rebellion is within the parameters of social approval. Brazilian youth are the most expressive of all, while Chinese youth are closest to the "repression" end of the scale, existing in an environment that is more repressive and rule-bound, with a high degree of control from powerful authorities, though not from nagging parents. They are moving in the direction of greater individualism, but not necessarily in a more expressive way; which presumably helps to explain their easier adoption of products to enable self-expression.

Achievement ranks very highly in Chinese society, as it does in Indian society, but in the rambunctious democracy that is India, there is more chaos than order in the process of getting ahead. Russian youth are also very achievement-oriented, but towards the fulfillment of personal goals. In India, on the other hand, achievement is strongly connected with making the family proud.

A Pressure-Cooked Generation

I once consulted for a gaming company, which had the license for an online multimedia game that was very successful in many markets, especially in the Philippines, Taiwan, and Brazil. The company's assumption was that once the game was introduced into India through cyber café, where the bulk of Internet penetration lay, it would explode. However, it did not. "What do young people do for relaxation?" the puzzled non-Indian managing director of the company asked. "They study, go for tuition, and try to get ahead," was the response he got from his Indian team. The key social drivers of this "generation next"—achievement and getting ahead; making your family proud of you; doing better than your peers—needed to be explained to him very carefully.

Young India lives in a world of unbelievable competition. There are more young people than there are opportunities, and everyone has been told from childhood that they have to study really hard, make their parents proud, and pay back all the things their parents have done for them, by being successful. There are 9.3 million young people wanting to go to college but only three million or so college seats. For admission to the premier engineering colleges, the Indian Institutes of Technology (IITs), there are 7,000 kids at each mark point in the entrance exam. My daughter got 92% in her school final exam but did not qualify for the premier colleges for a subject of her choice. The list can go on. This is a "grab any opportunity," self-made generation, who will conform and will not rebel or rock any boats for the rewards of success. The work market is equally competitive, but for graduates of the right colleges, life is good.

The atmosphere during exam season, especially for high school students is one of near frenzy. Every household with a child sitting for these exams sinks into exam mode: cable television is often cut off, visitors are discouraged, and extra tuition is the norm—not just for the exam period but for the whole year. The Common Entrance Test (CET) exams for college admissions and the Common Admission Test (CAT) exams for management schools, and the IIT entrance exam for the premier engineering colleges are national events where even the national news media telecast "how to crack the exam" programs.

It is often argued that achievement orientation is very high in many other emerging markets as well, but each of these societies has its own distinctive spin on it.

Pragmatism is the Key

Pragmatism and success-seeking are the core of this new generation. This was summed up in a study presented at an MTV youth conference several years ago:

1. Parents become democratic and friendly.

2. "You get oranges, enjoy. You get lemons, learn to make lemonade."

3. All things material are highly coveted.

4. No moral, sexual revolution here.

5. Youth icons are gilt-edged heroes.

6. Brand conscious but very value sensitive.

7. "Pubs aren't second homes; drugs are absurd."

They aren't too keen on love marriages, and parents finding them spouses, with the final choice left to them, of course, is their pragmatic solution for marriage, which they view as a life-business partnership, marching together, shoulder to shoulder, on the road to material success.

Indian Not Wannabe Western

A famous old Hindi film song has the hero singing "my shoes are Japanese, my trousers are English, the red cap on my head is Russian, but still my heart is Hindustani (Indian)." It was a very popular song in the '50s, '60s and '70s and while it may not be belted out in the market square anymore, it still does appear to resonate with how liberalization children feel. In 2006, Euro RSCG, a leading advertising agency, polled over 2,000 young people in the top eight cities in India. These people, aged between 15 and 30, were labeled "prosumers" or opinion spreaders, and are persuasive people, trusted by their peers, who pick up ideas and spread them as they interact with their peers. The key finding from the poll was that they preferred Indian brands, Indian looks, and Indian environments in which to bring up their children. They actually believed that personal-care products made for India worked better than their imported counterparts—a huge movement from the 1960s and 1970s, when there was a premium on imported goods. Some 90% of these young people said that they preferred taking up a job in India, and being with their family, rather than going abroad—as long as they made enough money to travel abroad. Mixing the best of the West and the East is what they like when it comes to music, and they believe that intellectually, Indians can hold their own against the best of elsewhere.

Young Indians have often been described as "dual passport holders," and as being a cultural *khichadi* (an Indian dish made from a mixture of many different grains). They are comfortable with their Indian-ness and are besotted with Hindi films.

An article in the *Business Standard*, March 30, 2006, talks of how trendsetters feel about their Indian identity. They define trendsetters as the nine million SEC A and B youth (12–25-years-old) in the top 35 cities of India. "The new young Indian is proud to be one, and is quite comfortable being one. He is as happy with Haldiram (a local snack brand) as he is with McDonald's, and Fab India (a local prêt line) as with FCUK…yet there is a global/western Indian emerging…some of the values they cherish (of the West) include the freedom to think, speak and act."

How can they, despite exposure to far better lifestyles of other countries, still prefer India? Because there is a real distinction between India and Indians—India has serious problems, they recognize, but they make a distinction between India and Indian. Indian is the brand they are proud to belong to and they aspire to make it even better.

Optimism, Success and Aspiration

While their parents' generation had very set views of what constituted success—becoming a doctor or engineer, securing a steady job, and so on—this generation recognizes that there are many routes to *Nirvana*. Any form of business ownership, including dog-grooming parlors, adventure tourism, counseling, or fitness instruction, is fine and respectable as long as they are making money. In the India of the past, identity was based on caste, community, and who your father was. Today, they see performance as something that can neutralize all these advantages (or lack of them) and their role models are first-generation, successful entrepreneurs, cricketers, newscasters, film stars, and so on.

In 2005, a blockbuster Hindi movie "Bunty aur (and) Babli" was made that perfectly explained the worldview of India's small-town young adults. What hits you hard in the movie is the force and nature of aspiration that drives small-town India and this has nothing to do with the old days of dreaming of being a famous film star, and not knowing how to go about it.

Babli, the heroine, is a small-town girl who wants to be a supermodel and decides that the route there is via the Miss India contest. She knows that trials are held in the bigger cities of Lucknow and Kanpur. Bunty, the hero, is another small-town person who knows that a financial-services business, involving small depositors and finance companies, could be a route to get rich. He is a wannabe entrepreneur who thinks of offbeat business models like selling "shower services" to people in his neighborhood, so that they can have a better bathing experience.

Babli and Bunty are united by a severe hunger to escape the expectations of their humdrum lives: the good daughter who becomes the good wife, and the good son with the modest, steady job with *izzat* and *imaandari* ("honor" and "integrity"). Rebellion is old-fashioned for the well-heeled, SEC A city kids, who do not need or want to rock the boat, because the good life is at hand. But the rest are willing to run away and escape into a newer and better orbit.

In focus groups with young people, an oft-repeated refrain is "It isn't where you have been born but what you can do with yourself. There are so many opportunities for the bold and the smart who seize them, look at all the [role models] who have proved it." There is no guilt about worrying the parents, no deep yearning for home, and just the pragmatism of missing home-cooked food.

The duo in the movie are voyagers, who are happy to experiment with things that would earlier have been the preserve of the bad: drinking doesn't make you a useless drunkard, and a cigarette is a useful accessory. They aren't one-way streets to hell, just harmless occasional fun. The accent is on being street smart to get what you want, on working the system from the inside, on experiencing and enjoying consumerist paradise when you can afford it.

The hip-and-happening clothes tell a story too. His "Nikee" T-shirt, jeans and sneakers are a good example of what the non-premium market is all about—not less style at a lower cost, but a more-affordable, though less-perfect clone. Her clothes are a good reflection of the broad spectrum that a modern young Indian woman's wardrobe spans—both East and West and often somewhere in between.

Have the values described in the film (corroborated in findings from consumer research), changed as rapidly as the attitudes to life, and the lifestyle of good living? Absolutely not. Babli and Bunti are *shareef* (well brought up), well-mannered, and really good kids at heart, despite external appearances. Loud and clear in the movie are evergreen Indian values, such as respect for elders—complete with the frequent ritual of touching elders' feet—and the family values of setting a good example for your child, and returning to live with your in-laws.

The wedding scene when Bunty and Babli get married echoes the theme of that "my shoes are Japanese but my heart is Hindustani" song mentioned earlier. They take the ritual seven steps around the fire but the vows that are traditionally taken with each step have been totally modernized. But she is a virgin till her wedding day, despite them living together before, and is not coy about the physicality, when it is permissible. The feminist statement about being an equal partner is a thread that runs right through, and the reasonable man is definitely taking over from the egoistic male.

However, the most telling part is in the end. They both agree that the dull life of disgusting domesticity is a very unhappy state to be in and the "this as well as that" resolution of their problem echoes what we hear from our focus groups all the time. So they go back to the exciting life of scams and stings, but as good, establishment guys who are using their considerable, dubious talent for creating a better world. To use that wonderful Indian phrase, "We are like that only," which means "things aren't really going to change out here, and we know its hard for you to understand it—just accept it!"

Liberalization Children: a Powerful Market Force

Defined in the classical sense, liberalization children are the "demographically disappointing" market, any other market is easy to shape. Shaping a failing market like this is the challenge yet to be achieved by marketers. However, the importance of the liberalization children is obvious if one were to look at household structure by age group (see Table 9.2).

% of households who have a family member aged…								
0–2 yrs	3–4 yrs	5–12 yrs	13–15 yrs	16–19 yrs	20–24 yrs	25–34 yrs	35–54 yrs	55+ yrs
24	21	52	28	31	35	53	71	42

Table 9.2: Breakdown of Households by Presence of Age Group

Source IRS, 2006

About six out of ten households have a liberalization child, who acts as a change agent in the household. They are not just a very attractive, niche-market opportunity but are also critical to the mainstream. The mainstream Indian market is a youth market.

WOMAN CONSUMER INDIA

What is Driving Change in Women's Behavior?

Popular theory has it that changes in household consumption behavior are happening rapidly because more women are now working outside the home. Hence, they are getting more independent as they earn their own money and see a wider world. They are also getting more assertive and are all set to bring about a consumption revolution and explosion. The truth of this, like everything else about Consumer India, is not so simple and straightforward. Yes, it is true that women are changing and this change will create new and different opportunities. But they are not changing because of a huge surge in the number working outside the home, as we will see.

Working Women: the Facts

Today, only 23% of housewives in urban India have a job outside the home. In rural India, where working in the fields is common for women, the figure is 42%. ("Housewives" pretty much covers, most adult women, since the age of marriage is still very low, as discussed in the section on Young India.) What is more, as households get richer, the proportion of women in the workforce falls (see Figure 9.2).

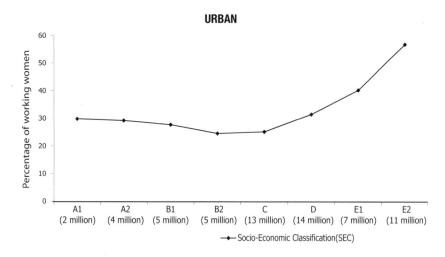

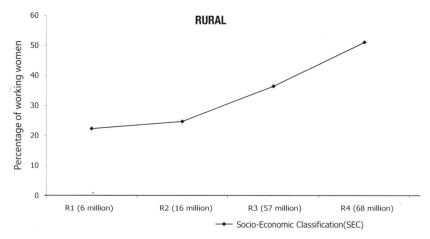

Figure 9.2: Working Women by Socio-Economic Classification (SEC), 2006
Source: IRS, 2006

In fact, even though there are more women working outside the home, this has not had the expected impact on consumption. The working woman tends to bend over backwards to play the traditional role at home, and in many ways is the last to change practices there, even as she blazes new trails outside it. Her own spending and saving patterns on personal products will change quite dramatically, but not her household behavior; at any rate, not in the same measure.

There is, however, a new category of working women just emerging, called micro-entrepreneurs, who run what they call a "home business."

They stay mostly at home, refer to themselves as "housewives" rather than working women, but run some sort of business: tailoring, cooking, catering, giving tuition to children, running a beauty parlor, and so on. A 2006 study conducted for The Indus Entrepreneurs (a not-for-profit organization to promote entrepreneurship) in six cities, among 1,200 women in the SECs of B, C and D, showed that 25% were already doing some work from home and another 30% intended to take up a home business. The desire to be productive and to improve self-worth by turning talent into money is huge, and this trend will actually accelerate.

Rena Bartos, an American demographer, has pointed out that the gender stereotypes of "working" and "non-working" women that marketers adopt are actually flawed. She pointed out, way back in the 1980s, that all working women are not the same: there are those for whom work is "just a job," and there are those who are actually pursuing careers. Similarly, women who "stay at home" are of two types: those that want to work and see themselves as working women, even though they do not work outside the home; and those that are happy to be at home.

I believe that in India, the increasing number of working women is not driving change as much as the increasing number of housewives who have acquired the "working woman" mindset.

Working from home or not, all women say they see themselves as "chief executives" of the household and coaches of children, ensuring the success of children in this ultra-competitive world. Furthermore, since around 60% of families, both urban and rural, are nuclear, with no elders living with them, the housewife sees herself as having a very important role to play. This has resulted in the rise of what I call "womanism," which is driving major change across households in Consumer India.

The Change Wave of Womanism

Gender equations have always been skewed in favor of men. "Your husband is your God, worship him" is what brides were routinely told. The ideal Indian woman was always told, "Yours is not to question why, yours is but to do … and die". Slowly but surely, this discourse is changing.

Womanism is about women saying: "I am a person too, I want my space and place"; "I want my opinion to count"; "I want to be productive/do something worthwhile and remunerative"; "I value my own time"; "I need to look after my own interests too; there is no glory in self denial." Womanism is a gentler and less individualistic form of feminism. It marks a change in the core of the woman's mind, and not on the periphery of her behavior—yet another example of the morphing change that is the hallmark of Consumer India. It is a change in the mental attitude of women to themselves and to their role in their world, and not just a change in how they dress or carry out their household chores. In fact, as one researcher put it, even for the most forward-looking Indian woman, the mental emancipation achieved in the past few years has been far greater than physical emancipation. This is another reason why this change is not easy to see, but will drive sustainable behaviour change over the next few generations.

This is the slow but definite wave of change happening in India. Women are on the move, inching their way away from being doormats, away from the socially ordained straitjacket that Hindi movies of yesteryear so glorified.

I deliberately used the words "inching their way away from being doormats" rather than saying "marching determinedly towards breaking free," to reflect the truth of the situation. So how does this slow burn qualify as a change wave? Because, as I have said in an earlier chapter, the force of change caused by a large mass of people moving even at a very slow speed is huge enough to qualify as a change wave

Various studies done by the advertising agency FCB ULKA and the Indian Market Research Bureau point out that urban women see their role as being a "value-added" one—that of the intellectual nurturer, helping her child to be competitive and achieving, and in being the "CEO" of the household.

Most women are re-evaluating the importance of each of their roles and activities, and are de-emphasizing those that are high on effort and low on appreciation. Cooking continues to occupy an important place in the portfolio, as it is high on payoff even if it is high on effort. It ensures health and nourishment for the family, enabling them to perform in this pressured world, and is a means of her self-expression and creativity. De-emphasizing certain traditional roles such as cleaning or shopping does not bring with it the stereotypical, old-world mountains of guilt, because the time released thereby is going towards fulfilling other more productive roles. It is in this churn of a woman's portfolio of roles and activities that marketers will find huge opportunities.

A McCann Advertising study in rural India says that the biggest change that struck the researchers was the changing role of the woman in villages, and how she was beginning to get a mind of her own and express her own opinions. Village girls insist on going to school, and their mothers are letting them do so, even if they have to go against the wishes of the father. The experience of ICICI Bank and Hindustan Lever with self-help groups in states like Andhra Pradesh and Tamil Nadu shows that networking and the availability of finance unleash a lot of woman power—resulting in a definite rise in self-esteem and a demand for recognition from the rest of the family. While self-help groups often do not last over time, they throw up the occasional, successful woman entrepreneur who serves as role model for the rest.

Many of the marketers who are busy tracking how many women work in offices outside the home are perhaps missing the big changes inside the home. Some understand, though: two-wheeler marketers, for example, have noticed the emergence of a whole new market for girls and women who want the freedom that comes with mobility.

There is a strong case for financial-services companies to specifically create a women's business cell, and go beyond offering the odd add-on credit card to her husband. The home manager is ready to manage finances better, and wants to know how. In almost every category, there is the opportunity for forward-looking companies to actively encourage this movement and secure a lion's share of the future of what will be an increasingly valuable target group.

The Many Shades of "Modernity"

According to Research International, the first step up the womanism ladder is when the traditional woman becomes "less traditional." She begins experimenting, seeks a better role for herself and her daughters, starts negotiating with the male, albeit tactfully, rather than blindly accepting his dominance, but is still suspicious of excessive modernity.

The next, and, usually final, step is for her to be "forward-looking." That means that she is still family-centered but individualistic, and her mental emancipation is far greater than her physical emancipation. She arrives at a balance of the modern and the traditional and there is no more movement after that.

The image that most of us have of western modernity is actually one that most Indian women do not aspire to. They call it "ultra modern," which refers to the small group of young people who have broken away from tradition and custom and are free, unshackled and unfettered —certainly not the picture of the modern Indian woman, at least not for several decades to come.

Understanding the Forces of Change

What are the forces driving this change wave? One is the increase in education amongst women of all social strata, especially urban women. At one level, the statistics on housewife education are dismal. Only 12% of urban housewives are college graduates and another 20% have completed school; 30% are illiterate and the remaining 40% or so have studied up to a maximum of grade IX. However, on adding up the number of years of school and college in the total pool of women, it is easy to see that the total "education capital" is definitely higher than before, and it is this that is helping to drive change.

With two-thirds of urban women living in nuclear families, the onus is on the woman to handle a lot of the outdoor chores that men in the family would have taken on in joint families—for example, visiting the bank, paying utility bills (has to be done in person), going to their children's schools for PTA meetings, running around government offices for ration cards or other official papers, and so on. To manage without the support of elders is giving her a new-found confidence.

The reservation of seats for women in the rural, local, self-governance bodies (called *panchayats*) has brought them into the public decision-making domain and a news report says that in Uttar Pradesh alone, there are 20,000 women who head these bodies. If the figure is right, that's a lot of role models to show the way to the rest.

Then, there is that most primordial force—television. Whatever may be our critical judgement on the retrograde stereotypes of women shown in serials, television has widened women's frame of reference and given them the information resources to imagine and aspire. While many people decry the soaps that are the staple of Indian television as regressive and brainless, the fact is that they all have a subversive, feminist discourse. The protagonists are all women, good or bad; they all take charge of situations, and they all deal with them in different ways. The virtuous heroine can, when required, be both vamp and vixen, and the message is that all is fair in the game of life and women have the power, if they choose to wield it.

Postscript

It is true that women are getting more of a say in homes, in families, and in their own lives, than they have had before. They are getting more educated, more entrepreneurial, and more gutsy about narrowing the gap between them and the authority figures in their lives (more so husbands and in-laws, than parents). This is going to keep increasing because once the worm turns, there is no stopping it.

The twist in the tale is that while it is true, by women's own admissions, that mothers-in-law are more tolerant and husbands less repressive, and she has equal voting rights on family issues, it isn't social evolution that is driving this change as much as the state of the economy. In other words, we have the phenomenon of EMI (Equated Monthly Installments, the name given to housing and other loan repayments) to thank for driving this change. The concept of family has changed from a predominantly social unit to an economic unit. The new truth about Indian marriages is the old truth—that its business model is based around a pragmatic "life-business" partnership rather than around romance. Ask any young man, or woman, and you will know.

Taking a loan, for whatever purpose, is the new Indian way of life. The EMI is here to stay. And everyone has to do whatever they can to contribute to family earnings, so that the quality of living can be improved or the house can be owned or made liveable.

What is the role of the woman in this? In the lower social class, she must either earn and be a co-contributor or she must look after the housework, and the children of the extended family, so that the men and the women who are working outside the home can maximize their earnings.

In the middle and upper-class households, she must take care of all home and "outdoor work" for the family so that she facilitates and insulates the man, who is better qualified and who has greater earning potential, to realize that potential with no distraction.

At the very top social class, if she can be an equal earning partner, she must contribute and do so. But only up to a point of "adequacy," because the idea is to optimize the family's earnings, not maximize the woman's earning. Therefore, predictably, 20% of SEC A housewives work outside the home, and this falls to 16% as you proceed towards SEC B and C. In SECs D and E this figure increases to almost 40%.

Have no doubt about it, the beleaguered wife and mother is here to stay. But rather than just having to worry about stains on the rugs or her husband's grumbling about the dinner, she now has to combine her old role as nurturer and her new role as provider-partner, either directly or indirectly contributing to the goddess EMI.

The good news is that as her economic role in the marriage becomes increasingly important, she receives better treatment and more freedom in what she does when she is outside the house, earning her living or doing "outdoor" chores for the family.

There is bad news, though, as a brief scan of the matrimonial ads show. In the "wanted brides" section, under "cosmopolitan," we find the following: "well-educated, beautiful, homely"/"convent-educated, charming, extremely beautiful." The emphasis on education is hard not to notice. Because in her new role as provider-facilitator, education helps for sure. Could this explain, at least in part, why female enrolment in college, even in the smaller towns, is increasing? Then there are these: "seeking career-oriented bride"/"seeks working, very beautiful bride"/ "seeks beautiful, professionally-qualified girl"/"working girl preferred". Need I say more on this subject? I went to look at the Brahmin brides section because I thought maybe those hidebound enough to stick to caste may have a different worldview on this. I should have known better. The following is a sample of what's there: "Preferable engineering graduate"/"suitable medico girl"/"seeks engineer/doctor /MBA beautiful, fair, slim girl from decent family"/"seeks qualified Maithil non vatsa (a very specific community and caste) bride…"

Yes, the times, they are a changing. But not exactly in the way we think they are!

10

Rural Consumer India

A MARKET IN TRANSITION—READY TO BE SHAPED

If there is any one part of Consumer India that epitomizes the line "every truism about India can be contradicted by another truism" it is rural Consumer India. Therefore, it is not surprising that despite masses of data available, it is not easy to form a clear picture of it. There is total truth to the view that rural Consumer India is large, poor, backward and made up of small farmers with handkerchief-sized farms, that do not fulfill the needs—forget about the wants—of the families they support. It houses most of India's poor, and a large number of the world's poor. It therefore constitutes a backward market but can, with a lot of persistent effort, brute force and some innovation, be dragged into the 21st century, and become a valuable market, as FMCG brands have shown

However, the story of rural India is how it is morphing under the cover of its poverty and backwardness, even as everyone watching it closely is missing the signals. Unfortunately, most people tend to look for the wrong metrics of change, and therefore miss the big opportunities that it harbors. While large parts of rural India continue to be abjectly poor and dependent on an archaic, unprofitable agriculture business, there is a new and large rural India that has quietly emerged, which is prosperous and urban-like in parts, fairly non-agricultural in nature, geographically scattered, and ripe for market shaping.

Rural India is a potential market that is generating large forces of change and seeing significant income growth for the first time in its history. It is becoming exposed to how things work elsewhere. Hence, it also wants such things and almost by definition offers enormous opportunity to be shaped. Rural India's per-capita income is growing at the same rate as urban India's and is far more exciting because there are three times as many people, representing a little over half of India's GDP. It is also exciting because it is generating tremendous forces of change as its large mass morphs, slowly transforming from within.

What is needed is the opposite of the usual in-depth descriptive consumer data on how rural India eats, breathes, lives, and shops. What is needed is a better bird's-eye view and understanding of the structure and segments of rural India, of how it is morphing, so that interested parties can visualise the new business opportunities that rural Consumer India can offer. That is what this chapter sets out to do.

READY TO BE SHAPED, BUT WHY SO FEW TAKERS?

Rural India is vastly under-served today because most businesses do not recognize the opportunity to shape it. This is partly because their perspective of rural India is incorrect and they don't *see* the opportunity to shape it; and partly because they do not have the capability or the vision to rise to the challenge of creating whole new business streams through innovating to meet the needs of a low-education, high-exposure, low-income, high-aspiration, mostly young consumer base.

Finding appropriately priced, smokeless, efficient and modern cooking fuel or cooking devices for rural India is a necessity. Rural consumers do know what cooking gas is—they see it on television all the time and women are becoming more educated about health, grooming, and home care. The cost of transportation and cylinders makes mini cylinders unviable for the manufacturers, and the unit cost makes large cylinders unaffordable for the consumers. The solution that some companies thought of was to produce an efficient wood stove or a smokeless stove. That is one possibility, but the question is, "Why can't they have LPG cooking gas? Why must they have better candles when they want electric lights?" The solution was shaped by Hindustan Petroleum, a public-sector company, which established community kitchens with eight gas-stove stations, a gas meter, and a pay-as-you-use system. Franchising this model to women entrepreneurs all over rural India will considerably enhance this business model and be my suggested "next steps" in this business. Once conceptualized, it is easy to adapt this idea to local customs, caste, and community idiosyncrasies and devise easy-pay token systems or pre-paid cards.

Another reason why rural markets are under-served is the assumption that as rural infrastructure and connectivity improve, rural India will automatically adopt urban products and urban business systems and models. This assumption is not always true, because we find time and again that rural India is not following the same trajectory of evolution as urban India any more than urban India is walking the same path taken by America 20 years ago. It leapfrogs. To someone who is illiterate, a computer screen with icons is the most basic device. However, to someone who can read, it is an advancement over the printed page. The most striking difference is that rural India is emerging as a growth market at a time when the government is stepping aside in favor of more efficient private players and when the Internet and wireless technology are now available, making hitherto unviable markets become very viable indeed.

For example, rural India used to be served by public-sector banks, which were forced to set up offices in rural areas as part of the socialist government's diktat. These offices were unprofitable and there was no motivation for them to innovate, nor was there the benefit of technology which could lower the costs of serving a scattered population. Today rural India can be served through state-of-the-art remote banking systems using business models of the hub-and-spoke kind, and of the small local rep-office kind, perhaps using manned machines—models that neither exist nor are useful in urban areas. Even the technology for ATMs may need to be different because, given the rural infrastructure, the cost of the ATMs and the specifications would also need to be different.

For example, rural healthcare needs can now be met through a distance healthcare system with state-of-the-art diagnostic equipment, and with no doctors on location but a number of local, not-very-well-educated paramedics in place, such as would not be acceptable in urban areas.

Some version of e-commerce, perhaps combined bricks-and-clicks business models, will develop faster in rural areas than in urban areas, because such models would offer enormous value advantage compared to the current way of doing things in the rural areas.

This chapter offers a better understanding—a bird's-eye view of rural Consumer India so that companies can understand how best to segment it, define their own target Rural India, and shape businesses for it.

The Changing Structure of the Rural Economy: Not Just Agriculture

The generally held, though erroneous, belief about rural India is that it is in the dark ages and getting darker. This belief is based on a set of incorrect assumptions about the structure of the rural economy. The arguments commonly advanced are as follows:

- Rural India is an economy comprising only agriculture and nothing else; therefore rural consumers consist of farmers, farm-related labor, and other services.
- Since the agricultural sector in India is growing very slowly, at a rate of 1.9% since 1995–96, so too is the rural economy, and hence there is no real improvement in rural per-capita incomes.
- Since India's total GDP growth is much higher for this period, the urban economy is growing much faster, at 7.3%, and urban India's per-capita income is rising steadily.
- 70% of India's population lives in rural areas and is supported by agriculture, which comprises only about 25% of India's GDP, growing at a mere 1.9%. And the 30% of India's population which is urban, is lording over the remaining 75% of India's GDP, growing at 7.3%.
- Obviously, therefore, the urban–rural income and lifestyle chasm is growing.

The conclusion is that the rural market must be approached with caution and that it will take a long while before the rural market shows any real potential for things like cell phones, consumer durables, and consumer goods and services.

The truth is quite different. The first hints of that this is so appeared as early as the end of the 1990s, when data began to show that the occupational profile of consumer-durables buyers in rural India was far more non-agricultural than the occupational profile of the rural population. Further, all anecdotal evidence of rural market behavior showed that it was far better than the commonly held beliefs about its backwardness.

In 2003, I was helping a leading Indian business house to develop its rural strategy and, as a first step, we needed to get a few fundamental facts together about the rural economy and about rural Consumer India. That's when it emerged that India did not actually have an official number in the government statistics for "Rural GDP." I worked with Subir Gokarn, the chief economist of Credit Rating Information Services of India Limited (CRISIL), and based on a 1993–94 one-off report from the Central Statistical Organization (CSO), which did a rural–urban classification of GDP, he constructed the rural GDP and its components for 2000–01. His numbers showed that 54% of India's GDP was rural, and 48% of the rural GDP was agricultural, down from 56% in 1993–94. It also showed that rural GDP had been growing at more or less the same pace as urban GDP. Since agriculture was growing far slower, it could only mean that the non-agricultural segment was growing much faster.

Omkar Goswami, economist and founder chairman of CERG Advisory, an economic research and consulting company, and I wrote in the *Business Standard* in July 2005, refuting an article that had the usual fallacious logic on rural Indians being poor, and getting poorer:

Our analysis shows that in 2000–01, out of India's NDP of Rs.1,062,400 crore at constant 1993–94 prices, the share of rural India was 52 per cent. This is how the rural NDP played out in 2000–01: agriculture accounted for 46 per cent; industry took up another 21 per cent; and services was 33 per cent. Between 1993–94 and 2000–01, rural NDP at constant prices grew at an average of 6.2 per cent per year. Since agriculture grew at around 2 per cent during this period, it is obvious that the rural economy has been much more than just agriculture.

Our second problem with the article under discussion is that it doesn't look at other evidence, much of which demonstrates the growth of non-agricultural activities throughout rural India. According to the Annual Survey of Industries, even in 1993–94, rural India accounted for 29% of the country's organised manufacturing units, 30% of its employees, 32% of its output and 30% of its net value added. In 2000–01, over a rising base, rural India could speak of 36% of organised manufacturing establishments, 38% of its employees, 43% of output and 41% of net value added.

Consider the Census of India 1991 and 2001. In 1991, 30.6% of rural households had *pucca* (permanent houses). By 2001, this had risen to 41%, over a base which was growing at 1.7% per year. Between 1991 and 2001, households that used liquified petroleum gas (LPG) for cooking rose from 1% to almost 6%, with Himachal Pradesh leading the pack at 22%. In 2001, almost 20% of rural households owned televisions, and the rural regions of ten states were significantly above the national average. Between 1991 and 2001, the percentage of rural households with electricity connections at their homesteads rose from a little over 30% to 43.5%, with eleven states being placed well over the national rural average. In 2001, over 30% of rural households kept their funds in banks or postal savings accounts. All this doesn't square up with the age-old dominant picture of rural India—that of highly indebted, underfed peasants ploughing their handkerchief-sized fields with emaciated bullocks under the blazing heat of the midday sun. That may be still be true of the agricultural economy; but not of the rural economy.

We could inundate you with more evidence, but we won't. We want to make four points.

- First, rural is much more than agriculture; it has a thriving and growing manufacturing and services sector.
- Second, per-capita rural income has grown at the same pace as that of urban between 1993–94 and 2000–01
- Third, the top quartile of rural India have been far higher spenders than the average, spending at least Rs.179,450 crore, with spending patterns that are similar to urban India.
- Finally, there is considerable pent-up demand for goods as well as services like education, communication, and medical treatment—so maybe it is time for celebration for cell phone and consumer durable manufacturers, with a large new market opportunity opening up.

COMPARISON OF SIZE AND PURCHASING POWER OF RURAL AND URBAN CONSUMER INDIA

The National Sample Survey (NSS) data of 2003–04 shows than 62% of consumer expenditure in India comes from rural India and only 38% from urban India. The NSS data also shows that while urban consumer expenditure grew at a rate of 8.3% between 1993–94 and 2003–04, at 7%, rural expenditure growth was not far behind.

Rural India's per-capita income of around US$530 is far lower than urban India's US$1,200 at current prices. Yet because rural India has three times as many people as urban India—750 million people as compared to 250 million—the rural market is larger than the urban market for many categories.

According to data compiled by Pradeep Kashyap of MART (a rural expert firm), Life Insurance Corporation (LIC), India's largest life insurer, sells more than half of its policies in rural India. Some 41 million *Kisan* credit cards were issued to farmers, which is almost double the 22 million credit and debit cards issued in urban India. Some 42 million rural households availed themselves of bank accounts, compared to 27 million urban households. These numbers sound very counter-intuitive, since we know that penetration of most products in rural India is actually very poor. However, as discussed earlier, the great Indian numbers trick, that usually surprises most marketers, is that a small penetration of a large population results in a very large actual market size.

Another indicator of the attractiveness of rural India is provided by a simple metric based on National Council of Applied Economic Research (NCAER) data. While the percentage of middle-income households (those earning between US$1,120 and US$5,330) in rural India is about 18%, the corresponding percentage for urban India is about 58%. The *number* of middle-income households in rural India, however, is around 27 million, while in urban India the number is a shade higher, at 29 million.

Looking into the future, this attractiveness remains, since per-capita income in rural India has grown at exactly the same rate as in urban India for the past 10 years

Indian Readership Survey (IRS) data also shows that between 2000 and 2005, there has a been a 5%–7% improvement in rural literacy and education levels, including those of women, and in television ownership and access to cable and satellite television. In addition, there are many government policy initiatives in the area of agriculture, and a public–private partnership movement is gaining increasing acceptance in several states, as are several technology-based services that enable rural services such as banking, telemedicine, and e-governance to become commercially viable.

This means that it is safe to assume that the rural market will continue to remain an attractive and very important market.

Marketing to rural India has its geographical and infrastructural challenges, which is why, despite being bigger in current market value than urban markets for many categories, it is still more expensive and less attractive to marketers.

SPENDING PATTERNS OF RURAL INDIA

The respective shares of food and non-food expenditure in any economy is one of the measures of consumption sophistication of the economy. On an aggregate basis, NSS data shows that in rural India the share of expenditure on food is still at a hefty 58.3% of total expenditure, while non-food expenditure is at 41.7%. For the top 5% of the rural population by income, this ratio is 50:50. For the bottom 5%, the share of food expenditure is as high as 65%.

The growth of food-related expenditure has been much slower than the growth of non-food expenditure: between 1993–94 and 2002–03, food expenditure grew at 5.7%, as compared to non-food expenditure growth at 9.8%.

The fastest-growing non-food expenditure categories, however, are education, healthcare, and conveyance. Education and healthcare increased their share of the rural consumer wallet from 9% to 11% in a the ten-year period from 1993–94 to 2003–04, during which total consumption expenditure doubled. Consumer durables are another category that is growing fast. FMCG expenditure share has, however, remained constant through the past ten years, perhaps explaining the pain of FMCG companies.

The emerging picture of the rural consumers is that they want life-improving "do-good" products and services of real quality; or consumer durables that enhance productivity and increase earning, such as motorcycles and cell phones. This is also a consumer base that has enough aspiration (70% of R1, R2 and R3 households, which account for about half of rural India, can be reached through the mass media) and not enough amenities, thanks to government neglect. Innovations in technology and service-delivery systems to deliver electricity, water, sanitation, health and other life-improving services will, therefore, be clear winners.

SEGMENTATION SCHEMES FOR RURAL INDIA: AFFLUENCE SEGMENTS, DEMAND SEGMENTS

Scattered Oases of Affluence: Rural India comprises 640,000 villages of varying sizes (see Table 10.1). Of these the 17% with populations of over 2,000, have 50% of the total rural population and 60% of the wealth. A little over one-third have hardly any developed distribution in the form of shops.

Viewed through the consumer expenditure window, 20% of rural India accounts for 43% of expenditure, and the top 10% by income are higher spenders, far removed from the overall trend line. However, these pockets of affluence, and, hence, a higher-quality market opportunity, are scattered over a wide geographic area, with no apparent logic.

Population	Number of villages	% of total villages
Less Than 200	92,541	15.6
200–500	127,054	21.4
501–1,000	144,817	24.4
1,001–2,000	129,662	21.9
2,001–5,000	80,313	13.5
5,001–10,000	18,758	3.2
Total number of villages	593,154*	100.0

Table 10.1: Distribution of Villages by Population

*Inhabited villages. Total number of villages is 638,691
Source: Census 2001, Pradeep Kashyap, MART

Rural India has deserts and oases within it that form no discernible pattern. The average statistics on any count are quite dismal, but the total numbers of opportunity are very heartening. Even at the state level there is huge heterogeneity and the patterns of oases and deserts are not driven by any particular development design logic, but by a series of localized happenstances. Therefore, one model of winning in rural consumer markets is to undertake micro-market planning—map each geographic sub-segment, a district or even its sub-unit, a *taluka*, or in some cases even villages, and undertake distribution and other market development activities. LG and other Korean companies do this very well, painstakingly isolating pockets of demand that are under-served and moving in to mop it up. Hindustan Lever looks for growth by micro-market, mapping media-dark and distribution-dark areas for development. It is also in the process of developing a women's network to really penetrate such villages.

There are at least 150 rural districts that have assets and amenities equivalent to urban India.

Developed and Developing States: Rural India, in the more progressive, higher-GDP-growth states, is far more prosperous and well-developed and fairly close to the levels of urban India. The higher-growth, better-developed states such as Punjab, Haryana, Gujarat, Maharashtra, Goa, Karnataka, Kerala, and Tamil Nadu account for one-third of the population of rural India. The developed rural Consumer India has a diamond-shaped income distribution. For the rest of rural India it is triangle-shaped, with the maximum number of people in the lowest income group. Media reach is significantly higher, as is product penetration.

NON-AGRICULTURAL RURAL CONSUMER INDIA

According to NSS data, 35% of households in rural India are engaged in non-agricultural activities. The data also shows that these households are far higher spenders than the "agricultural" households. Households are classified as agricultural or non-agricultural depending on their major source of income. However, an analysis of the occupation of individual household members shows that many households are engaged in both. As the sons grow up, the inability of the farm to support all of them forces them to move out of agriculture. Gradually, as the proportion of non-agricultural income increases and predominates, the character of the household changes, as do its consumption patterns. This was a major factor that contributed to the sustained growth in motorcycle sales in rural India between 1999 and 2003.

It is also this wave that changed the agricultural-equipment market: as families started to engage in other businesses, they wanted greater productivity and time away from the farm to earn more; rather than lowest-cost, lower-productivity equipment.

As discussed in an earlier chapter, this non-agricultural rural segment is an interesting demand segment with many sub-segments, and one that has not yet been specifically targeted by marketers, for whom emerging new segments provide huge opportunity across sectors to create new businesses. This segment is neither quite urban nor quite rural in mindset and needs and, hence, requires custom-built products and services.

AGRICULTURAL CONSUMER INDIA

The best segmenting variable for agricultural Consumer India is how the farmer thinks about his farming business.

In a study done for Mahindra and Mahindra several years ago, one segment that emerged were "return-on-investment" farmers who thought of farming as a business and were willing to spend more to earn more. Then there was a segment that is gradually turning to non-agricultural businesses as well, who are looking at maximizing productivity. Thirdly, there is a segment for whom farming is inescapable in that they have neither the skills nor the mindset to diversify away from it. To them, the accent is on cash-flow minimization.

This objective function drives not just their orientation to agriculture-related products, but also to all other products and to living and spending in general. All this will again change as laws governing the agricultural sector become liberalized.

FUTURE SHIFTS: LIBERALIZING AGRICULTURE, SPECIAL ECONOMIC ZONES (SEZS)

Laws governing the sale of agricultural commodities and relating to corporate contract farming are in the process of being modified. As is usual of India, individually these changes seems limited and minor, but over a period of five years, we have seen significant changes, sufficient to encourage the rise of new businesses and new business models.

The newest growth business, that most large corporates are looking at, is related to agriculture and food. ITC Ltd has demonstrated that with the use of IT they can create virtual markets for agricultural produce and farmers are ready to do far-more-sophisticated transactions because they have more information. The government's acceptance of the fact that ITC can buy directly from the farmers (till recently the law said they had to sell at a government marketplace called a *mandi*), as long as it pays a *mandi* tax, has inspired more corporates to test the system.

Supplying modern retailers, and the recent entry of Wal-Mart into the cash-and-carry segment of the market, have changed the vision of agricultural supply chains altogether, and will hopefully change the landscape as well.

All these changes, when they start kicking in very soon, will change farmers' mindsets—in different ways for different types of farmers in different states—creating a new pattern of rural Consumer India, with yet another shake of the kaleidoscope.

And still another shake of the kaleidoscope could come from special economic zones (SEZs), which are islands of world-class infrastructure, industry and residential townships in the middle of rural areas. The jury is still out on how many and what scale of SEZs we may have. But that could change agriculture, young people, and rural India forever— or not. It all depends on how they are structured, and how much local talent they use.

A senior bureaucrat once said that when things finally happen in India, they happen with a big thud, leaving most people unprepared. It is possible that we will soon have a "rural" market which is totally different from the "morphing rural" and urban markets, creating many more Indias with different market opportunities.

11

Understanding the "Bottom of the Pyramid" Consumer India

Ever since the release of Professor C K Prahalad's book *Fortune at the Bottom of the Pyramid*, there has been a sort of skeptical scramble from large global companies to find the Holy Grail—a business model that can give the consumer all that he wants, at the price he can afford, and still be profitable. Several leading-edge global companies have undertaken experimental projects in India to try and figure out how best to engage with the Bottom of the Pyramid (BOP) consumer.

Having been a part of many of these projects, I am not convinced that there is enough conviction amongst operating managers, no matter how senior, about the need to construct such a challenging and risky business model. Serving the BOP consumer is seen to be part of corporate social responsibility, and, hence, essential and noble, but not part of mainstream business. It is seen to be part of sustainable development and, hence, important, but not urgent—the planet must be saved, but not at the cost of displeasing Wall Street? The general feeling is that finding ways to serve the BOP consumer is about buying some kind of option on an amorphous eventuality—a bit like prayer; essential but not critical to everyday living.

Partly because of this lower level of conviction, companies have not invested a great deal of effort or energy in understanding the BOP consumer as a starting point to develop appropriate business models. Most of the time, the effort is in the form of blinkered, "inside-out" approaches. At worst, it comes in the form of tinkering, to strip features and create "no frills" cheaper versions of a feature-rich expensive product, with no concern for what consumers would consider to be a "frill" and what an "essential." At best, it has been in the form of letting R&D loose in their spare time to invent things that the poor could use—based on the stereotypical image of the poor as illiterate, uninformed and primitive. The result has been specially created new products which are low-priced but light-years behind in sophistication. In either case, they usually fail to connect with the market.

No discussion on Consumer India's potential and strategies to unlock it would be complete without a customer-centered discussion on the BOP consumer.

The first part of this chapter addresses the question of whether there really is a fortune at the bottom of the Indian pyramid for anyone to seriously bother about. The second part discusses the characteristics, attitudes, and value-processing methods of low-income consumers in India, to enable the development of keys that could unlock their market potential.

WHY BOTHER ABOUT THE BOTTOM OF THE PYRAMID (BOP) CONSUMER INDIA?

Large Value: The size of the BOP market in India is 650 million people who, individually, earn less than a dollar a day, but who, collectively, account for 30% of national income, a little over 33% of consumption expenditure and a little over 20% of India's savings. At current prices, in 2004–05, this amounts to a market with an aggregate income of about US$165 billion (US$840 billion on a purchasing power parity (PPP) basis), and consumption expenditure of about US$125 billion (US$630 billion on a PPP basis).

The total income of BOP Consumer India is 1.4 times that of Malaysia, 1.6 times that of Singapore, equal to that of South Africa and 90% of that of Hong Kong. The per-capita incomes are very low, and therein lies the strategic and economic challenge of the BOP: an interesting-sized market on the aggregate, pathetic on per-capita incomes. The answer to the question of "why bother with consumers at the bottom of the pyramid?" is, therefore, that there is a reasonable-sized fortune at the bottom of the Indian pyramid, but it isn't easy to access it with current business models.

A Dollar a Day Per Capita is a Reasonable Income in India: One US dollar a day per capita translates into about Rs.6,750 per month for an average family of five. On a PPP basis, this would convert to a comfortable middle-class living, with all the basic consumer durables and the ability to service a mortgage. Even assuming no conversion to PPP, at just Rs.6,750, this will buy only shanty dwelling in big cities, but it can buy better living conditions in the smaller towns. Two months of this salary can buy a good color television, which is why it is not unusual to see homes with lots of consumer durables but no individual toilets. Five months of salary can buy a good second-hand motorcycle, and half a month's salary can get a cell phone connection for life, with the instrument and incoming calls free for life. Another Rs.200 (US$5) per month can buy a pre-paid card.

Our experience of BOP consumers in India thus far has been that the bottom 250 million of the 650 million may be very hard to integrate into the mainstream market economy, as Professor Prahalad urges in *Fortune at the Bottom of the Pyramid.*

However, the other 400 million are full of surprises, challenging all our mental images of what poor consumers are really like. The fact that bears yet another repetition is that there has never been a consumer group like this ever before in the world. Never before in the history of humanity have so many poor people been subjected to so much real-time information and so much technology, bringing newer benefits more frequently. This creates a unique new market, which needs to be understood if it is to be innovated for. It is not about transplanting best practices from the past of other markets, but about creating "next practices" for a totally new kind of future.

Sensible Investment for the Future: BOP markets in growing economies are very good investments to make because, firstly, brand emotions and aspirations that are established when consumers are poor tend to stick as they get richer, provided, of course, that relevant product offerings are available. Secondly, securing the loyalty of 400 million consumers, who are in an economy where real national income doubles every decade, if not earlier, makes for a very good business case for investment. This investment can be either in finding the right business models that can generate a profit today and/or in settling for lower profits from this target group today, to secure the future.

Guaranteed Income Growth: Is there enough evidence that the fruits of economic growth are trickling down, and will continue to do so, to lower-income Consumer India? Have the incomes of the lowest income groups actually improved in this past 15 years, and what are they likely to be in the future?

As we saw in the chapter on purchasing power, when compared on a like-to-like inflation-adjusted basis, the size of the lowest income group has actually declined sharply, showing that upward income mobility is very much a fact.

In the early years of liberalization, say between 1995–96 and 2001–02, the number of households in the lower income group declined at an average annual growth rate of 8.5% in urban India, but by only 2.7% in rural India, since the fruits of liberalization were not evenly distributed. In the next phase, between 2001–02 and 2005–06, however, both urban and rural lower income households declined at between 5–6% each year. For the period 2005–06 and 2009–10, the fruits of liberalization will reach rural India more sharply, with the number of rural lower-income households set to decline at 14% annually. The number of lower-income households in urban India will decline at 9% annually. On an all-India basis, this translates into a 10% annual average decline in the number of lower-income households. The bottom of the pyramid is rising quite fast in terms of absolute quantum of income earned. This data comes from National Council of Applied Economic Research (NCAER), and has been described more fully in the chapter on purchasing power.

Favorable Change in Social Attitudes: Ever since liberalization, there has been a perceptible change in the social attitudes of the poor, as documented in the Hindi movies. The biggest change has been a move away from demanding social justice to grabbing economic opportunity. The fear of authority (and of the rich man) has now been replaced by reducing power distances and the language is one of striving, aspiration, and self-esteem. The key driving force is escape velocity for their children and the entire language is about "how to" rather than "why not." The hunger for information and knowledge is extreme.

All these, taken together, make for a very fertile environment to invest in this consumer group.

CHARACTERISTICS OF THE BOP CONSUMER

Poor but No Longer Backward

BOP Consumer India has seen significant shifts in its consumption orientation in the last decade (see Table 11.1). These consumers are aware of what is happening in the rest of the world as it happens, in real time. They are knowledgeable about the product options available to others, and are hence, unwilling to settle for less. They prefer to stretch for more and better.

In the pre-liberalization, socialist era, the poor were resigned to their fate and unexposed to the world around them. With no informational resources to imagine a better life, they were destiny-driven. Today, however, they maximize benefits, like any other income group. This is where most of the "no frills" offerings to poor consumers go wrong. What suppliers consider to be a "frill," consumers consider to be a necessity. A better wood stove is not good enough in a world of LPG, nor is a black-and-white television or even a color one without a remote.

FROM (pre-Liberalization poor)	TO (post-Liberalization poor)
Settle for less	Stretch for more
Reluctance, avoidance	Seeking experience
Abstemiousness ("not for us")	Affordable indulgence
Destiny-driven, resigned to fate	Struggling and aspiring for a better life
Simple needs	State-of-the-art needs too!

Table 11.1: Changing Consumption Orientation of BOP Consumers

They live in a fast-growing economy and have witnessed a rapid change, in less that one generation, in their economic status. This makes them confident about the future and quite comfortable about aspiring for a better life, because it will, in all likelihood, happen within their lifetime. Therefore the accent is not on abstemiousness and rationalizing that "all these things are not for us", but, rather, on affordable indulgence—of the kind that rich people have.

There is no avoidance of experiences; rather, there is experience-seeking, and the struggle is to have interesting consumption experiences within the constraints of the purse. What we said earlier about Consumer India's cultural shifts applies to this group too—the new life-view that "life is not a condition to be endured, but a product to be experienced" (Santosh Desai). On special occasions like weddings, low-income consumers will serve the more expensive colas rather than the cheaper squashes they usually consume. However, the glasses used are usually smaller, in order to make it affordable and not the usual cheaper, non-fizzy orange drink in somewhat larger glasses.

They want illnesses diagnosed with x-rays and other tests—they are no longer satisfied solely with the doctor's intuition. Poor consumers would rather defer making a purchase and get a better product than settle for something of a far lower standard today: not a new moped, but a second-hand motorcycle, when they can afford it.

They Value All Kinds of Productivity Devices That Help Them Earn More

Poor consumers see access to information, knowledge, healthcare, education, transportation, and communication as the means to earn more. They simply see all these as methods by which they can widen their operations, get more done in a day, and work smarter.

I once did a study on motorcycles in the villages, and was puzzled to find that as the availability of public transport increased, the sales of motorcycles also went up. On investigating, we were told by the rural consumers that when they had no public transport, they did not have anywhere to go. The arrival of public transport enabled them to do business or go to work outside of their village; and the more they started doing that, the more they wanted to go at times that suited them, in order to maximize their productivity—hence the need for private transport.

Most of the loans taken by poor consumers are related to medical problems. Every illness has the potential to cause a drop in income and increase the burden of loans. Health insurance, preventive medical measures and timely control and cure of illness are therefore services that they value greatly. It is this need that Philips India is trying to tap into with a distance healthcare service.

ITC *e-chaupal*, an IT-enabled multiple-services provider in the villages, decided to provide information free to rural consumers so that the total desire to do business transactions would increase. And they were confident that their superior execution skills would get them the lion's share of the new market thus created.

It is entirely likely that the poor will be faster adopters of e-commerce and reverse auctions than the rich.

Poor Consumers Do Complicated Value Processing, Have Complicated Financial Models

Banks often assume that complex financial transactions are done by the rich, and simple ones by the poor. This is part of the "no frills" train of thought that companies pursue when developing products for the poor. In actual fact, because of the limited resources and complicated financial balancing acts that poor people need to do, their financial transactions are a lot more complex: borrow from several sources at several interest rates; lend when needed at different terms depending on the exigencies involved; constantly revolve sources and uses of funds, and so on. It is interesting that default rates on loan repayments are extremely low for poor consumers.

This complicated model of sources and uses of funds that poor consumers work with, with their income generation and consumption activities totally intertwined, defies many of the banking sector's ideas of loans being for consumption or for income generation.

Poor consumers don't think that way. They calculate the value of the cable television channels they pay for against a how much more the family would spend if they had to step out of the house to entertain themselves. They weigh the value of the interest that might appear usurious against how the use of those funds will help improve earnings in the longer term.

Poor Consumers are Very Innovative—They Innovate Their Own Product Solutions to Make Them "Value-Right"

Necessity is the mother of innovation. The need to make a little bit of money go a long way is a powerful driver of smart solutions. Poor countries are innovative. The Hindi word for this is *jugaad*—to somehow cobble together a solution. The CEO of an Indian company that does outsourced research for a large US pharmaceutical company said that, ironically, his competitive advantage over developed countries came from the fact that most of his researchers had gone to colleges where the equipment available was far less than what was needed for the number of students enrolled. So they had learnt to do experiments in the quickest possible time, a skill that they brought to the workplace, making the Indian business faster and cheaper. The CEO of a company manufacturing blood-glucose monitoring equipment was shocked to find that consumers in India had figured out how to cut up the glucometer strips into the minimum useable size, thus converting one strip into three.

By the same logic, we find that poor consumers are far more innovative than the folks that design products and services for them. The following are examples of some of such innovations by poor consumers, each one more interesting than the previous one.

• Poor consumers with cell phones do not use them to make calls— outgoing calls cost money, incoming calls are free. So if they need to get in touch with you, they will tell you that they will give you a "missed call", and you should call them back. (*Madam I will give you missed call at 11 a.m. tomorrow.*")

• It is not unusual in rural India to have a form of community lighting where the headlights of a jeep or a tractor are turned on, and the fuel used is a mixture of the more expensive petrol and the cheaper kerosene.

• Micro-glasses to serve cold drinks at weddings are an innovation (*"Let us not look bad serving a quarter of a glass of cola; let us just reduce the size of the glass itself."*) Poor consumers can refill, recycle and reuse almost anything. As an exasperated consumer durables marketer once said, "It seems that the last thing that you Indians ever threw out was the British!"

• The Grassroots Innovations Augmentation Network (GIAN) is an organization that encourages innovation, and its work offers interesting insights into how the poor create solutions to their problems, since big businesses either do not feel the need or do not have the orientation to do so. I had been working with a tractor company which was engaged in developing a new small tractor that would help small farmers mechanize their farms—thus expanding the served market beyond what existing tractors could do. At the same time, I noticed that GIAN innovators had created and were selling locally a whole slew of farm mechanization equipment: post-harvest groundnut separators, areca nut cutters, cotton-picking machines, paddy-threshing machines, 10HP tractors, motorcycle-driven ploughs, bicycle hoes, and a tilting bullock cart. Other GIAN innovations include a washing machine operated by pedaling a stationary bicycle. The poor do not want a better stick with which to beat their clothes, but an affordable washing machine that can operate without electricity.

Poor Consumers Embrace Technology

The poor might be illiterate but they are totally comfortable with technology and can find innovative ways to use it.

n-Logue is a company that has a low-cost technology enabling it to put up kiosks in villages with one Internet connection and one telephone connection for around Rs.50,000 (less than US$1000). Each kiosk is franchised to a kiosk operator—typically, a not-very-well-educated young woman from a low-income family—who have to earn about Rs.4,500 per month (approximately US$100) in order for the kiosk to be financially viable. Consumers found several applications for this, and soon the computer kiosk network was being used as a movie theatre and as a public address system for the local politician. With the help of a webcam, veterinary doctors were able to provide distance treatment for cattle and a whole host of other applications were created. The young women were providing technological support to one another via Yahoo chats in Tamil, saving the company the cost of a traditional technological support team. Now, the children are able to use to practice their lessons for their exams, since content for this has been made available.

Poor consumers, like children, have no preconceived notions or fear when it comes to dealing with technology. To them, technology is the great democratizer, free from human prejudices.

This is indeed good news for companies who want to mine the profit at the bottom of the pyramid, because technology-driven consumer interfaces will be an integral part of keeping costs low when servicing a network of remote locations, or when having to do a large number of small transactions.

A GENERIC FRAMEWORK FOR UNDERSTANDING LOW-INCOME CONSUMERS BETTER

Linda Alwitt and Thomas Donley, in their outstanding book *Low Income Consumer—Adjusting the Balance of Exchange* (Sage Publications) make a compelling case for marketers to think about the low-income consumer as a distinct market, rather than as just one more consumer segment, differentiated from the rest only in terms of income.

They suggest that marketers recognize that low-income consumers are heterogeneous and need to be further segmented, that they view life differently because of their circumstances and, hence, have different needs, behaving totally differently as consumers. "Affluent consumers" they say, "worry about size, style, color, and flavor. Poor consumers worry about the basic necessities—'For *which* child should I buy shoes'?"

The book presents a lot of research on low-income consumers in the US, who are a world apart from those here, but there is much that is relevant to the Indian context.

Segmenting Low-Income Consumers

The age, education, and occupation segments are the most obvious places to start since they are clearly likely to influence consumption attitudes and values. However, these can be combined into a more interesting segmenting variable—"spell length in low income" or how long the household or individual is likely to remain in the low-income group.

They define two low-income segments—transitory and persistent. Transitory consumers are particularly valuable long-term assets for a business, where efforts to build brand equity work better. Sylvester Research Ltd, in their document *World Waves*, say, "The consumer may be poor, but he is living in a society that is growing faster than at any time in its history. At 8% growth, income will double in the next seven years. They are deciding how to spend it now. Decisions made when poor really count."

In the Indian context, the transitory segment could include a low-income family unit with young, relatively better educated, sons who are beginning to earn. Their disposable income may not change immediately but investing in them makes sense since they are clearly transitory. Or it may include older people at the stage when their children are a few years away from being settled, who will then have a sudden increase in disposable income.

Understanding Spending Power and Patterns Beyond Annual Income

First, since the bulk of low-income Consumer India is rural and does not have a steady source of income, total annual income is not the best measure to use to understand their affluence. Other variables such as per-capita income, number of earning members, and rules of household spending, especially in joint families, need to be factored in. Secondly, there are often swings in the income of a given family unit which cause frequent changes in spending patterns. Agricultural income is one such example that we are familiar with.

New household configurations (for example, the earning son who leaves to set up his own home, or an earning daughter getting married) change the spending patterns of both the old unit and the new. The practice of borrowing also stretches income—while formal credit is often not available to this group, they are borrowing informally against future income, not by way of planning for the future but for more immediate needs. It is either the retailer who captures this value, or the pawn shop owner. Furthermore, given the interdependent nature of our society, there is a lot of borrowing from friends and relatives.

Improving Buyer Power: It is well known and well documented that existing retail environments extract more from the poor customers (poor neighborhoods have less-competitive retail environments, pushing up prices. Low-income consumers are dependent on the retailer for credit and end up paying more as they buy in small quantities, and get poorer service). There is a case for opening a set of thrift stores, offering credit as well a relevant merchandise to lower-income consumers, who will reward this empowerment with loyalty. Another interesting suggestion is the creation of buying groups, modeled on the borrowing circles set up by Dr Mohammad Yunus of the Grameen Bank in Bangladesh.

Understanding Value Processing and Budget Balancing: Consumer durables are obviously far more attractive items for low-income consumers than FMCG. The Indian low-income consumer is struggling to up-trade on consumer durables and is down-trading on FMCG. While they carefully look at ways to stretch budgets with no-frills FMCG products, there are occasional gratification purchases—for children, around festival time and occasional treats for the family. Sylvester Research says that "it isn't practicable [for them] to buy houses and cars [and the big stuff] and "so how do you flaunt new disposable income?" Their answer is "labels." The low-end branding game has latent potential, in the area of store brands, perhaps?

SUICIDAL MOVES BY GLOBAL COMPANIES IN SERVING LOW-INCOME CONSUMERS

India has seen a lot of efforts from global companies to roll out products that are affordable for poor consumers. They have reduced the price by reducing performance and assumed that this combination would work; because they thought that everybody would expect and accept that for a lower price one has to settle for lower performance. They reduced functionality, reduced styling, and offered old and obsolete products with no adaptation. When the consumer rejected all of this, they blamed the consumer and the country for not being evolved; in actual fact, the consumer was way ahead in sophistication.

So now we need to move to the next stage of learning—trying to achieve acceptable performance at affordable prices through real innovation of either product or business system, perhaps by co-creating them with the consumers themselves, for best results.

12

Winning in the Indian Market

—»·0·«—

THE "CLASS VS. MASS" DILEMMA

Most multinational companies (MNCs), especially those which are recent entrants into the Indian market, voice their disappointment with the total mismatch between the size of the Indian economy and the size of their own business in India. The explanation for this usually lies in the different perspectives they have when assessing market opportunity and setting financial expectations, and when developing business strategy. Their financial expectations are based on the fact that India is a nearly US$1-trillion economy, with one billion people, mostly young. They forget, however, that India is a large market made up of many poor consumers, and insist on deploying their tried and tested "global" strategy, one designed for far richer markets with different consumer psyches. This severely truncates the canvas of opportunity available to them.

Despite some concessions and adaptations in the name of localization, strategies transplanted from developed markets are relevant only to about 20 million households, which represent the top 10% of all Indian households, or the top 30% of urban Indian households, often labeled the "class" market. These 20 million households account for less than one-third of India's consumer expenditure, which is equivalent to the gross domestic product (GDP) of a small economy like Thailand, though with lower per-capita income. Targeting this India can typically result in a small business enjoying revenue of around US$50–100 million today, with average profitability by global standards. In order to boost these numbers, targeting the rest of the Indian consumer base, the "mass" market, is necessary. However, this requires the development of whole new strategies, especially the creation of unprecedented price-performance points. Making this choice between the comfort of a familiar strategy and a modest-sized business or the discomfort of a new untested strategy and a potentially large business is what most MNCs agonize over. I call it the "class versus mass dilemma," and it sits at the heart of what winning in the Indian market entails.

The argument put forward by companies reluctant to depart from their tried-and-tested business models is that there is no need to go through the considerable pain of designing new, tailor-made strategies for the mass market, since the class market is one of the fastest-growing consumer groups in the economy. The inevitable comparisons are made with China, where this strategy of targeting the top end of the income pyramid and growing with it results in far bigger businesses. However, in India, while a strategy designed only for the class market can deliver a business growth of a minimum of 30–35% over the next five years, given the low starting point, these numbers will still be far short of the expectations triggered by the idea of a one-trillion-dollar economy with one billion consumers—and far smaller than the results in China.

The math is simple. The "creamy layer" of high-income consumers is far thicker and creamier in China than it is in India. Furthermore, since India is about ten years behind China in per-capita income terms, it will take far longer to achieve equivalent-sized businesses. By 2015, China will have about 110 million households with an annual household income of over US$20,000 (in purchasing power parity (PPP) terms), while the corresponding number for India will only be about 30 million.

Therefore, building a business in India that is in line with India's large GDP and population requires winning in the mass market too. In order to do that, businesses must design special keys to unlock the potential of the mass market, and to accept that these keys could be quite different from those already in existence in other parts of the world.

Another argument that is put forward by companies who do not buy the "make for India" prescription is that they will run a small and profitable operation in the class market, and wait until the mass market gets rich enough to become a part of this. This is a deeply flawed argument because mass markets do not sit around and wait with primitive products and unfulfilled needs until they get rich enough to afford the "real thing." The risk of not addressing the needs of this market today is that these consumers could be lost forever as they embrace other kinds of solutions that someone else innovates for them. In the first chapter, we discussed the personal computer (PC) business and how, instead of waiting until they got rich enough to buy big-brand PCs, consumers were buying PCs assembled in the local electronics market, and moving to increasingly powerful cell phones that were still cheaper than PCs or shared grid-computing services. In other markets, it could be the retailer's store brand, or a smart local company with a better understanding of customers' needs, that starts to develop and capture the mass market well before it becomes a class market.

There is an interesting window of opportunity, that will remain open for a while longer, for companies to establish dominant positions in the Indian mass market. This is because Indian businesses are, as yet, not focused on, or capable of, seizing the opportunity to step in and own this market and lock out competition. For most of them this is not currently possible, because to build a large, sustainable and profitable business needs global competencies and global access to raw materials, labor, markets, and money — which few Indian companies have as yet. Those who can are very focused on establishing a global footprint for themselves in developed markets; consequently, their focus on making a big push in the domestic Indian market is low. Therefore, the party is yet to begin, and the prize is still up for grabs.

THE CHALLENGE OF "GETTING IT RIGHT" FOR THE INDIAN MARKET

Winning in the Indian mass market is not about finding ways to squeeze or coax revenue and/or profitability from it using a suboptimal strategy compensated for by marketing aggression, discounted pricing, for old generation products, or new "no-frills" products with cheaper prices but drastically reduced functionality and style.

India is a long-haul market, as was pointed out in the first chapter, and what it offers is cheap entry tickets into a guaranteed long-term, slow-burn growth story. Winning in the Indian market is about being able to design the right business machine which can profitably deliver adequate quality at affordable process to serve the mass market, which is a large base of consumers with modest incomes but sophisticated needs and demands. This machine, if correctly designed, will be robust enough to run on autopilot and, over the next decade, capture the fruits of automatic growth of the Indian economy, locking out competition for a long while or raising their cost of entry significantly.

There are Three Big Factors to "Getting it Right" for the Indian Market

Creating "Blockbuster" Relevance: This can be done by defining business arenas in ways that make them relevant to the aspirations and problems of most Indians. For example, the heartbeat of the new India is about education, healthcare, productivity improvement, work-saving, entertainment, income improvement, better management of assets, and so on. As I said once to a team of R&D experts from one of the world leaders in lighting and semiconductors, "What is the point of defining your business as light bulbs of various sizes and shapes, and waiting for my government to first put electricity into villages? Can you not address the pressing need for lighting by marrying your LED, solar-energy and nanotechnology capabilities to create low-cost community lighting for us, before electricity gets there? Or persuade the government to use smart cards of some kind to administer a corruption-free subsidy program, by devising robust and simple devices that will stand up to the rigors of rural India?" Equally, e-governance, education and healthcare are the arenas for IT companies like Microsoft to enter in order to win in the Indian market, rather than waiting for home PC penetration to pick up, and fretting over piracy levels. And cola companies would definitely win in the Indian market if they defined their core business in India as water and nutrition-based drinks for young children.

Creating Perceived Value Advantage: It would be a positive step to achieve this for consumers and customers who have modest incomes but are not backward in their thinking and their aspirations, in an environment where innovative direct competition exists and offers low costs and high benefits, and where aggressive indirect competition for the customer rupee abounds from other product categories.

Getting the Business Economics Right: This is important for determining what business model (especially what pricing model) to go to market with, and how to produce and deliver the better-value offer at the lowest possible cost. It is necessary to keep in mind that India has; a fundamentally different demand structure from that of the developed markets (see Chapter 3); a consumer base which expects high functionality at low cost; and a patchy "ecosystem" where all elements of what is needed to support a business are not equally well developed. Often, there are no ready-made support systems such as appropriate retailing or specialized service providers, and creating these will require investment and partnerships.

The business economics challenge, the value challenge and the patchy-ecosystem challenge can only be resolved by designing and implementing strategies specifically made for India; strategies which represent the "next" practice, rather than the best practice so far. This could entail new business models, new products, new pricing models, new price-performance points, new low-cost business and distribution systems, and partnerships with the existing network of small service providers in the "ecosystem," or with other companies addressing the same target group or value spaces, and so on.

Are Global Companies Ready to Create "Made for India" Businesses?

Despite the overwhelming evidence of the need to create innovative business models and new value propositions to win both the classes and masses in a different kind of market, in my experience MNCs are most reluctant to do so.

The mindset and organizational structure by which global companies are held captive makes it very hard for them to do anything differently in new markets. It requires too much dismantling of existing planning processes and governance practices.

In addition, they have a deeply ingrained belief that all emerging markets will grow up to become just like America or Europe—that the ugly duckling will grow up to become the beautiful swan. However, as we have seen in this book, there is more than enough evidence to suggest that ugly ducklings are valuable in their own right.

Until recently, I believed that with all the information available from the experiences of early MNC entrants into India prospective new entrants would accept the need to develop, from a zero base, a customized business strategy. However, each new wave of MNCs exploring India seems to tread the same old path of assuming that best practices for emerging markets are the historical best practices from developed markets. In fact, I would argue that the early entrants, being the pioneers, were far more open to fresh approaches than the middle majority who are now beginning to explore emerging markets.

What Can MNCs Do Differently in Their Approach to the Indian Market?

Ask the Right Question: Not "When will this market be ready for my 'global' strategy?", but "What is the right strategy to unlock the potential of this market, given my competencies and comparative advantages?"

Just as there are many companies who have exaggerated financial expectations from the Indian market based on the macro numbers of GDP and population, equally, there are several others that come into India armed with their tried-and-tested strategies and business models and ask: "What is the size of opportunity for this?"

Usually the answer is "not much"; and the company then decides that the market is underdeveloped and that they will come back later. The fact is that they have just thrown the baby out with the bathwater by asking the wrong strategic question. The question is not "What sort of market for this [global] strategy?", but "What sort of strategy for this [local] market?"

This is illustrated perfectly by the story of a healthcare company, with impeccable global leadership credentials, in the business of making glucometers to measure the blood-glucose levels of diabetics. The company explored coming into India around 1999, and decided that there wasn't enough opportunity to justify anything more than setting up a distribution outpost for global products.

Here are the facts—according to World Health Organization (WHO) statistics, at that time India had (and continues to have) the highest diabetic population in the world. However, it also had the world's smallest blood-glucose monitoring market, for a variety of reasons. Doctors were not asking patients to monitor their blood glucose as regularly as they do in the developed world, where the accent is on maintaining the quality of life and aggressively managing the disease. In fact, many of the general practitioners belonged to the old school and asked patients not to get too obsessed with their blood-sugar count and to lead a "normal" life by not paying too much attention to the disease and letting their morale down. Patients were fatalistic and were thus casual about managing their illness. Though they knew sugar was bad for them, they felt obliged to eat the dessert served by close relatives because they did not wish to give offence.

The reasons for the small monitoring market also lay in the difficulty and expense involved in getting a two-stage glucose test. For consumers, there was more than just the cost of the test itself involved: they also had to factor in the costs of traveling to and from the pathology lab to give blood and collect results, and to the doctor to discuss the results. There was also the casual leave that they had to take from work to do all this. Existing blood-glucose meters for self-testing were too expensive for most people to buy. In other markets, the company provided the machine virtually free, and made money from recurrent use of strips; but this would not work in India. Here, people not only monitored their blood-sugar levels a lot less often, but also cut the strips into two to use them twice.

It was not difficult to see in this case that the obvious answer to the question "Is this market ready for my global strategy?" was a resounding "No." As the president of the business said, "If the Government of India does not think this is a priority disease, if there are so few diabetes specialists, if the general practitioners are so old fashioned and the consumer so poor, we have no market here."

But had the question been "Is the market fundamentally attractive?" the obvious answer just had to be a resounding "Yes." Not only did India have the world's highest number of diabetics, it was also poised for a large growth in its diabetic population, thanks to changes in occupation and income and an increase in urbanization which, in turn, led to changes for the worse in the eating habits and lifestyle of the average Indian. With a predicted diabetic population of 32 million by 2005, soaring to 57 million by 2025, this was the chance of a lifetime for a company that knew how to make glucometers of all shapes and sizes for all kinds of usage. However, the question that needed to be asked was: "What kind of strategy and business model is needed to profitably serve a market with a demand structure that is different from the 'usual' (that is, rather than one comprising a few people testing a lot, one consisting of a lot of people testing a little bit each)?"

One model that could have worked was to shift the business focus from serving the end-consumer to serving pathology labs — setting up these machines as "instamatic" monitoring stations in pathology labs, which would enable the lab to charge more for instant results, and yet would save the patient money from having to make fewer trips to the lab. The model could also include establishing testing centers in the clinics of a new emerging breed of modern, young general practitioners who were just beginning to build their practice and needed an additional source of income that would fit with their image.

However, the company would not even engage in this discussion, let alone evaluate the option seriously. It made it quite clear that "the world over" it made money by targeting the pathology labs, and taking their business away. It also made it clear that this line of the company's business was about "statistical monitoring of blood glucose at home," and not about instant monitoring in a pathology lab. It had a range of equipment meant for the institutional market, but that was designed for hospitals and Indian hospitals, it felt, were not sophisticated enough or rich enough to use it.

There are several other examples that tell the same tale. As discussed in the introductory chapter, PC and microchip makers, software companies, and the rest of that "ecosystem" repeatedly ask the question: "When will PC penetration in India increase, so that India will be ready for our global strategy?" The likelihood is that the cell phone revolution may overtake PCs, and the country may never be ready for their global strategy. Mass markets, like time and tide, wait for no one.

Johnson & Johnson operates in the world's most child-centric market, where the largest number of babies is produced. Yet, given the potential size of the opportunity, the length of time it has been in the Indian market, and how much brand respect it enjoys even with the poor, its baby-products business is miniscule. The prices it sets for its products are such that even those families that use them for the first child do not do so for the second child. The company could have created a larger, more vibrant business for India if it had asked the strategy question "What do I need to do in order to fully exploit the potential of this market?"

On the other hand, there is Nokia, which, in addition to offering a range of affordable instruments, has also focused on promoting Hindi-language text messaging despite not being a service provider. And there is Honda that has done an aggressive "made for India" play and built a large and profitable business, and continues to innovate, as households evolve and infrastructure contexts change. The Korean MNCs came, adapted and have, as a result, captured significant parts of the white-goods market and established a decent position in the small-car market.

Eschew Value Arrogance, a Mindset That Says "Who Can Resist Progress? Consumers Don't Know What They Don't Know Until You Show Them Better": In the late 1990s, I worked in the Indian office of one of the "Big five" management-consulting firms. The expatriate partner I worked with was the quintessential corporate imperialist, who firmly believed in the uniform world that MNCs would, and should, create wherever they went. He would nip in the bud every discussion about whether MNCs should review their global strategy for its applicability to the Indian market by demanding "Why do you believe that India is different? Do Indians wear their noses on their ears? Does water flow uphill in India?"

Citing examples of the onward march of Kelloggs, Coca-Cola, United Distillers, and of organized retailers all over Southeast Asia, he would opine that "people don't know what they don't know" and that demand invariably followed supply in emerging markets. "Who can resist progress?" was the subtext to his firm belief that India would soon join the ranks of "global–standard" consumers, and we would all forget the fact that we thought we were different.

A decade later, I notice that there are a lot of consumers out there who have resisted progress. Breakfast cereals never managed to make significant consumer inroads over the years, and it isn't for lack of presence, push or advertising spends from the big brands.

Kellogg's, for example, entered the Indian market with a range of breakfast cereals promoted with the proposition that they were nutritious, fat-free, cereal-based and a very convenient way of (not) cooking breakfast in the morning. However, the consumers' general response is typified by that of housewives in a focus group in south India who pointed out that, in their opinion, the humble *idli* (rice and lentil steamed cakes that form the staple diet in south India) was also cereal-based, nutritious and fat-free. What's more, it was far most cost-effective in terms of "cost per full stomach for a family of four."

As for the convenience benefit of breakfast cereal, Indian consumers did not attach much value to the benefit of there being "no need to cook" Kellogg's products, because the Indian kitchen is a hive of activity in the mornings, and cooking one or two more dishes for breakfast does not really add to the work load. A full, hot meal has to be cooked early in the morning to be packed into lunch boxes for office- and school-goers, since a snacky cold meal is considered unhealthy. Any additional cooking for those who eat lunch at home, such as old people or pre-schoolers, is also done at that time. Ironic isn't it? Here is a huge consumer base all eating cereal for breakfast in some form or other but with little desire to switch to the progressive world's breakfast habit. But then cold breakfasts do not cut much ice in a holistic, health-food culture that is obsessed with the heating and cooling qualities of foods, with dos and don'ts for each kind of weather. Cold milk was not a preferred accompaniment, and with hot milk, the overall experience was, well, mushy.

The right time for cereal could well have been in the evening when kids come home from school, and when mothers are busy getting the evening organized. But then, if your business description is breakfast cereals, that would be a hard transition to make. The company would have to make up its mind that its business was to leverage its core competence in cereal nutrition delivered the convenient way, whenever and however the consumer would like it. It would have to know that localizing the product but not the mindset, and offering mango-flavored breakfast cereal, would not be the solution to winning in this market.

Smuggled Scotch whisky abounds in the Indian market. The old joke is that there is more Scotch drunk in India than is distilled in Scotland. The early MNC entrants into the Scotch market just assumed that nobody would want to drink the smuggled variety of questionable origin, rather than the real thing, just because it was cheaper. In actual fact, the Indian market is divided between the "label pourers," a phrase used to describe those who flaunt the brand of the whisky they serve at home in order to signal their own status and impress visitors, and the true connoisseurs, who appreciate and savor the qualities of the whisky they drink. The former want an impressive brand label at the lowest possible cost, and are not too concerned about the genuineness of the whisky they serve. The latter are usually rich enough to travel abroad frequently and buy the real thing from their trips abroad, at cheaper duty-free prices. Neither wanted genuine Scotch whisky, now available in India at two-and-a-half times the price of smuggled Scotch, or at a price higher than duty free.

Recognize and Accept That India is a Multi-Tiered and Multi-Layered Market and Needs a Multi-Pronged Strategy: There seems to be an implicit paradigm in the minds of MNC strategists that low-income or developing markets require less-complex strategies than richer or better-developed markets. India, however, does not fit neatly into that equation because the most fundamental characteristic of the Indian market is its plurality. It is poor, and developing, but has many sub-Indias that are very different in size, in consumer sophistication and in their future evolution.

Therefore, no one segment of the market is deep enough to provide the value that makes a business financially vibrant. A one-size-fits-all, unsegmented strategy will not pull in the numbers—nor will it hedge against different levels of growth that the different sub-segments will show in any given year.

Recognize and Accept That Emerging Markets are Not the Way Developed Markets Were in Their Infancy: As I have said several times in this book, the analogy school, in which the big consulting firms love to take comfort, is not valid in India. To assume that per-capita GDP increases over the period from 1995 to 2005 would produce exactly the same changes in consumption as occurred between 1975 and 1985 is not logical: available options are different, as are theories of consumption. History cannot repeat itself. Markets evolve in different ways—there is no set pattern of evolution, and leapfrogging happens.

Mercedes-Benz first launched in India with an old model, which was not good enough for well-heeled Indians. Liquor companies launched with faded old brands that were once famous but well past their heyday, and were also rejected. In fact, local Indian admixes were preferred as better options. An Internet-surfing 15-year-old in India will not play with a Rubik's cube today just because it was all the rage in America 15 years ago; and poor rural Indians are not queuing up to buy a black-and-white television rather a color one, willing to settle for old styling on motorcycles, or wait for landline phones before they "graduate" to cell phones.

Therefore, the winning game for companies is about leveraging present competencies and historical experiences in order to create for the new world.

Forget About Thresholds of Income Above Which Consumption "Takes Off": There is a favorite theory entrenched in the world of business and economics that there is a magic number called the "threshold level" of income above which consumption "takes off." This threshold has been pegged variously at a per-capita income of US$1,100 or US$2 per day per person, and so on. This threshold theory however, is based on the notion that prices of delivered goods and services will remain unchanged, and will conform to existing "global" standards of existing companies. But consider the facts: poor people or those below the designated thresholds of income still have the same desires as those above the threshold—to eat well, educate their children, own a television, buy at a well-laid out store, and so on. However, if someone were able to drop prices sharply *and* make products that satisfied customer expectations, then consumption could "take off" at income levels far below the thresholds currently assumed and the market would blossom at any given income level. The threshold theory assumes that no smart new business models are possible which can achieve this. As Shakespeare would say:

"The fault, dear Brutus, is not in our stars,
  But in ourselves, that we are underlings."

The "Global vs. Local" Power Struggle: One of the most persistent business battles being fought in India is not between competitors in the marketplace, but between MNC head offices in America or Europe and local managers in India. Local managers (even non-Indians based in India) are keen to get access to the considerable global competencies and resources (especially in R&D) that exist in developed markets, and to develop customized products and services for the Indian market. Head-office folk are not convinced that fresh effort is needed to create for India, reasoning that whatever is available on shelves or in the archives of developed markets is good enough for an emerging market. What's more, head offices often believe that these products must be sold at international prices or thereabouts, because all markets must measure up to a global income standard.

Local managers feel that margin sacrifices or significant investments in market development must be considered because there are enormous volumes available for value-right products; it is a growth market and the payoff will be handsome, though slow. Head offices believe that if there isn't purchasing power available in this market, then it has no right to demand better benefits for its consumers at lower prices. Local managers feel that a zero-base approach could help create the right price-performance points, and the right business model. Head office feels that re-inventing the wheel is quite unnecessary, and is not easily persuaded that there is lost opportunity in not doing so.

The odd thing is that this inflexible mindset exists alongside amazing pieces of thought leadership on strategy that everyone in head office celebrates—"Blue Ocean Strategy," "Competing for the Future," "Seeing the Future First," "Creative Destruction," "Creating Industry Revolution," and so on. The implicit assumption seems to be that the only strategic challenges caused by changes in market conditions that head office will respond to are those that happen in the developed world, not the developing world.

POSTSCRIPT

The Changing Center of Gravity of "Global"

A critical question that links with all of these issues is: "What is 'global'? What is the 'global' standard that every new market must measure up to?"

Out of every 100 people in the world of the future, at least two-thirds will be in Asia, and most of them in India and China. One-third will be illiterate; perhaps one-fifth will have a college education, and about a quarter will be developed-market consumers from Europe or the US. Between now and 2025, 95% of the increase in global population will be in emerging markets and their increase in consumption will be greater than that of the traditional top six developed markets.

The inescapable conclusion to be drawn from this is that the center of gravity of what constitutes "global" is changing, as is the picture of the typical "global" consumer. So why should global strategy that has worked in the past, work in the future too? Consumer India requires companies to create the "next practice," and that goes beyond current best practice. It requires the creation of new solutions, rather than the transplanting of strategies from other markets. It requires companies to leverage their core competence, things that they are very good at doing, and apply it to new markets — to *create winning "made for India" solutions: new solutions for a new and different world.*

Bibliography

Appadurai, Arjun, *Modernity at Large: Cultural Dimensions of Globalization,* University of Minnesota Press, 224pp, 1996.

Bery, Suman, Bosworth, Barry, and Panagariya, Arvind (editors), *India Policy Forum,* Sage Publications Pvt Ltd, 360pp, 2006.

Dreze, Jean, and Sen, Amartya, *India: Economic Development and Social Opportunity,* Oxford University Press, 312pp, 1999.

Ghoshal, Sumantra, Piramal, Gita, and Budhiraja, Sundeep, *World Class in India: A Casebook of Companies in Transformation,* Penguin Books, 652pp, 2001.

Guide to Indian Markets 2006, MRUC, Hansa Research.

Jhabvala, Renana, Sudarshan, Ratna M, and Unni, Jeemol, *Informal Economy Centrestage,* Sage Publications Pvt Ltd, 288pp, 2003.

Kashyap, Pradeep, and Siddharth, Raut, *The Rural Marketing Book (2007 Edition),* Dreamtech Press, 354pp, 2007.

Khilnani, Sunil, *The Idea of India,* Penguin Books Ltd, 304pp, 2003.

Pelle, Stefano, *Understanding Emerging Markets: Building Business Bric by Brick,* Sage Publications Pvt. Ltd, 248pp, 2007.

Prahalad, C K, *The Fortune At The Bottom of The Pyramid: Eradicating Poverty Through Profits,* Wharton School Publishing, 496pp, 2004.

Silverstein, Michael J, and Stalk, George (editors), *Breaking Compromises: Opportunities for Action in Consumer Markets from The Boston Consulting Group,* John Wiley & Sons, 227pp, 2000.

Tharoor, Shashi, *India: From Midnight to Millennium,* Arcade Publishing, 416pp, 1998.

The Great Indian Middle Class, NCAER, *Business Standard,* New Delhi, 2005.

Varma, Pavan K, *Being Indian,* Penguin Books, India, 238pp, 2006.

Index

"made for India" businesses, 1, 4, 7, 168, 207, 211, 216
"popular" segment, 37, 50, 55, 68
"sachet" strategy, 48

accelerating consumption, 79
advertising, 5, 65, 119, 134, 167, 174, 175, 211
affluence, 10, 18, 34, 65, 69, 71-76, 80, 187, 201
affluent consumers, 200
affordable prices, 55, 202
age cohorts, 90, 94, 96, 115, 116, 134
agricultural Consumer India, 189
agricultural economy, 25, 184
agriculture, 19, 26, 27, 39, 90, 131, 180, 182, 183, 184, 186, 188, 189, 190
air conditioners, 2, 35, 53, 76, 129
America, 95, 143, 159, 181, 207, 214
annual household income, 68, 74, 83, 204

Appadurai, Arjun, 36, 146
aspirants, 54, 56, 57, 58, 59, 61
aspiration, 33, 34, 36, 92, 108, 131, 146, 150, 152, 168, 169, 187, 194
ATM, 113, 148, 181
Average annual growth rate, 25, 83, 194

B2B, 49, 50
Bangalore, 96, 114
benefit-maximizers, 55, 56, 58, 59, 94
Bharat, 89, 90, 132, 149
Biyani, Kishore, 112, 113, 120
Booz Allen Hamilton, 9
Bottom of the Pyramid (BOP), 8, 12, 30, 81, 191, 192, 193, 194, 200
Boston Consulting Group, India, 41
brands, 2, 3, 4, 5, 37, 54, 56, 58, 60, 61, 67, 98, 99, 104, 110, 111, 113, 114, 116, 119, 155, 158, 159, 161, 162, 164, 179, 213
BRIC(Brazil, Russia, India, China) economies, 12, 43, 44, 80, 82, 164

bricks-and-clicks business models, 182
business economics, 2, 207
business models, 7, 44, 81, 150, 169,
181, 182, 189, 192, 193, 194, 204,
207, 208, 214
business planning, 69
Business Standard, 33, 168, 183
business strategy, 7, 21, 92, 203, 208
Business Today, 33
Business World, 11, 49, 84

capitalism, 2
car manufacturers, 72
car markets, 65
cash-constrained benefit
maximizers, 58, 94
cash-flow minimizer, 57
caste system, 101, 103
cell phones, 6, 16, 17, 19, 33, 38, 60,
68, 84, 87, 103, 112, 125, 128, 165,
183, 187, 198, 205, 214
central government, 26, 128, 142, 151
Central Statistic Organization (CSO),
183
change confluence, 27, 28, 124, 125,
126, 158
Chennai, 96
Chidambaram P, 30
Chief Wage Earner (CWE), 102, 160
child-centricity, 152
China, 4, 5, 8, 12, 13, 14, 18, 21, 23,
25, 28, 38, 40, 41, 43, 44, 80, 94, 95,
97, 101, 139, 140, 152, 165, 204, 215
Churchill, Winston, 21
chocolate market, 134
class market, 203
climbers, 54
Coca-Cola, 159
communication revolution, 145
community consumption, 62, 145
comparative advantages, 208

competition, 3, 4, 16, 35, 51, 89, 93,
126, 166, 205
complexity of strategy, 97
connectivity, 36, 39, 145, 147, 181
consolidation, 130
consumer behavior, 21, 32, 139
Consumer China, 5
consumer classes, 53, 54, 58, 94
consumer confidence, 3, 17, 35, 86, 89,
93, 125
consumer credit, 16, 18, 35, 49, 125
consumer demand, 13, 44, 86
consumer durables, 16, 75, 78, 109,
125, 183, 186, 193, 198, 202
consumer economy, 67
consumer expenditure, 185, 187, 203
consumer finance, 16
consumer goods, 16, 35, 47, 54, 65, 68,
79, 104, 109, 124, 183
Consumer India, 1, 3, 4, 5, 7, 8, 9, 10,
13, 16, 17, 18, 21, 23, 24, 25, 26,
27, 28, 37, 43, 45, 53, 61, 65, 78, 91,
117, 131, 140, 152, 171, 189, 216
consumer interfacing, 61
consumer market, 15, 19, 21, 27, 33,
48, 54, 69, 77, 129, 140, 154, 157,
188
consumerism, 5, 13, 21, 37, 66, 89,
142, 147
consuming class, 54, 57, 58, 60, 65, 68,
90, 107, 160
consuming power, 68, 81, 109
consumption "takes off ", 47
consumption behavior, 73, 78, 81, 88,
101, 111, 115, 131, 171
consumption data, 72, 81, 145
consumption expenditure, 49, 186, 192
consumption ideology, 96, 115
consumption increase, 33, 36, 79
consumption intensity, 75, 76, 109
consumption potential, 109

consumption-oriented, 157
continuity with change, 6, 127, 129, 130
corporate imperialism, 133
cost-benefit optimizers, 55, 56, 59
cost-benefit orientations, 54
creeping trends, 124, 131
cross-cultural classification system, 113
cultural future, 134, 139, 140
cultural issues, 71
cultural meanings, 6, 140
cultural orientations, 85
cultural sensitivity, 3, 7
cultural shifts, 140, 196
culture shock, 87
customer-relationship, 21
customization, 7, 93
customized strategy, 7
cyber cafés, 62

data sources, 70, 82
Desai, Santosh, 129, 142, 152, 154, 196
demand analysis, 72
demand environment/market potential, 72
demand segments, 50, 86, 87, 91, 94, 187
demand structure, 8, 43, 47, 50, 61, 207, 210
democracy, 27, 128, 147, 165
demographics, 12, 27, 102, 160
developed markets, 6, 12, 19, 27, 40, 44, 52, 203, 205, 207, 213
Diageo, 3
digital divide, 19
discount segments, 52, 106
discount-segment manufacturers, 52
disposable income, 84, 88, 201
distribution, 5, 14, 31, 58, 61, 71, 81, 119, 161, 187, 207

distribution strategies, 119
diversity, 5, 25, 85, 91, 101, 121
Diwali, 134, 135, 154
DNA of Indian society, 134, 136
down-trading, 16, 52, 60, 125, 202

e-commerce, 182, 197
economic growth, 4, 10, 15, 18, 24, 59, 82, 84, 89, 95, 127, 157, 194
economic liberalization, 1, 2
economic policy, 128
economic status, 195
education, 7, 23, 30, 40, 46, 57, 72, 87, 92, 96, 102, 106, 132, 144, 145, 149, 151, 160, 176, 178, 186, 196, 200, 206
E-governance, 186, 206
electronics market, 57, 205
emerging economies, 44
emerging markets, 4, 6, 133, 144, 159, 167, 207, 211, 213, 215
empowerment, 149, 202
enablement, 149
entrepreneurs, 87, 97, 152, 169, 172, 181
equated monthly installment (EMI), 36, 177
ethnicity, 118
European Union (EU), 98, 118
expenditure share, 186
extended families, 176

farmer, 20, 57, 90, 96, 189
fast-moving consumer goods (FMCGs), 16, 47, 48, 50, 54, 56, 109, 113, 125
feminism, 132, 174
financial services, 93, 104, 121, 125
financial-service solutions, 31
fixed price, 94
food market, 135
force of liberalization, 140

forecasting, 86, 94
Foreign Direct Investment (FDI), 13, 128
Fortune 500, 12
France, 25, 81
free market economy, 65
Future Group, 112, 120

Gandhi, Mahatma, 1, 116, 141
Gandhi, Rajiv, 2, 116, 141
Gandhi, Indira, 2, 19, 141, 146
garibi hatao, 2, 141
Gateway of India, 17
GDP distribution, 79, 80, 81
GDP growth rate, 3, 14, 26, 87, 140,
GDP per capita, 21, 44, 49, 66, 79-82, 132, 133
generation next, 157, 163, 166
geographical clusters, 39, 146
Grassroots Innovations Augmentation Network (GIAN), 199
global best-practice strategy, 12
global brands, 2
global businesses, 9
global retailers, 4, 45
global strategy, 6, 12, 203, 208, 216
globalization, 19, 87
Goldman Sachs, 44, 82
government employees, 87, 88
Government of India, 71, 209
Grameen Bank, 202
Great Indian Middle Class, 14, 16, 66
Gross Domestic Product (GDP), 1, 10, 23, 43, 65, 86, 131, 140, 159, 203
guaranteed growth, 27
guaranteed income, 194

Hansa Research, 67, 70, 73, 109, 111
healthcare, 30, 39, 72, 90, 93, 111, 144, 182, 186, 196, 206
Heinz, 3

highest income group, 34, 38, 47, 72, 83
Hindu rate of growth, 13, 141
Hindu way of life, 136, 150
Hindustan Lever, 48, 55, 69, 78, 92, 108, 175, 188
home loan, 36
Honda, 3, 33, 106, 114, 211
household consumption behavior, 47, 171
household earnings, 71
household surveys, 71
housewives, 21, 63, 117, 135, 171, 173, 176, 178, 212
hybrid models, 151
hyped expectation, 13

ICI India, 69
ICICI Bank, 92, 93, 175
income class, 58, 71, 74
income data, 49, 70, 71, 79, 82, 84
income distribution, 32, 33, 71, 79, 188
income growth, 15, 24, 33, 35, 89, 180, 194
income label, 73, 104
income percentile, 73, 106
income pyramid, 204
income strata, 72
income surveys independence, 2, 143
India, 2, 23, 31, 111, 131
Indian consumers, 5, 21, 46, 98, 101, 212
Indian culture, 134, 140, 152
Indian economy, 3, 11, 36, 91, 203, 206
Indian Institute of Management (IIM), 142
Indian Institute of Technology (IIT), 143, 165

Indian market, 9, 10, 11, 12, 14, 17, 21, 28, 45, 48, 52, 55-7, 61-3, 66, 67, 85, 98, 99, 119, 157, 161, 162, 171, 203, 204, 206, 208, 210, 212, 214
Indian Readership Survey (IRS), 38, 67, 73, 109, 185
Indian women, 90, 138, 158, 176
Information technology, communication and entertainment (ICE), 144
infrastructure and operational capability, 92
infrastructure and technology, 95
innovation, 5, 12, 30, 40, 46, 48, 51, 79, 81, 179, 187, 198, 199, 202
Institute of Development Studies, 147
institutions, 19, 27, 41, 67, 127, 142, 151
inter-category competition, 16
Internet, 6, 20, 39, 62, 87, 97, 133, 144, 166, 181, 199, 213
investment, 11, 13, 27, 28, 57, 62, 66, 82, 95, 98, 129, 142, 189, 193, 207, 215
IT, 90
IT economy, 90
IT India, 86, 87

Jayate, Satyameva, 21
jeans, 4, 67, 116, 129, 130, 161, 162, 169

Kapoor, Ekta, 118
Karnataka, 96, 148, 188
Kellogg's, 3, 9, 33, 211, 212
Khilnani, Sunil, 91

Lakshmi, 155
Levi's, 159, 161, 163

liberalization, 5, 13, 24, 37, 50, 54, 89, 101, 115, 125, 134, 139, 140, 157, 167, 170, 191
liberalization children, 37, 90, 115, 117, 157, 167, 170,
lifestyle, 30
literacy, 37
Liquefied Natural Gas (LNG), 98
low acceleration change, 124
lowest income group, 32, 34, 38, 47, 83, 127, 188, 194
low-income consumer, 192
Liquefied Petroleum Gas (LPG), 34, 107, 181, 184, 195
luxury brands, 54, 104, 110

Made for India, 4, 7, 168, 207, 211
mainstreamers, 113
management consulting firms, 211
Maira, Arun, 40
Market Information Survey of Households (MISH), 32, 46, 47
market planning, 188
market potential, 40, 46, 97, 192
Market Research Society of India (MRSI), 102
market segmentation, 187
market structure, 21, 48, 50, 53, 130, 160
Maruti, 34
mass market, 16, 48, 111, 204
McCann-Erickson, 129
McDonald's, 135, 168
McKinsey, 14
McKinsey Quarterly, 40
megatrends, 124
Mercedes, 3, 9, 20, 54, 213
middle class, 8, 14, 16, 37, 66, 88, 106, 149
middle-income group, 33
middle-income consumer, 37

"Midnight's Children", 115
"Midway children, " 115
Mini-Indias, 91
multinational companies (MNCs), 2, 9,
28, 203
mobility, 107
modernity, 136
molting change, 127
mom-and-pop shops, 4
morality, 152
morphing change, 127, 129, 131, 174
motorcycles, 20, 72, 76, 111, 127, 196
MTV, 3
Mumbai, 4
My Target India, 21, 24, 92, 97, 102,
110, 121
Murthy, Narayana, 148

National Accounting Statistics of the
Government of India, 71
National Association for Computer
Training, 145
National Council for Applied Economic
Research (NCAER), 13, 53, 68, 72,
82, 83, 194
national income, 3, 16, 68, 89, 128,
131, 192, 194
Naipaul, V S, 121
Nehru, Jawaharlal, 1
negotiation, 150
New Delhi, 2, 12, 125
new entrants into consumption, 56
New York Times, 65
no frills, 192, 206
Nokia, 3
nominal income, 35
non-agricultural activity, 39
non-agricultural economy, 130
non-food expenditure, 186
Non-governmental organization
(NGOs), 39

not yet into consumption, 56
National Sample Survey (NSS) data,
185, 186

occupation, 39
outsourcing, 4, 10, 40, 88, 135
Prahalad, C K, 5, 7, 28, 191
P&L, 16
PC, 6, 206
penetration, 33, 47, 62, 84, 111
pent-up demand, 14
per-capita consumption, 23
per-capita income, 23, 13, 201
Philippines, 6, 159, 166
plurality, 85, 91, 128, 136, 213
politics, 15, 18, 26, 91, 139
popular culture, 6, 147
popular market, 48, 50
popular segment, 37, 50, 54
popular theory, 171
population, 31
post-independence generation, 25
post-liberalization generation, 25
poverty effect, 36
power distance, 132, 147
pragmatism, 112, 141, 142, 151, 167,
169
pre-independence generation, 90
premium market, 48, 61, 170
premium segment, 50, 60, 86
premium-popular-discount construct
price-performance points, 4
private consumption, 28, 154
privatization, 38, 88
Procter & Gamble (P&G), 14
productivity, 196
psychographic determinants of
consumption, 113
public-private partnership, 31
purchasing power, 8, 10, 43, 65, 69, 75,
81, 108, 185, 192, 194, 204, 215

purchasing power index, 76
Purchasing Power Parity (PPP), 1, 10, 43, 72, 192

research and development (R&D), 40, 126, 192
Research International, 175
rich brats, 160, 161
rock table, 15, 24
rope trick of numbers, 45, 47, 49, 75
rural Consumer India, 39, 58, 179
rural economy, 182
rural expenditure growth, 185
rural GDP, 183
rural income distribution, 33
rural India, 83, 87, 95, 107
rural market, 39, 58, 182
rural SEC system, 104, 107
rural teens, 162
Rushdie, Salman, 115
Russia, 6, 159

sales patterns, 86
Sen, Amartya 25
Samsung, 3
savings, 81
schizophrenic India, 85, 89
self-employed, 27
self-reliance, 140
Semiotic Solutions, 115, 139
service economy, 38, 91, 96
shampoo, 16, 35, 47, 56, 60, 76, 78, 79, 125
small towns, 87, 107
social development, 25, 95
social policy, 27
socio-economic classification (SEC), 102
sociocultural diversity, 85
socio-economic development, 25

special economic zones (SEZs), 189, 190
spending patterns, 184, 186, 201
state government, 26
status, 16
status signals, 151
strategic business segmentation, 97
strategic challenges, 9, 215
strategic objectives, 93
strategy developers, 70
stratification scheme, 73
Subhiksha, 45
sub-segment, 98
Supermarkets, 4, 60
Swadeshi, 116, 141

Tamil Nadu, 30, 95, 175, 188
Tata Motors, 52
Tharoor Shashi, 21, 26
tech-led democracy, 148
technology, 20, 29, 39, 57, 72, 95, 141, 144, 163, 166, 181, 186, 193, 199
telephone, 21, 62, 74, 145, 164, 199
televisions, 2, 20
The Times of India, 121
traditional, 4, 32, 47, 92, 112, 127, 172, 174, 199, 215
trucks, 130
two-wheelers, 46, 56, 72, 76, 111, 127, 196
undeclared income, 89

Unilever India, 92, 133
urban economy, 182
urban GDP, 183
urban income distribution, 32
urban India, 25, 30, 32, 34, 38, 58, 73, 78, 83, 88, 90, 94, 95, 102, 104, 106, 107, 146, 157, 163, 171, 181, 194, 203

urban market, 39, 58, 185, 186, 190
urban SEC system, 104, 105
urbanization, 209
USA, 18, 23, 43, 44, 116, 120, 133
Uttar Pradesh, 30, 114, 176

value advantage, 52, 182, 206
value growth, 13, 59, 60, 61
value orientation, 53, 54, 55, 56, 94,
value processing, 197, 202
value-optimizing, 55
value right, 60, 73, 198
Valentine, Virginia, 115, 139
Varma, Pavan K, 66
Videshi, 143
virgin markets, 4
visible consumption, 33, 34
volume growth, 13, 59, 60

Wal-Mart, 162, 190
Walt Disney, 6
wealth management, 92

western values, 152, 153
westernization, 23, 134, 140
Woman Consumer India, 171
Woman India, 157
womanism, 132, 173, 174, 175
working women, 171, 172, 173
World Bank, 66, 95
World Health Organization (WHO),
  208
World Trade Organization (WTO), 87

Yadav, Laloo, 132
Young and Rubicam, 113
young Consumer India, 158, 160
Young India, 157, 159, 166, 168, 170,
  171
younger generation, 130, 137, 143
youth brands, 158, 164
youth culture, 158, 159
youth demographics, 160
youth market, 117, 126, 158, 159, 161,
  164, 171

GEORGE BROWN COLLEGE
ST. JAMES CAMPUS
LIBRARY LEARNING COMMONS
200 KING ST. E.
TORONTO, ON
M5A 3W8